Asmodeus: or,
The Devil on Two Sticks
By Alain René Le Sage
Edited by Anthony Uyl

Devoted Publishing
Ingersoll, Ontario, 2025

Asmodeus; or, The Devil on Two Sticks
Asmodeus: or, The Devil on Two Sticks
By Alain René Le Sage
With a biographical notice of the author, by Jules Jann
Edited by Anthony Uyl

Originally Published by:
George Routledge and Sons, London: Broadway, Ludgate Hill. New York: 416 Broome Street. 1879.

The text of *Asmodeus: or, The Devil on Two Sticks* is all protected under Copyright ©2025 Devoted Publishing. The covers, background, layout and Devoted Publishing logo are Copyright ©2025 Devoted Publishing. This edition is published by Devoted Publishing a division of 2165467 Ontario Inc.

Contact us at: devotedpub@hotmail.com
Visit us on X (Twitter): @AnthonyDevPub
Published in Ingersoll, Ontario, Canada 2025

ISBN: 978-1-77356-552-1

Alain René Le Sage

TRANSLATOR'S PREFACE.

    When I first determined on the publication of a new edition of "THE DEVIL ON TWO STICKS," I had certainly no idea of engaging in a new translation. I had not read an English version since my boyhood, and naturally conceived that the one which had passed current for upwards of a century must possess sufficient merit to render anything beyond a careful revision, before passing it again through the press, unnecessary. However, on reading a few pages, and on comparing them with the much-loved original, I no longer wondered, as I had so often done, why LE DIABLE BOITEUX was so little esteemed by those who had only known him in his English dress, while Gil Blas was as great a favourite with the British public as any of its own heroes of story. To account for this, I will not dwell on the want of literal fidelity in the old version, although in some instances that is amusing enough; but the total absence of style, and that too in the translation of a work by one of the greatest masters of verbal melody that ever existed, was so striking as to induce me, rashly perhaps, to endeavour more worthily to interpret the witty and satirical ASMODEUS for the benefit of those who have not the inestimable pleasure of comprehending him in his native tongue--for, as Jules Janin observes, he is a Devil truly French.

    In the translation which I here present, I do not myself pretend, at all times, to have rendered the words of the 'graceful Cupid' with strict exactness, but I have striven to convey to my reader the ideas which those words import. Whether I have succeeded in so doing is for others to determine; but, if I have not, I shall at all events have the satisfaction of failing in company,--which, I am told, however, is only an Old Bailey sort of feeling after all.

    I have not thought it necessary to attempt the Life of the Author; it will be enough to me, for fame, not to have murdered one of his children. I have therefore adopted the life, character, and behaviour of Le Sage from one of the most talented of modern French writers, and my readers will doubtless congratulate themselves on my resolve. Neither have I deemed it needful to enter into the controversy as to the originality of this work, except by a note in page 162: and this I should probably not have appended, had I, while hunting over the early editions there referred to, observed the original dedication of Le Sage to 'the illustrious Don Luis Velez de Guevara,' in which are the following words: "I have already declared, and do now again declare to the world, that to your Diabolo Cojuelo I owe the title and plan of this work ...; and I must further own, that if the reader look narrowly into some passages of this performance, he will find I have adopted several of your thoughts. I wish from my soul he could find more, and that the necessity I was under of accommodating my writings to the genius of my own country had not prevented me from copying you exactly." This is surely enough to exonerate Le Sage from the many charges which have been urged against him; and I quote the concluding sentence of the above, because it is an excuse, from his own pen, for some little liberties which I have, in my turn, thought it necessary to take with his work in the course of my labours.

    JOSEPH THOMAS.

NOTICE OF LE SAGE

  I shall at once place LE SAGE by the side of Molière; he is a comic poet in all the acceptation of that great word,--COMEDY. He possesses its noble instincts, its good-natured irony, its animated dialogue, its clear and flowing style, its satire without bitterness, he has studied profoundly the various states of life in the heights and depths of the world. He is perfectly acquainted with the manners of comedians and courtiers,--of students and pretty women. Exiled from the Théâtre-Français, of which he would have been the honour, and less fortunate than Molière, who had comedians under his direction, and who was the proprietor of his own theatre, Le Sage found himself obliged more than once to bury in his breast this Comedy, from want of a fitting stage for its exhibition, and actors to represent it. Thus circumstanced, the author of "Turcaret" was compelled to seek a new form, under which he might throw into the world the wit, the grace, the gaiety, the instruction which possessed him. In writing the biography of such men, there is but one thing to do, and that is to praise. The more humble and obscure have they been in their existence, the greater is the duty of him who tells the story of their lives, to heap upon them eulogy and honour. This is a tardy justice, if you will, but it is a justice nevertheless; and besides, of what importance, after all, are these vulgar events? All these biographies are alike. A little more of poverty, a little less of misery, a youth expended in energy, a manhood serious and filled with occupation, an old age respected, honourable; and, at the end of all these labours, all these troubles, all these anguishes of mind and heart, of which your great men alone have the secret,--the Académie-Française in perspective. Then, are you possessed of mediocre talents only? all doors are open to you;-- are you a man of genius? the door opens with difficulty;--but, are you perchance one of those excelling spirits who appear but from century to century? it may turn out that the Académie-Française will not have you at any price. Thus did it with the great Molière; thus also has it done for Le Sage; which, by-the-bye, is a great honour for the illustrious author of "Gil Blas."

  René Le Sage was born in the Morbihan, on the 8th of May, 1668:[1] and in that year Racine produced "Les Plaideurs," and Molière was playing his "Avare." The father of Le Sage was a man slightly lettered,--as much so as could be expected of an honourable provincial attorney, one who lived from day to day like a lord, without troubling himself too much as to the future fortunes of his only son. The father died when the child was only fourteen years of age; and soon afterwards the youthful René lost his mother. He was now alone, under the guardianship of an uncle, and he was fortunate enough to be placed under the tutelage of those learned masters of the youth of the seventeenth century, the Jesuits who subsequently became the instructors of Voltaire, as they have been of all France of the great age. Thanks to this talented and paternal teaching, our young orphan quickly penetrated into the learned and poetical mysteries of that classic antiquity, which is yet in our days, and will be to the end of time, the exhaustless source of taste, of style, of reason, and of good sense. It is to praise Le Sage to say that he was educated with as much care and assiduity as Molière and Racine, as La Fontaine and Voltaire; they one and all prepared themselves, by severest study, and by respect for their masters, to become masters in their turn; and they have themselves become classic writers, because they reverenced their classic models,--which may, in case of need, serve as an example for the beaux-esprits of our own time.

  But what matters poverty when one is so young,--when our hopes are so vast, our thoughts so powerful and rich? You have nothing, it is true; but the world itself belongs to you,--the world is your patrimony; you are sovereign of the universe; and around you, the twentieth year touches every thing with its golden wand. Your clear and sparkling eye may look in the sun's bright face as dauntless as the eagle's. It is accomplished: all the powers of your soul are awakened, all the passions of your heart join in one swelling choir, to chant Hosanna in excelsis! What matter then that you are poor! A verse sublime, a noble thought, a well-turned phrase, the hand of a friend, the soft smile of some bright-eyed damsel as she flits across your path,--there is a fortune for a week. Those who, at the commencement of every biography, enter into all sorts of lamentation, and deplore with pathetic voice the mournful destiny of their hero, are not in the secret of the facile joys of poetry, of the exquisite happiness of youth,--the simpletons! They amuse themselves in counting, one by one, the rags that cover yonder handsome form; and they see not, through the holes of the cloak which envelopes it, those Herculean arms, or that athletic breast! They look with pity on that poor young man with well-worn hat, and beneath that covering deformed they see not those abundant, black, and tended locks, the flowing diadem of youth! They will tell you, with heart-rending sighs, how happy Diderot esteemed himself, when to his crust of bread he joined the luxury of cheese, and how this poor René le Sage drank at his repasts but pure spring water;--a lamentable matter, truly! But Diderot, while he ate his cheese, already meditated the shocks of his "Encyclopædia"; but this same clear fountain from which you drink, at twenty, in the hollow of your hand, as pure, will intoxicate more surely than will, after twenty other years, alas! the sparkling produce of Champagne, poured out in cups of crystal.

This is sufficient reason why we should not trouble ourselves overmuch as to the early life of Le Sage; he was young and handsome, and as he marched, his head upturned like a poet, he met as he went along with those first loves which one always meets when the heart is honest and devoted. A charming woman loved him, and he let her love him to her heart's content; and, without concerning himself as to his good fortune, more than would master Gil Blas have done on a similar occasion, these first amours of our poet lasted just as long as such sort of amours ought to last--long enough that they should leave no subject for regret, not enough that they should evoke hatred. When, therefore, they had loved each other as much as they could, she and he, they separated, still to please themselves; she found a husband of riper age and better off than her lover; he took a wife more beauteous and less wealthy than his mistress. And blessings on the amiable and devoted girl who consented, with a joyous heart, to encounter all the risks, all the vexations, and also to expose herself to the seducing pleasures of a poetic life! Thus Le Sage entered, almost without thinking of it, into that laborious life in which one must daily expend the rarest and most charming treasures of his mind and soul. As a commencement, he made a translation of the Letters of Calisthenes, without imagining that he was himself possessed of more wit than all the Greeks of the fourth century. The work had no success, and it ought not to have had. He who has the genius of Le Sage must create original works, or not meddle in the craft. To translate is a trade of manual skill--to imitate, is one of plagiary. However, the failure of this first book rendered Le Sage less proud and haughty; and he accepted, what he would never have done had he at once succeeded, a pension from M. l'Abbé de Lyonne. This pension amounted to six hundred francs; and thereupon the biographers of our author are in extacies at the generosity of the Abbé de Lyonne.

Six hundred francs! and when we reflect that had Le Sage lived in our day, depending only on his Théâtre de la Foire, he would have gained thirty thousand francs a year! In our days, a romance like "Gil Blas" would not be worth less than five hundred thousand francs; "Le Diable Boiteux" would have brought him a hundred thousand, at least: still, we must not be angry with M. l'Abbé de Lyonne, for having bestowed a pension of six hundred on the author of "Gil Blas." The abbé did more; he opened to Le Sage an admirable treasure of wit, of imagination, and of poetry; he taught him the Spanish tongue, that lovely and noble instructress of the great Corneille; and it is doubtless no slight honour for the language of Cervantes to have given birth in our land to "The Cid" and to "Gil Blas." You may imagine with what delight Le Sage accepted this instruction, and how perfectly at home he found himself in those elegant and gracious manners; with what good will he studied that smiling gallantry, that loyal jealousy; those duennas in appearance so austere, in reality so accessible; those lovely women, their feet ensatined, their head in the mantilla; those charming mansions, all carved without, and within all silence; those exciting windows, lighted by smiles above, while concerts murmur at their feet! You may imagine if he adopted those lively and coquetish waiting-women, those ingenious and rascally valets, those enormous mantles so favourable to love, those ancient bowers so friendly to its modest blisses! Thus, when he had discovered this new world of poesy, of which he was about to be the Pizarro and the Fernando Cortes, and of which Corneille had been the Christopher Columbus, René le Sage clapped his hands for joy. In his noble pride, he stamped his feet on this enchanted land; he began to read, you may fancy with what delight, that admirable epic, "Don Quixote," which he studied for its grace, its charms, its poetry, its passion; putting for the time aside its satire, and the sarcasm concealed in this splendid drama, as weapons for a later use, when he should attack the financiers. Certainly, the Abbé de Lyonne never dreamt that he was opening to the light this exhaustless mine for the man who was to become the first comic poet of France--since Molière is one of those geniuses apart, of whom all the nations of the earth, all literary ages, claim alike with equal right the honour and the glory.

The first fruit of this Spanish cultivation was a volume of comedies which Le Sage published, and in which he had translated some excellent pieces of the Spanish stage. It contained only one from Lopez de Vega, so ingenious and so fruitful; that was certainly too few: there was in it not one of Calderon de la Barca; and that was as certainly not enough. In this book, which I have read with care, in search of some of those luminous rays which betoken the presence of the man of genius wherever he has passed, I have met with nothing but the translator. The original writer does not yet display himself: it is because style is a thing which comes but slowly; it is because, in this heart of comedy more especially, there are certain secrets of trade which no talent can replace, and which must be learned at whatever cost. These secrets Le Sage learned, as every thing is learned, at his own expense. From a simple translator as he was, he became an arranger of dramatic pieces, and in 1702 (the eighteenth century had begun its course, but with timid steps, and none could have predicted what it would become) Le Sage brought out at the Théâtre Français a comedy in five acts, "Le Point d'Honneur:" it was a mere imitation from the Spanish. The imitation had small success, and Le Sage comprehended not this lesson of the public; he understood not that something whispered to the pit, so reserved in its applause, that there was in this translator an original poet. To avenge himself, what did Le Sage? He fell into a greater error still: he set to work translating--will you believe it?--the continuation of "Don Quixote," as if "Don Quixote" could have a continuation; as if there were a person in the world, even Cervantes himself, who had the right to add a chapter to this famous history! Verily, it is strange, indeed, that with his taste so pure, his judgment so correct, Le Sage should have ever thought of this unhappy continuation. This time, therefore, again his new attempt had no success; the Parisian public, which, whatever may be said to the contrary, is a great judge, was more just for the veritable Quixote than Le Sage himself; and he had once more to begin anew. However, he yet once more attempted this new road, which could lead him to nothing good. He returned to the charge, still with a Spanish comedy, "Don César Ursin," imitated from Calderon. This piece was played for the first time at Versailles, and applauded to the skies by the court, which deceived itself almost as often as the town. Le Sage now thought that the battle at last was won. Vain hope! it was again a battle lost, for, brought from Versailles to Paris, the comedy of "Don César Ursin" was hissed off the stage by the Parisian pit, which thus unmercifully annihilated the eulogies of the court, and the first victory of the author. It was now full time to yield to the force of evidence. Enlightened by these rude instructions, Le Sage at last comprehended that it was not permitted to him, to him less than to all others, to be a plagiarist; that originality was one of the grand causes of success; and that to confine himself for ever to this servile imitation of the Spanish poets was to become a poet lost.

Now, therefore, behold him, determined in his turn to be an original poet. This time he no longer copies, he invents; he arranges his fable to his mind, and seeks no further refuge in the phantasmagoria of Spain. With original ideas, comes to him originality of style; and he at last lights on that wondrous and imperishable dialogue which may be compared to the dialogue of Molière, not for its ease, perhaps, but unquestionably for its grace and elegance. He found at the same time, to his great joy, now that he was himself--that he walked in the footsteps of nobody, he found that the business was much more simple; this time he was at his ease in his plot, which he disposed as it pleased him; he breathed freely in the space which he had opened to himself; nothing constrained his march, any more than his poetical caprice. Well! at last then we behold him the supreme moderator of his work, we behold him such as the pit would have him, such as we all hoped he was.

This happy comedy, which is, beyond all doubt, the first work of Le Sage, is entitled "Crispin, Rival de son Maître." When he had finished it, Le Sage, grateful for the reception which the court had given to "Don César Ursin," was desirous that the court should also have the first hearing of "Crispin, Rival de son Maître." He remembered, with great delight, that the first applauses he had received had been echoed from Versailles! Behold him then producing his new comedy before the court. But, alas! this time the opinion of the court had changed: without regard for the plaudits of Versailles, the pit of the Paris theatre had hissed "Don César Ursin"; Versailles in its turn, and as if to take its revenge, now hissed "Crispin, Rival de son Maître." We must allow that, for a mind less strong, here was enough to confound a man for ever, and to make him comprehend nothing either as to the success or the failure of his productions. Happily, Le Sage appealed from the public of Versailles to the pit of Paris; and as much as "Crispin, Rival de son Maître" had been hissed at Versailles, so much was this charming comedy applauded at Paris. On this occasion, it was not alone to give the lie to the court, that the pit applauded; Paris had refound, in truth, in this new piece, all the qualities of true comedy,--the wit, the grace, the easy irony, the exhaustless pleasantry, a noble frankness, much biting satire, and a moderate seasoning of love.

As to those who would turn into accusation the hisses of Versailles, they should recollect that more than one chef-d'oeuvre, hissed at Paris, has been raised again by the suffrages of Versailles;--"Les Plaideurs" of Racine, for instance, which the court restored to the poet with extraordinary applause, with the bursting laughter of Louis XIV., which come deliciously to trouble the repose of Racine, at five o'clock in the morning. Happy times, on the contrary, when poets had, to approve them, to try them, this double jurisdiction; when they could appeal from the censures of the court to the praises of the town, from the hisses of Versailles to the plaudits of Paris!

Now we behold René le Sage, to whom nothing opposes: he has divined his true vocation, which is comedy; he understands what may be made of the human race, and by what light threads are suspended the human heart. These threads of gold, of silver, or of brass, he holds them at this moment in his hand, and you will see with what skill he weaves them. Already in his head, which bears Gil Blas and his fortune, ferment the most charming recitals of "Le Diable Boiteux." Silence! "Turcaret" is about to appear,--Turcaret, whom Molière would not have forgotten if Turcaret had lived in his day; but it was necessary to wait till France should have escaped from the reign, so decorous, of Louis XIV., to witness the coming, after the man of the Church, after the man of the sword, this man without heart and without mind,--the man of money. In a society like our own, the man of money is one of those bastard and insolent powers which grow out of the affairs of every day, as the mushroom grows out from the dunghill. We know not whence comes this inert force,--we know not how it is maintained on the surface of the world, and nothing tells how it disappears, after having thrown its phosphorus of an instant. It is necessary, in truth, that an epoch should be sufficiently corrupt, and sufficiently stained with infamy, when it replaces, by money, the sword of the warrior, by money the sentence of the judge, by money the intelligence of the legislator, by money the sceptre of the king himself. Once that a nation has descended so low, as to adore money on its knees--to require neither fine arts, nor poesy, nor love, it is debased as was the Jewish people, when it knelt before the golden calf. Happily, of all the ephemeral powers in the world, money is the most ephemeral; we extend to it our right hand, it is true, but we buffet it with our left; we prostrate ourselves before it as it passes along,--yes; but when it has passed, we kick it with our foot! This is what Le Sage marvellously comprehended, like a great comic poet as he was. He found the absurd and frightful side of those gilded men who divide our finances, menials enriched overnight, who, more than once, by a perfectly natural mistake, have mounted behind their own coaches. And such is Turcaret. The poet has loaded him with vices the most disgraceful, with follies the most dishonouring; he tears from this heart, debased by money, every natural affection; and nevertheless, even in this fearful picture, Le Sage has confined himself within the limits of comedy, and not once in this admirable production does contempt or indignation take the place of laughter. It was then with good cause that the whole race of financiers, as soon as they had heard of Turcaret, caballed against this chef-d'oeuvre; the cry resounded in all the rich saloons of Paris; it was echoed from the usurers who lent their money to the nobles, and re-echoed by the nobles who condescended to borrow from the usurers; it was a general hue and cry.

"Le Tartufe" of Molière never met with greater opposition among the devotees than "Turcaret" experienced from financiers; and, to make use of the expression of Beaumarchais in reference to "Figaro," it required as much mind for Le Sage to cause his comedy to be played as it did to write it. But on this occasion, again, the public, which is the all-powerful manager in these matters, was more potent than intrigue; Monseigneur le Grand Dauphin, that Prince so illustrious by his piety and virtue, protected the comedy of Le Sage, as his ancestor, Louis XIV., had protected that of Molière. On this, the financiers, perceiving that all was lost as far as intrigue was concerned, had recourse to money, which is the last reason of this description of upstarts, as cannon is the ultima ratio of kings. This time again the attack availed not: the great poet refused a fortune that his comedy might be played, and unquestionably he made a good bargain by his resolve, preferable a hundred thousand times to all the fortunes which have been made and lost in the Rue Quincampoix.[2] The success of "Turcaret" (1709) was immense; the Parisian enjoyed with rare delight the spectacle of these grasping money-hunters devoted to the most cruel ridicule. What if Le Sage had deferred the production of this masterpiece! These men would have disappeared, to make room for others of the kind, and they would have carried with them into oblivion the comedy they had paid for. It would have been a chef-d'oeuvre lost to us for ever; and never, that we know of, would the good men on 'Change have dealt us a more fatal blow.

Who would credit it, however? After this superb production, which should have rendered him the master of French comedy, Le Sage was soon compelled to abandon that ungrateful theatre which understood him not. He renounced,--he, the author of "Turcaret,"--pure comedy, to write, as a pastime, farces, little one-act pieces mingled with couplets, which made the life of the Théâtre de la Foire Saint Laurent, and of the Théâtre de la Foire Saint Germain. Unfortunate example for Le Sage to set, in expending, without thought, all his talent, from day to day, without pity for himself, without profit for anyone. What! the author of "Turcaret" to fill exactly the same office as M. Scribe; to waste his time, his style, and his genius upon that trifling comedy which a breath can hurry away! And the French comedians were all unmoved, and hastened not to throw themselves at the feet of Le Sage, to pray, to supplicate him to take under his all-powerful protection that theatre elevated by the genius and by the toils of Molière! But these senseless comedians were unable to foresee anything.

Nevertheless, if he had renounced the Théâtre Français, Le Sage had not abandoned true comedy. All the comedies which thronged his brain, he heaped them up in that grand work which is called "Gil Blas," and which includes within itself alone the history of the human heart. What can be said of "Gil Blas" which has not already been written? How can I sufficiently eulogise the only book truly gay in the French language? The man who wrote "Gil Blas" has placed himself in the first rank among all the authors of this world; he has made himself, by the magic of his pen, the cousin-german of Rabelais and Montaigne, the grandfather of Voltaire, the brother of Cervantes, and the younger brother of Molière; he takes his place, in plenitude of right, in the family of comic poets, who have themselves been philosophers. In the same vein, he has further composed the "Bachelier de Salamanque," which would be a charming book if "Gil Blas" existed not, if above all, before writing his "Gil Blas," he had not written this charming book, "LE DIABLE BOITEUX."

And now, sauve qui peut! the Devil is let loose upon the town, a devil truly French, who has the wit, the grace, and the vivacity of Gil Blas. Beware! Look to yourselves, you the ridiculous and the vicious, who have escaped the high comedy of the stage, for, by the virtue of this all-potent wand, not alone your mansions but your very souls shall in a twinkling change to glass. Beware! I say; for Asmodeus, the terrible scoffer, is about to plunge his pitiless eye into those mysterious places which

Asmodeus; or, The Devil on Two Sticks

you deemed so impenetrable, and to each of you he will reveal his secret history; he will strike you without mercy with that ivory crutch which opens all doors and all hearts; he will proclaim aloud your follies and your vices. None shall escape from that vigilant observer, who, astride upon his crutch, glides upon the roofs of the best secured houses, and divines their ambitions, their jealousies, their inquietudes, and, above all, their midnight wakefulness. Considered with relation to its wit without bitterness, its satire which laughs at everything, and with regard to its style, which is admirable, "Le Diable Boiteux" is perhaps the book most perfectly French in our language; it is perhaps the only book that Molière would have put his name to after "Gil Blas."

Such was this life, all filled with most delightful labour, as also with the most serious toil; thus did this man, who was born a great author, and who has raised to perfection the talent of writing, go on from chef-d'oeuvre to chef-d'oeuvre without pause. The number of his productions is not exactly known; at sixty-five years of age, he yet wrote a volume of mélanges, and he died without imagining to himself the glories which were reserved for his name. An amiable and light-hearted philosopher, he was to the end full of wit and good sense; an agreeable gossiper, a faithful friend, an indulgent father, he retired to the little town of Boulogne-sur-Mer, where he became without ceremony a good citizen, whom everybody shook by the hand without any great suspicion that he was a man of genius. Of three sons who had been born to him, two became comedians, to the great sorrow of their noble father, who had preserved for the players, as is plainly perceptible in "Gil Blas," a well-merited dislike. However, Le Sage pardoned his two children, and he even frequently went to applaud the elder, who had taken the name of Monmenil; and when Monmenil died, before his father, Le Sage wept for him, and never from that time (1743) entered a theatre. His third son, the brother of these two comedians, was a good canon of Boulogne-sur-Mer; and it was to his house that Le Sage retired with his wife and his daughter, deserving objects of his affection, and who made all the happiness of his latest days.

One of the most affable gentlemen of that time, who would have been remarkable by his talents, even though he had not been distinguished by his nobility, M. le Comte de Tressan, governor of Boulogne-sur-Mer, was in the habit of seeing the worthy old man during the last year of his life; and upon that fine face, shaded with thick white hairs, he could still discern that love and genius had been there. Le Sage rose early, and his first steps took him to seek the sun. By degrees, as the luminous rays fell upon him, thought returned to his forehead, motion to his heart, gesture to his hand, and his eyes were lighted with their wonted fire: as the sun mounted in the skies, this awakened intelligence appeared, on its side, more brilliant and more clear; so much so, that you beheld again before you the author of "Gil Blas." But, alas! all this animation drooped in proportion as the sun declined; and, when night was come, you had before your eyes but a good old man, whose steps must be tended to his dwelling.

Thus died he, one day in summer. The sun had shown itself in heaven's topmost height on that bright day; and it had not quite left the earth when Le Sage called the members of his family around to bless them. He was little less than ninety when he died (1747).

To give you an idea of the popularity that this man enjoyed even during his life-time, I will finish with this anecdote: When the "Diable Boiteux" appeared, in 1707, the success of this admirable and ingenious satire upon human life was so great, the public esteemed the lively epigrams it contains so delightful, that the publisher was obliged to print two editions in one week. On the last day of this week, two gentlemen, their swords by their sides, as was then the custom, entered the bookseller's shop to buy the new romance. A single copy remained to sell: one of these gentlemen would have it, the other also claimed it; what was to be done? Why, in a moment, there were our two infuriate readers with their swords drawn, and fighting for the first blood, and the last "Diable Boiteux."

But what, I pray you, had they done, were it a question then of the "DIABLE BOITEUX" illustrated by TONY JOHANNOT?

JULES JANIN.

Footnotes:
1. According to Moreri, in his "Grand Dictionnaire Historique," (folio, Paris, 1759,) and he cites as his authority M. Titon de Tillet's second supplement to the "Parnasse Français," Le Sage was born at Ruis in Brittany, in 1677. There is, however, every reason to believe that M. Jules Janin is correct, both as to the year and the place of his birth, notwithstanding that Mr. Chalmers, in his "Biographical Dictionary," while he assigns to the former the year 1668, places the latter at Vannes, as does also the "Biographie Universelle," which he appears to have followed.

But, when this preliminary education was completed, and when he left these learned mansions, all filled with Greek and Latin, all animated with poetic fervour, Le Sage encountered those terrible obstacles that await invariably, as he emerges from his studies, every young man without family, and destitute of fortune. The poet Juvenal has well expressed it, in one of his sublimest verses: "They with difficulty rise, whose virtues are opposed by the pinching wants of home."

Alain René Le Sage

*"Haud facile emergunt, quorum virtutibus obstat
   Res angusta domi."*

2. In this street, in 1716, the famous projector Law established his bank; and the rage for speculation which followed, made it for a time the Bourse of Paris. A hump-backed man made a large fortune by lending himself as a desk, whereon the speculators might sign their contracts, or the transfer of shares. The Rue Quincampoix is still a leading street for business, but its trade is now confined to more honest wares, such as drugs and grocery.

CHAPTER I

WHAT SORT OF A DEVIL HE OF THE TWO STICKS WAS--WHEN AND BY WHAT ACCIDENT DON CLEOPHAS LEANDRO PEREZ ZAMBULLO FIRST GAINED THE HONOUR OF HIS ACQUAINTANCE.

A night in the month of October covered with its thick darkness the famous city of Madrid. Already the inhabitants, retired to their homes, had left the streets free for lovers who desired to sing their woes or their delights beneath the balconies of their mistresses; already had the tinkling of guitars aroused the care of fathers, or alarmed the jealousy of husbands; in short, it was near midnight, when Don Cleophas Leandro Perez Zambullo, a student of Alcala, suddenly emerged, by the skylight, from a house into which the incautious son of the Cytherean goddess had induced him to enter. He sought to preserve his life and his honour, by endeavouring to escape from three or four hired assassins, who followed him closely, for the purpose of either killing him or compelling him to wed a lady with whom they had just surprised him.

Against such fearful odds he had for some time valiantly defended himself; and had only flown, at last, on losing his sword in the combat. The bravos followed him for some time over the roofs of the neighbouring houses; but, favoured by the darkness, he evaded their pursuit; and perceiving at some distance a light, which Love or Fortune had placed there to guide him through this perilous adventure, he hastened towards it with all his remaining strength. After having more than once endangered his neck, he at length reached a garret, whence the welcome rays proceeded, and without ceremony entered by the window; as much transported with joy as the pilot who safely steers his vessel into port when menaced with the horrors of shipwreck.

He looked cautiously around him; and, somewhat surprised to find nobody in the apartment, which was rather a singular domicile, he began to scrutinize it with much attention. A brass lamp was hanging from the ceiling; books and papers were heaped in confusion on the table; a globe and mariner's compass occupied one side of the room, and on the other were ranged phials and quadrants; all which made him conclude that he had found his way into the haunt of some astrologer, who, if he did not live there, was in the habit of resorting to this hole to make his observations.

He was reflecting on the dangers he had by good fortune escaped, and was considering whether he should remain where he was until the morning, or what other course he should pursue, when he heard a deep sigh very near him. He at first imagined it was a mere phantasy of his agitated mind, an illusion of the night; so, without troubling himself about the matter, he was in a moment again busied with his reflections.

But having distinctly heard a second sigh, he no longer doubted its reality; and, although he saw no one in the room, he nevertheless called out,--"Who the devil is sighing here?" "It is I, Signor Student," immediately answered a voice, in which there was something rather extraordinary; "I have been for the last six months enclosed in one of these phials. In this house lodges a learned astrologer, who is also a magician: he it is who, by the power of his art, keeps me confined in this narrow prison." "You are then a spirit?" said Don Cleophas, somewhat perplexed by this new adventure. "I am a demon," replied the voice; "and you have come in the very nick of time to free me from slavery. I languish in idleness; for of all the devils of hell, I am the most active and indefatigable."

These words somewhat alarmed Signor Zambullo; but, as he was naturally brave, he quickly recovered himself, and said in a resolute tone: "Signor Diabolus, tell me, I pray you, what rank you may hold among your brethren. Are you an aristocrat, or a burgess?" "I am," replied the voice, "a devil of importance, nay, the one of highest repute in this, as in the other world." "Perchance," said Don Cleophas, "you are the renowned Lucifer?" "Bah," replied the spirit; "why, he is the mountebank's devil." "Are you Uriel then?" asked the Student. "For shame!" hastily interrupted the voice; "no, he is the patron of tradesmen; of tailors, butchers, bakers, and other cheats of the middle classes." "Well, perhaps you are Beelzebub?" said Leandro. "Are you joking?" replied the spirit; "he is the demon of duennas and footmen." "That astonishes me," said Zambullo; "I thought Beelzebub one of the greatest persons at your court." "He is one of the meanest of its subjects," answered the Demon; "I see you have no very clear notions of our hell."

"There is no doubt then," said Don Cleophas, "that you are either Leviathan, Belphegor, or Ashtaroth." "Ah! those three now," replied the voice, "are devils of the first order, veritable spirits of

Alain René Le Sage

diplomacy. They animate the councils of princes, create factions, excite insurrections, and light the torches of war. They are not such peddling devils as the others you have named." "By the bye! tell me," interrupted the Scholar, "what post is assigned to Flagel?" "He is the soul of special pleading, and the spirit of the bar. He composes the rules of court, invented the law of libel, and that for the imprisonment of insolvent debtors; in short, he inspires pleaders, possesses barristers, and besets even the judges.

"For myself, I have other occupations: I make absurd matches; I marry greybeards with minors, masters with servants, girls with small fortunes with tender lovers who have none. It is I who introduced into this world luxury, debauchery, games of chance, and chemistry. I am the author of the first cookery book, the inventor of festivals, of dancing, music, plays, and of the newest fashions; in a word, I am ASMODEUS, surnamed THE DEVIL ON TWO STICKS."

"What do I hear," cried Don Cleophas; "are you the famed Asmodeus, of whom such honourable mention is made by Agrippa and in the Clavicula Salamonis? Verily, you have not told me all your amusements; you have forgotten the best of all. I am well aware that you sometimes divert yourself by assisting unhappy lovers: by this token, last year only, a young friend of mine obtained, by your favour, the good graces of the wife of a Doctor in our university, at Alcala." "That is true," said the spirit: "I reserved that for my last good quality. I am the Demon of voluptuousness, or, to express it more delicately, Cupid, the god of love; that being the name for which I am indebted to the poets, who, I must confess, have painted me in very flattering colours. They say I have golden wings, a fillet bound over my eyes; that I carry a bow in my hand, a quiver full of arrows on my shoulders, and have withal inexpressible beauty. Of this, however, you may soon judge for yourself, if you will but restore me to liberty."

"Signor Asmodeus," replied Leandro Perez, "it is, as you know, long since I have been devoted to you: the perils I have just escaped will prove to you how entirely. I am rejoiced to have an opportunity of serving you; but the vessel in which you are confined is undoubtedly enchanted, and I should vainly strive to open, or to break it: so I do not see clearly in what manner I can deliver you from your bondage. I am not much used to these sorts of disenchantments; and, between ourselves, if, cunning devil as you are, you know not how to gain your freedom, what probability is there that a poor mortal like myself can effect it?" "Mankind has this power," answered the Demon. "The phial which encloses me is but a mere glass bottle, easy to break. You have only to throw it on the ground, and I shall appear before you in human form." "In that case," said the Student, "the matter is easier of accomplishment than I imagined. But tell me in which of the phials you are; I see a great number of them, and all so like one another, that there may be a devil in each, for aught I know." "It is the fourth from the window," replied the spirit. "There is the impress of a magical seal on its mouth; but the bottle will break, nevertheless." "Enough," said Don Cleophas; "I am ready to do your bidding. There is, however, one little difficulty which deters me: when I shall have rendered you the service you require, how know I that I shall not have to pay the magician, in my precious person, for the mischief I have done?" "No harm shall befall you," replied the Demon: "on the contrary, I promise to content you with the fruits of my gratitude. I will teach you all you can desire to know; I will discover to you the shifting scenes of this world's great stage; I will exhibit to you the follies and the vices of mankind; in short, I will be your tutelary demon: and, more wise than the Genius of Socrates, I undertake to render you a greater sage than that unfortunate philosopher. In a word, I am yours, with all my good and bad qualities; and they shall be to you equally useful."

"Fine promises, doubtless," replied the Student; "but if report speak truly, you devils are accused of not being religiously scrupulous in the performance of your undertakings." "Report is not always a liar," said Asmodeus, "and this is an instance to the contrary. The greater part of my brethren think no more of breaking their word than a minister of state; but for myself, not to mention the service you are about to render me, and which I can never sufficiently repay, I am a slave to my engagements; and I swear by all a devil holds sacred, that I will not deceive you. Rely on my word, and the assurances I offer: and what must be peculiarly pleasing to you, I engage, this night, to avenge your wrongs on Donna Thomasa, the perfidious woman who had concealed within her house the four scoundrels who surprised you, that she might compel you to espouse her, and patch up her damaged reputation."

The young Zambullo was especially delighted with this last promise. To hasten its accomplishment, he seized the phial; and, without further thought on the event, he dashed it on the floor. It broke into a thousand pieces, inundating the apartment with a blackish liquor: this, evaporating by degrees, was converted into a thick vapour, which, suddenly dissipating, revealed to the astonished sight of the Student the figure of a man in a cloak, about two feet six inches high, and supported by two crutches. This little monster had the legs of a goat, a long visage, pointed chin, a dark sallow complexion, and a very flat nose; his eyes, to all appearance very small, resembled two burning coals; his enormous mouth was surmounted by a pair of red mustachios, and ornamented with two lips of unequalled ugliness.

The head of this graceful Cupid was enveloped in a sort of turban of red crape, relieved by a plume of cock's and peacock's feathers. Round his neck was a collar of yellow cloth, upon which were embroidered divers patterns of necklaces and earrings. He wore a short white satin gown, or tunic, encircled about the middle by a large band of parchment of the same colour, covered with talismanic characters. On the gown, also, were painted various bodices, beautifully adapted for the display of the fair wearers' necks; scarfs of different patterns, worked or coloured aprons, and head-dresses of the newest fashion;--all so extravagant, that it was impossible to admire one more than another.

But all this was nothing as compared with his cloak, the foundation of which was also white satin. Its exterior presented an infinity of figures delicately tinted in Indian ink, and yet with so much freedom and expression that you would have wondered who the devil could have painted it. On one side appeared a Spanish lady covered with her mantilla, and leering at a stranger on the promenade; and on the other a Parisian grisette, who before her mirror was studying new airs to victimize a young abbé, at that moment opening the door. Here, the gay Italian was singing to the guitar beneath the balcony of his mistress; and there, the sottish German, with vest unbuttoned, stupefied with wine, and more begrimed with snuff than a French petit-maître, was sitting, surrounded by his companions, at a table covered with the filthy remnants of their debauch. In one place could be perceived a Turkish bashaw coming from the bath, attended by all the houris of his seraglio, each watchful for the handkerchief; and in another an English gentleman, who was gallantly presenting to his lady-love a pipe and a glass of porter.

Besides these there were gamesters, marvellously well portrayed; some, elated with joy, filling their hats with pieces of gold and silver; and others, who had lost all but their honour, and willing to stake on that, now turning their sacrilegious eyes to heaven, and now gnawing the very cards in despair. In short, there were as many curious things to be seen on this cloak as on the admirable shield which Vulcan forged for Achilles, at the prayer of his mother Thetis; with this difference however,--the subjects on the buckler of the Grecian hero had no relation to his own exploits, while those on the mantle of Asmodeus were lively images of all that is done in this world at his suggestion.

CHAPTER II
WHAT FOLLOWED THE DELIVERANCE OF ASMODEUS.

Upon perceiving that his appearance had not prepossessed the student very greatly in his favour, the Demon said to him, smiling: "Well, Signor Don Cleophas Leandro Perez Zambullo, you behold the charming god of love, that sovereign master of the human heart. What think you of my air and beauty? Confess that the poets are excellent painters." "Frankly!" replied Don Cleophas, "I must say they have a little flattered you. I fancy, it was not in this form that you won the love of Psyche." "Certainly not," replied the Devil: "I borrowed the graces of a little French marquis, to make her dote upon me. Vice must be hidden under a pleasing veil, or it wins not even woman. I take what shape best pleases me; and I could have discovered myself to you under the form of the Apollo Belvi, but that as I have nothing to disguise from you, I preferred you should see me under a figure more agreeable to the opinion which the world generally entertains of me and my performances." "I am not surprised," said Leandro, "to find you rather ugly--excuse the phrase, I pray you; the transactions we are about to have with each other demand a little frankness: your features indeed almost exactly realise the idea I had formed of you. But tell me, how happens it that you are on crutches?"

"Why," replied the Demon, "many years ago, I had an unfortunate difference with Pillardoc, the spirit of gain, and the patron of pawnbrokers. The subject of our dispute was a stripling who came to Paris to seek his fortune. As he was capital game, a youth of promising talents, we contested the prize with a noble ardour. We fought in the regions of mid-air; and Pillardoc, who excelled me in strength, cast me on the earth after the mode in which Jupiter is related by the poets to have tumbled Vulcan. The striking resemblance of our mishaps gained me, from my witty comrades, the sobriquet of the Limping Devil, or the Devil on Two Sticks, which has stuck to me from that time to this. Nevertheless, limping as I am, I am tolerably quick in my movements; and you shall witness for my agility.

"But," added he, "a truce to idle talk; let us get out of this confounded garret. My friend the magician will be here shortly; as he is hard at work on rendering a handsome damsel, who visits him nightly, immortal. If he should surprise us, I shall be snug in a bottle in no time; and it may go hard but he finds one to fit you also. So let us away! But first to throw the pieces, of that which was once my prison, out of the window; for such 'dead men' as these do tell tales."

"What if your friend does find out that you are 'missing?'" "What!" hastily replied the Demon; "I see you have never studied the Treatise on Compulsions. Were I hidden at the extremity of the earth, or in the region where dwells the fiery salamander; though I sought the murkiest cavern of the gnomes, or plunged in the most unfathomable depths of the ocean, I should vainly strive to evade the terrors of his wrath. Hell itself would tremble at the potency of his spells. In vain should I struggle: despite myself should I be dragged before my master, to feel the weight of his dreaded chains."

"That being the case," said the Student, "I fear that our intimacy will not be of long duration: this redoubtable necromancer will doubtless soon discover your flight." "That is more than I know," replied the Spirit; "there is no foreseeing what may happen." "What!" cried Leandro Perez; "a demon, and ignorant of the future!" "Exactly so," answered the Devil; "and they are only our dupes who think otherwise. However, there are enough of them to find good employment for diviners and fortune-tellers, especially among your women of quality; for those are always most eager about the future who have best reason to be contented with the present, which and the past are all we know or care for. I am ignorant, therefore, whether my master will soon discover my absence; but let us hope he will not: there are plenty of phials similar to the one in which I was enclosed, and he may never miss that. Besides, in his laboratory, I am something like a law-book in the library of a financier. He never thinks of me; or if he does, he would think he did me too great an honour if he condescended to notice me. He is the most haughty enchanter of my acquaintance: long as he has deprived me of my liberty, we have never exchanged a syllable."

"That is extraordinary!" said Don Cleophas; "what have you done to deserve so much hatred or scorn?" "I crossed him in one of his projects," replied Asmodeus. "There was a chair vacant in a certain Academy, which he had designed for a friend of his, a professor of necromancy; but which I had destined for a particular friend of my own. The magician set to work with one of the most potent talismans of the Cabala; but I knew better than that: I had placed my man in the service of the prime minister; whose word is worth a dozen talismans, with the Academicians, any day."

Asmodeus; or, The Devil on Two Sticks

While the Demon was thus conversing, he was busily engaged in collecting every fragment of the broken phial; which having thrown out of the window, "Signor Zambullo," said he, "let us begone! Hold fast by the end of my mantle, and fear nothing." However perilous this appeared to Leandro Perez, he preferred the possible danger to the certainty of the magician's resentment; and, accordingly, he fastened himself as well as he could to the Demon, who in an instant whisked him out of the apartment.

CHAPTER III

WHERE THE DEVIL TRANSLATED THE STUDENT; AND THE FIRST FRUITS OF HIS ECCLESIASTICAL ELEVATION.

Cleophas found that Asmodeus had not vainly boasted of his agility. They darted through the air like an arrow from the bow, and were soon perched on the tower of San Salvador. "Well, Signor Leandro," said the Demon as they alighted; "what think you now of the justice of those who, as they slowly rumble in some antiquated vehicle, talk of a devilish bad carriage?" "I must, hereafter, think them most unreasonable," politely replied Zambullo. "I dare affirm that his majesty of Castile has never travelled so easily; and then for speed, at your rate, one might travel round the world nor care to stretch a leg."

"You are really too polite," replied the Devil; "but can you guess now why I have brought you here? I intend to show you all that is passing in Madrid; and as this part of the town is as good to begin with as any, you will allow that I could not have chosen a more appropriate situation. I am about, by my supernatural powers, to take away the roofs from the houses of this great city; and notwithstanding the darkness of the night, to reveal to your eyes whatever is doing within them." As he spake, he extended his right arm, the roofs disappeared, and the Student's astonished sight penetrated the interior of the surrounding dwellings as plainly as if the noon-day sun shone over them. "It was," says Luis Velez de Guevara, "like looking into a pasty from which a set of greedy monks had just removed the crust."

The spectacle was, as you may suppose, sufficiently wonderful to rivet all the Student's attention. He looked amazedly around him, and on all sides were objects which most intensely excited his curiosity. At length the Devil said to him: "Signor Don Cleophas, this confusion of objects, which you regard with an evident pleasure, is certainly very agreeable to look upon; but I must render useful to you what would be otherwise but a frivolous amusement. To unlock for you the secret chambers of the human heart, I will explain in what all these persons that you see are engaged. All shall be open to you; I will discover the hidden motives of their deeds, and reveal to you their unbidden thoughts.

"Where shall we begin? See! do you observe this house to my right? Observe that old man, who is counting gold and silver into heaps. He is a miserly citizen. His carriage, which he bought for next to nothing at the sale of an alcade of the Cortes, and which to save expense still sports the arms of its late owner, is drawn by a pair of worthless mules, which he feeds according to the law of the Twelve Tables, that is to say, he gives each, daily, one pound of barley: he treats them as the Romans treated their slaves--wisely, but not too well. It is now two years since he returned from the Indies, bringing with him innumerable bars of gold, which he has since converted into coin. Look at the old fool! with what satisfaction he gloats over his riches. And now, see what is passing in an adjoining chamber of the same house. Do you observe two young men with an old woman?" "Yes," replied Cleophas, "they are probably his children." "No, no!" said the Devil, "they are his nephews, and, what is better in their opinion, his heirs. In their anxiety for his welfare, they have invited a sorceress to ascertain when death will take from them their dear uncle, and leave to them the division of his spoil. In the next house there are a pair of pictures worth remarking. One is an antiquated coquette who is retiring to rest, after depositing on her toilet, her hair, her eyebrows and her teeth; the other is a gallant sexagenarian, who has just returned from a love campaign. He has already closed one eye, in its case, and placed his whiskers and peruke on the dressing table. His valet is now easing him of an arm and one leg, to put him to bed with the rest."

"If I may trust my eyes," cried Zambullo, "I see in the next room a tall young damsel, quite a model for an artist. What a lovely form and air!" "I see," said the Devil. "Well! that young beauty is an elder sister of the gallant I have just described, and is a worthy pendant to the coquette who is under the same roof. Her figure, that you so much admire, is really good; but then she is indebted for it to an ingenious mechanist, whom I patronise. Her bust and hips are formed after my own patent; and it is only last Sunday that she generously dropped her bustle at the door of this very church, on the occasion of a charity sermon. Nevertheless, as she affects the juvenile, she has two cavaliers who ardently dispute her favour;--nay, they have even come to blows on the occasion. Madmen! two dogs fighting for a bone.

"Prithee, laugh with me at an amateur concert which is performing in a neighbouring mansion; an after-supper offering to Apollo. They are singing cantatas. An old counsellor has composed the air; and the words are by an alguazil, who does the amiable after that fashion among his friends--an ass who writes verses for his own pleasure, and for the punishment of others. A harpsichord and clarionet form the accompaniment; a lanky chorister, who squeaks marvellously, takes the treble, and a young girl with a hoarse voice the bass." "What a delightful party!" cried Don Cleophas. "Had they tried expressly to get up a musical extravaganza, they could not have succeeded better."

"Cast your eyes on that superb mansion," continued the Demon; "and you will perceive a nobleman lying in a splendid apartment. He has, near his couch, a casket filled with billets-doux; in which he is luxuriating, that the sweet nothings they contain may lull his senses gently to repose. They ought to be dear to him, for they are from a signora he adores; and who so well appreciates the value of her favours, that she will soon reduce him to the necessity of soliciting the exile of a viceroyalty, for his own support. Let us leave him to his slumbers, to watch the stir they are making in the next house to the left. Can you distinguish a lady in a bed with red damask furniture? Her name is Donna Fabula. She is of high rank, and is about to present an heir to her spouse, the aged Don Torribio, whom you see by her side, endeavouring to soothe the pangs of his lady until the arrival of the midwife. Is it not delightful to witness so much tenderness? The cries of his dear better-half pierce him to the soul: he is overwhelmed with grief; he suffers as much as his wife. With what care,--with what earnestness does he bend over her!" "Really," said Leandro, "the man does appear deeply affected; but I perceive, in the room above, a youngster apparently a domestic, who sleeps soundly enough: he troubles himself not for the event." "And yet it ought to interest him," replied Asmodeus; "for the sleeper is the first cause of his mistress's sufferings.

"But see,--a little beyond," continued the Demon: "in that low room, you may observe an old wretch who is anointing himself with lard. He is about to join an assembly of wizards, which takes place to-night between San Sebastian and Fontarabia. I would carry you thither in a moment, as it would amuse you; but that I fear I might be recognised by the devil who personates the goat."

"That devil and you then," said the Scholar, "are not good friends?" "No, indeed! you are right," replied Asmodeus, "he is that same Pillardoc of whom I told you. The scoundrel would betray me, and soon inform the magician of my flight." "You have perhaps had some other squabble with this gentleman?" "Precisely so," said the Demon: "some ten years ago we had a second difference about a young Parisian who was thinking of commencing life. He wanted to make him a banker's clerk; and I, a lady-killer. Our comrades settled the dispute by making him a wretched monk. This done, they reconciled us: we embraced; and from that time have been mortal foes."

"But, have done with this belle assemblée," said Don Cleophas; "I am not at all curious to witness it: let us continue our scrutiny into what is before us. What is the meaning of those sparks of fire which issue from yonder cellar?" "They proceed from one of the most absurd occupations of mankind," replied the Devil. "The grave personage whom you behold near the furnace is an alchymist; and the flames are gradually consuming his rich patrimony, never to yield him what he seeks in return. Between ourselves, the philosopher's stone is a chimera that I myself invented to amuse the wit of man, who ever seeks to pass those bounds which the laws of nature have prescribed for his intelligence.

"The alchymist's neighbour is an honest apothecary, who you perceive is still at his labours, with his aged wife and assistant. You would never guess what they are about. The apothecary is compounding a progenerative pill for an old advocate who is to be married to-morrow; the assistant is mixing a laxative potion; and the old lady is pounding astringent drugs in a mortar."

"I perceive, in the house facing the apothecary's," said Zambullo, "a man who has just jumped out of bed, and is hastily dressing." "Pshaw!" replied the Spirit, "he need not hurry himself. He is a physician; and has been sent for by a prelate who since he has retired to rest--about an hour--has absolutely coughed two or three times.

"But look a little further, in a garret on the right, and try if you cannot distinguish a man half dressed, who is walking up and down the room, dimly lighted by a single lamp." "I see," said the Student; "and so clearly that I would undertake to furnish you with an inventory of his chattels,--to wit, a truckle-bed, a three-legged stool, and a deal table; the walls seem to be daubed all over with black paint." "That exalted personage," said Asmodeus, "is a poet; and what appears to you black paint, are tragic verses with which he has ornamented his apartment, being obliged, for want of paper, to commit his effusions to the wall." "By his agitation and phrenzied air, I conclude he is now busily engaged on some work of importance," said Don Cleophas. "You are not far out," replied the Devil: "he only yesterday completed the last act of an interesting tragedy, intitled The Universal Deluge. He cannot be reproached with having violated the unity of place, at all events, as the entire action is limited to Noah's ark.

"I can assure you it is a first-rate drama: all the animals talk as learnedly as professors. It of course must have a dedication, upon which he has been labouring for the last six hours; and he is, at this moment, turning the last period. It will be indeed a masterpiece of adulatory composition: every social and political virtue; every grace that can adorn; all that tends to render man illustrious, either by his own deeds or those of his ancestors, are attributed to its object;--never was praise more lavishly bestowed, never was incense burnt more liberally." "For whom, then, of all the world, is so magnificent an apotheosis intended?" "Why," replied the Demon, "the poet himself has not yet determined that; he has put in every thing but the name. However, he hopes to find some vain noble who may be more liberal than those to whom he has dedicated his former productions; although the purchasers of imaginary virtues are becoming every day more rare. It is not my fault that it is so; for it is a fault corrected in the wealthy patrons of literature, and a great benefit rendered to the public, who were certain to be deluged by trash from the Swiss of the press, so long as books were written merely for the produce of their dedications.

"Apropos of this subject," added the Demon, "I will relate to you a curious anecdote. It is not long since an illustrious lady accepted the honour of a dedication from a celebrated novelist, who, by the bye, writes so much in praise of other women, that he thinks himself at liberty to abuse the one peculiarly his own. The lady in question was anxious to see the address before it was printed; and not finding herself described to her taste, she wisely undertook the task, and gave herself all those inconvenient virtues, which the world so much admires. She then sent it to the author, who of course had weighty reasons for adopting it."

"Hollo!" cried Leandro, "surely those are robbers who are entering that house by the balcony." "Precisely so," said Asmodeus; "they are brigands, and the house is a banker's. Watch them! you will be amused. See! they have opened the safe, and are ferreting everywhere; but the banker has been before them. He set out yesterday for Holland, and has taken with him the contents of his coffers for fear of accidents. They may make a merit of their visit, by informing his unfortunate depositors of their loss."

"There is another thief," said Zambullo, "mounting by a silken ladder into a neighbouring dwelling." "You are mistaken there," replied the Devil; "at all events it is not gold he seeks. He is a marquis, who would rob a young maiden of the name, of which, however, she is not unwilling to part. Never was 'stand and deliver' more graciously received: he of course has sworn he will marry her, and she of course believes him; for a marquis's 'promises' have unlimited credit upon Love's Exchange."

"I am curious to learn," interrupted the Student, "what that man in a night-cap and dressing-gown is about. He is writing very studiously, and near him is a little black figure, who occasionally guides his hand." "He is a registrar of the civil courts," replied the Demon; "and to oblige a guardian, is, for a consideration, altering a decree made in favour of the ward: the gentleman in black, who seems enjoying the sport, is Griffael the registrars' devil." "Griffael, then," said Don Cleophas, "is a sort of deputy to Flagel; for, as he is the spirit of the bar, the registrars are doubtless included in his department." "Not so," replied Asmodeus; "the registrars have been thought deserving of their peculiar demon, and I assure you they find him quite enough to do."

"Near the registrar's house, you will perceive a young lady on the first floor. She is a widow; and the man, whom you see in the same room, is her uncle, who lodges in an apartment over hers. Admire the bashfulness of the dame! She is ashamed to put on her chemise before her aged relative; so, modestly seeks the assistance of her lover, who is hidden in her dressing-room.

"In the same house with the registrar lives a stout graduate, who has been lame from his birth, but who has not his equal in the world for pleasantry. Volumnius, so highly spoken of by Cicero for his delicate yet pungent wit, was a fool to him. He is known throughout Madrid as 'the bachelor Donoso,' or 'the facetious graduate;' and his company is sought by old and young, at the court and in the town: in short, wherever there is, or should be, conviviality, he is so much the rage, that he has discharged his cook, as he never dines at home; to which he seldom returns until long after midnight. He is at present with the marquis of Alcazinas, who is indebted for this visit to chance only." "How, to chance?" interrupted Leandro. "Why," replied the Demon, "this morning, about noon, the graduate's door was besieged by at least half-a-dozen carriages, each sent for the especial honour of securing his society. The bachelor received the assembled pages in his apartment, and, displaying a pack of cards, thus addressed them:--'My friends, as it is impossible for me to dine in six places at one time, and as it would not appear polite to show an undue preference, these cards shall decide the matter. Draw! I will dine with the king of clubs.'"

"What object," said Don Cleophas, "has yonder cavalier, who is sitting at a door on the other side of the street? Is he waiting for some pretty waiting-woman to usher him to his lady's chamber?" "No, no," answered Asmodeus; "he is a young Castilian, whose modesty exceeds his love; so, after the fashion of the gallants of antiquity, he has come to pass the night at his mistress's portal. Listen to the twang of that wretched guitar, with which he accompanies his tender strains! On the second floor you may behold his inamorata: she is weeping as she hears him;--but it is for the absence of his rival.

"You observe that new building, which is divided into two wings. One is occupied by the proprietor, the old gentleman whom you see now pacing the apartment, now throwing himself into an easy chair." "He is evidently immersed in some grand project," said Zambullo: "who is he? If one may judge by the splendour which is displayed in his mansion, he is a grandee of the first order." "Nevertheless," said Asmodeus, "he is but an ancient clerk of the treasury, who has grown old in such lucrative employment as to enable him to amass four millions of reals. As he has some compunctions of conscience for the means by which all this wealth has been acquired, and as he expects shortly to be called upon to render his account in another world, where bribery is impracticable, he is about to compound for his sins in this, by building a monastery; which done, he flatters himself that peace will revisit his heart. He has already obtained the necessary permission; but, as he has resolved that the establishment shall consist of monks who are extremely chaste, sober, and of the most Christian humility, he is much embarrassed in the selection. He need not build a very extensive convent.

"The other wing is inhabited by a fair lady, who has just retired to rest after the luxury of a milk bath. This voluptuary is widow of a knight of the order of Saint James, who left her at his death her title only; but fortunately her charms have secured for her valuable friends in the persons of two members of the council of Castile, who generously divide her favours and the expenses of her household."

"Hark!" cried the Student; "surely I hear the cries of distress. What dreadful misfortune has occurred?" "A very common one," said the Demon: "two young cavaliers have been gambling in a hell (the name is a scandal on the infernal regions), which you perceive so brilliantly illuminated. They quarrelled upon an interesting point of the game, and I naturally drew their swords to settle it: unluckily, they were equally skilful with their weapons, and are both mortally wounded. The elder is married, which is unfortunate; and the younger an only son. The wife and father have just come in time to receive their last sighs; and it is their lamentations that you hear. 'Unhappy boy,' cries the fond parent over the still breathing body of his son, 'how often have I conjured thee to renounce this dreadful vice!--how often have I warned thee it would one day cost thee thy life. Heaven is my witness, that the fault is none of mine!' Men," added the Demon, "are always selfish, even in their griefs. Meanwhile the wife is in despair. Although her husband has dissipated the fortune she brought him on their marriage; although he has sold, to maintain his shameful excesses, her jewels, and even her clothes, not a word of reproach escapes her lips. She is inconsolable for her loss. Her grief is vented in frantic exclamations, mixed with curses on the cards, and the devil who invented them; on the place in which her husband fell, and on the people who surround her, and to whom she fondly attributes his ruin."

"How much to be lamented," interrupted the Student, "is the love of gaming which possesses so large a portion of mankind; in what an awful state of excitement does it plunge its victims. Heaven be praised! I am not included in their legion." "You are in high feather," replied the Demon, "in another, whose exploits are not much more ennobling, and scarcely less dangerous. Is the conquest of a courtezan a glory worth achievement? Is the possession of charms common to a whole city worth the peril of a life? Man is an amusing animal! The vision of a mole would enable him to discover the vices of his fellows, while that of the vulture could scarce detect a folly of his own. But let us turn to another affecting spectacle. You can discern, in the house just beyond the one we have been contemplating, a fat old man extended on a bed: he is a canon, who is now in a fit of apoplexy. The two persons, whom you see in his room, are said to be his nephew and niece: they are too much affected by his situation to be able to assist him; so, are securing his valuable effects. By the time this is accomplished, he will be dead; and they will be sufficiently recovered, and at leisure, to weep over his remains.

"Close by, you may perceive the funeral of two brothers; who, seized with the same disorder, took equally successful but different means of ensuring its fatality. One of them had the most utter confidence in his apothecary; the other eschewed the aid of medicine: the first died because he took all the trash his doctor sent him; the last because he would take nothing." "Well! that is very perplexing," said Leandro; "what is a poor sick devil to do?" "Why," replied Asmodeus, "that is more than the one who has the honour of addressing you can determine. I know, for certain, that there are remedies for most ills; but I am not so sure that there are good physicians to administer them when necessary."

"And now I have something more amusing to unriddle. Do you not hear a frightful din in the next street? A widow of sixty was married this morning to an Adonis of seventeen; and all the merry fellows of that part of the town have assembled to celebrate the wedding by a concert of pots and pans, marrow-bones and cleavers." "You told me," said the Student, "that these matches were under your control: at all events, you had no hand in this." "No, truly," answered the Demon, "not I. Had I been free, I should not have meddled with them. The widow had her scruples; and has married for no better reason than that she may enjoy, without remorse, the pleasures she so dearly loves. These are not the unions I care to form; I prefer troubling people's consciences to setting them at rest."

"Notwithstanding this charming serenade," said Zambullo, "it seems to me that it is not the only concert performing in the neighbourhood." "No," said the cripple; "in a tavern in the same street, a lusty Flemish captain, a chorister of the French opera, and an officer of the German guard are singing a trio. They have been drinking since eight in the morning; and each deems it a duty to his country, to see the others under the table."

"Look for a moment on the house which stands by itself, nearly opposite to that of the apoplectic canon: you will see three very pretty but very notorious courtezans enjoying themselves with as many young courtiers." "They are, indeed, lovely!" exclaimed Don Cleophas. "I am not surprised that they should be notorious: happy are the lovers who possess them! They seem, however, very partial to their present companions: I envy them their good fortune." "Why, you are very green!" replied the Demon: "their faces are not disguised with greater skill than are their hearts. However prodigal of their caresses, they have not the slightest tenderness for their foolish swains; their affection is bounded to the purses of their lovers. One of them has just secured the promise of a liberal establishment; and the others are prepared with settlements which they are in expectation of securing ere they part. It is the same with them all. Men vainly ruin themselves for the sex: gold buys not love. The well-paid mistress soon treats her lover as a husband: that is a rule which I found necessary to establish in my code of intrigue. But we will leave these fools to taste the pleasures they so dearly purchase; while their valets, who are waiting in the street, console themselves with the pleasing anticipation of enjoying them gratis."

"Tell me," interrupted Leandro Perez, "what is passing in that splendid mansion on the left. The house is filled with well-dressed cavaliers and ladies; and all seems dancing and conviviality. It is indeed a joyous festival." "It is another wedding," said Asmodeus; "and happy as they now are, it is not three days since that house witnessed the deepest affliction. It is a story worth hearing: it is rather long, certainly; but it will repay your patience." The Devil then began as follows.

CHAPTER IV
STORY OF THE LOVES OF THE COUNT DE BELFLOR AND LEONORA DE CESPEDES.

Leonora de Cespedes was passionately beloved by the young Count de Belflor, one of the most distinguished nobles of the court. He had, however, no thoughts of suing for her hand; the daughter of a private gentleman might command his love, but had no pretensions in his eyes to rank above his mistress; and such was the honour he designed for her.

Accordingly, he followed her everywhere; and lost no opportunity of testifying by his glances the extent of his affection for her person; but he was unable to converse with her, or even to communicate by letter, so incessantly and vigilantly was she guarded by an austere duenna, the lady Marcella. He was almost in despair; yet, incited by the obstacles which were thus opposed to his desires, he was constantly occupied in devising means for their attainment, and for deceiving the Argus who so carefully watched his Io.

In the meanwhile, Leonora had perceived the attention with which the Count regarded her; and flattered by that first homage, so delightful to the unworn heart, she soon yielded to the soft persuasion of his eyes, and insensibly formed for him a passion as violent as his own. The flames of love are seldom kindled at the altar but they burn the temple. I did not, however, fan those thus lighted in her bosom, for the magician had put a stopper on my operations; but Nature, and woman's nature especially, is generally potent enough in such cases, without my assistance. Indeed, I doubt if she does not manage these matters best by herself; the only difference in our modes of procedure being, that Nature saps the heart by slow degrees, while I love to carry it by storm.

Affairs were in this posture, when Leonora, and her eternal governante, going one morning to church, were accosted by an old woman, carrying in her hand one of the largest chaplets ever framed by hypocrisy. "Heaven bless you!" said she, addressing herself, with a saintly smile, to the duenna, "the peace of God be with you! Have I not the honour of speaking to the lady Marcella, the chaste widow of the lamented Signor Martin Rosetta?" "You have," replied the governante. "How fortunate!" exclaimed the old hypocrite; "I have a relation, at this moment lying at my house, who would see you ere he dies. He was intimately acquainted with your dear husband, and has matters of the utmost importance to communicate to you. It is only three days since he arrived in Madrid, from Flanders, for the express purpose of seeing you; but scarcely had he entered my house when he was stretched on a bed of sickness, and he has now, I fear, but a few hours to live. Let us hasten, while there is yet time, to soothe the pangs of his passing spirit: a few steps will bring us to his side."

The wary duenna, who had seen enough of the world to be suspicious of the best even of her own sex, still, however, hesitated to follow: which the old lady perceiving, "My dear lady Marcella," said she, "surely you do not doubt me. You must have heard of La Chichona. Why! the licentiate Marcos de Figuerna and the bachelor Mira de Mesqua would answer for me as for their grandmothers. If I desire that you accompany me to my house, it is for your good only. Heaven forbid that I should touch the smallest portion of that which is your due, and which my poor relation is so anxious to repay to the wife of his friend!" At the word "repay," the lady Marcella hesitated no longer: "Let us go, my child," said she to Leonora; "we will see this good woman's relation;--to visit the sick is among the first of our duties." "Verily," said the Demon, "charity does cover a multitude of sins!"

They soon arrived at the house of La Chichona, who introduced them to a mean apartment, where they found a man in bed: he had a long beard, and if he were not really desperately ill, he at least appeared to be so. "See, cousin!" said the old woman, presenting the governante; "behold the person whom you sought so anxiously; this is the lady Marcella, the respected widow of your friend Rosetta." At these words, the old man raised himself on his pillow with apparent difficulty; and, making signs for the duenna to approach him, said with a feeble voice,--"Heaven be praised, for its mercy in permitting me to live till now!--to see you, my dear lady, was all that I desired upon earth. Indeed, I feared to die, without the satisfaction of seeing you, and of rendering into your hands the hundred ducats which your late husband, my dearest friend, so kindly lent me in my dire necessity, at Bruges, when but for that assistance my honour had been for ever lost:--but you must have often heard of me and my adventures."

"Alas! no," replied Marcella, "he never mentioned it to me. God rest his soul! he was ever so generous as to forget the services he rendered to his friends; and so far from boasting of such kindnesses as these, I can declare that I even never heard of his doing a good action in his life." "His was indeed a noble mind," replied the sick man, "as I have perhaps better reason to know than most persons; and to prove this to you I must relate the history of the unfortunate affair from which his liberality so happily released me. But as I shall have to speak of things which should be disclosed to no other ears than thine, honourable as they are to the memory of my deceased friend, it were better that we should be alone."

"Oh, certainly!" cried Chichona, "though it would delight me to hear of the good Rosetta, whom you are always praising, we will retire to my closet;" saying which, she led Leonora into the next apartment. No sooner had she done so, and closed the door, than without ceremony the old woman thus addressed her companion:--"Charming Leonora, our moments are too precious to be wasted. You know the young Count de Belflor, at least by sight. Need I say how long he has loved you, and how ardently he desires to tell you so? Driven to despair by the vigilance and austerity of Marcella, he has had recourse to my assistance to procure him an interview; and I, who could refuse nothing to so handsome a cavalier, have dressed up his valet as the sick man you have just seen, that I might engage your governante's attention and bring you hither."

As she finished speaking, the Count, who was concealed by the drapery of a little window, discovered himself, and, falling at the feet of Leonora: "Madam," said he, "pardon the stratagem of a lover, who could no longer conceal from you the passion that is destroying the life to which it alone gives value:--but for this good woman's kindness, I had perished in despair." These words, uttered with respectful earnestness, by a man whose appearance was far from displeasing, affected, while they perplexed Leonora, and she remained for some time speechless. But at length recovering herself, she looked, or endeavoured to look, haughtily on her prostrate lover, and replied: "Truly you are deeply indebted to your obliging confidante for this attention, but I am not so sure that I have equal reason to be thankful, or that you will gain by her kindness the object you desire."

In saying these words, she moved towards the door; but the Count, gently detaining her, exclaimed: "Stay, adorable Leonora! deign to listen to me but for an instant. Be not alarmed! my affection for you is pure as your own thoughts. I feel that the artifice to which I have descended must revolt you; but consider how vainly I have striven by more honourable means to address you. You cannot be ignorant that for many months, at the church, in the public walk, at the theatre, I have vainly sought to confirm with my lips that passion which my eyes could not disguise. Alas! while I implore pardon for a crime to which the cruelty of the merciless duenna has compelled me, let me also entreat your pity for the torments I have endured; and judge, by the charms which your happy mirror discloses, of the extent of his wretchedness who is banished from their sight."

Belflor did not fail to accompany these words with all the arts of persuasion commonly practised with so much success by my devotees: tender looks, heart-broken sighs, and even a few tears were not wanting; and Leonora was of course affected. Despite herself, she began to feel those little flutterings of the heart, which are the usual preludes of capitulation with woman; but far from yielding without a struggle to her tenderness, or pity, or weakness, the more sensible she became of treason in the garrison, the more hastily she resolved to vacate the place. "Count," she exclaimed, "it is in vain you tell me this. I will listen no longer. Do not attempt to detain me: let me leave a house in which my honour is exposed to suspicion; or my cries shall alarm the neighbourhood, and expose your audacity which has dared to insult me." This she uttered with so resolute an air that Chichona, who was on very punctilious terms with the police, prayed the Count not to push matters to extremity. Finding his entreaties useless, he released Leonora, who hastened from the apartment, and, what never happened to any maiden before, left it as she had entered it.

"Let us quit this dangerous house," said Leonora, on rejoining her governante: "finish this idle talk,--we are deceived." "What ails you, child?" cried Marcella in reply; "and why should we leave this poor man so hastily?" "I will tell you," said Leonora; "but let us fly: every instant I remain here but adds to my affliction." However desirous was the duenna to learn the cause of her ward's anxiety, she saw that the best way to be satisfied was to yield to her entreaties; and they quitted the apartment with a celerity which quite discomposed the stately governante, leaving Chichona, the Count, and his valet as much disconcerted as a company of comedians, when the curtain falls on a wretched farce, which the presiding deities of the pit have consigned to a lower deep.

When Leonora found herself safely in the street, she related, as well as her extreme agitation, and Marcella's exclamations of astonishment, would permit, all that had passed in the chamber with the Count and Chichona. "I must confess, child," said the duenna, when they had reached home, "that I am exceedingly mortified to hear what you have just been telling me. To think that I have been the dupe of that wicked woman! You will allow, however, that I was not without my doubts. Why did I yield them? I should have been suspicious of so much kindness and honesty. I have committed a folly which is absolutely inexcusable in a person of my sagacity and experience. Ah! why did you not tell me this in her presence? I would have torn her eyes out: I would have loaded the Count de Belflor with reproaches for his perfidy: and as for the scoundrel with his ducats and his beard, he should not have had a hair left on his head. But I will return, this instant, with the money which I have received as a real restitution; and if I find them still together, they shall not have waited for nothing." So saying, the enraged widow of the generous Rosetta folded her mantilla around her, and left Leonora to weep over the treachery of mankind.

Marcella found the Count with Chichona, in despair at the failure of his design. Most of my pupils, in his place, would have been abashed at seeing her: it is extraordinary what scruples I have to overcome. But Belflor was of another stamp: to a thousand good qualities, he added that of yielding implicit obedience to my inspirations. When he loved, nothing could exceed the ardour with which he followed the devoted object of his affections; and though naturally what the world calls an honourable man, he was then capable of violating the most sacred duties for the attainment of his desires. No sooner, therefore, did he perceive Marcella, than, as he saw that their fulfilment could only be completed through the duenna's agency, he resolved to spare nothing to win her to his interests. He shrewdly guessed that, rigidly virtuous as the lady appeared, she, like her betters, had her price; and as he was disposed to bid pretty liberally, you will own he did no great injustice to a duenna's fidelity: for so rare a commodity will only be found where lovers are not over-rich, or not sufficiently liberal.

The instant Marcella entered the room, and perceived the three persons she sought, her tongue went as though possessed; and while she poured a torrent of abuse on the Count and Chichona, she sent the restitution flying at the head of the valet. The Count patiently endured the storm; and throwing himself on his knees before the duenna, to render the scene more moving, he pressed her to take back the purse she had rejected; and offering to add to it a thousand pistoles, he besought her compassion on his sufferings. As Marcella had never before been so earnestly entreated, it is no wonder that she was, on this occasion, not inexorable: her invectives, therefore, speedily ceased; and on comparing the tempting sum now offered to her, with the paltry recompence she expected from Don Luis de Cespedes, she was not slow in discovering that it would be much more profitable to turn Leonora from her duty, than to keep her in its path. Accordingly, after some little affectation, she again received the purse, accepted the offer of the thousand pistoles, promised to assist the Count in his designs, and departed at once to labour for their accomplishment.

As she knew Leonora to be strictly virtuous, she was extremely cautious of exciting the least suspicion of her intelligence with the Count, lest the plot should be discovered to Don Luis, her father; so, desirous of skilfully effecting her ruin, she thus addressed her on her return: "My dear Leonora, I have revenged myself on the wretches who deceived us. I found them quite confounded at your virtuous resolution; and, threatening the infamous Chichona with your father's resentment, and the most rigorous severity of the law, I bestowed on the Count de Belflor all the insulting epithets that my anger could suggest. I warrant that the Signor will make no more attempts of this kind on you; and that henceforth his gallantries will cease to engage my attention. I thank Heaven that, by your firmness, you have escaped the snare that was laid for you. I could weep for joy to think that the deceiver has gained nothing by his stratagem; for these noble signors make it their amusement to seduce the young and innocent. Indeed, the greater part even of those who pique themselves on their honourable conduct have no scruples on this point, as though it were no disgrace to carry ruin into virtuous families. Not that I think the Count absolutely of this character, nor even that he intends studiously to deceive you: we should not judge too harshly of our neighbours; and perhaps, after all, he meant you honourably. Although his rank would give him pretensions to the hand of the noblest at our court, your beauty may yet have induced him to resolve on marriage with yourself. In fact, I recollect that in his answers to my reproaches, which I heeded not at the time, I might have perceived something of the sort."

"What say you, dear Marcella?" interrupted Leonora. "If that were his intention, he would have sought me of my father, who would never have refused his daughter to a person of his rank." "What you say is perfectly just," replied the governante, "and I am quite of your opinion; the Count's proceedings are certainly suspicious, or rather his designs cannot be good: for a trifle, I would return and scold him again." "No, good Marcella," replied Leonora, "we had better forget the past, and revenge ourselves by contempt." "Very true," said the duenna; "I believe that is the best plan: you are more prudent than myself. But, after all, may we not do the Count injustice? Who knows that he has not been actuated by the purest and most delicate motives? It is possible that, before obtaining your father's consent, he may have resolved to deserve and to please you; to render your union more delightful by first gaining your heart. If that were so, child, would it be a very great sin to listen to him? Tell me your thoughts, love; you know my affection: does your heart incline towards the Count, or would it be very disagreeable to marry such a man?"

To this malicious question, the too-sincere Leonora replied, with down-cast eyes, and face suffused with blushes, by avowing that she had no aversion to the Count; but, as modesty prevented her explaining herself more openly, the duenna still pressed her to conceal nothing from her; and at last succeeded, by affected tenderness, in obtaining a full confession of her love. "Dearest Marcella," said the unsuspicious girl, "since you desire me to speak to you without disguise, I must confess that Belflor has appeared to me not unworthy of my love. I was struck by his appearance; and I have heard him so much praised, that I could not remain insensible to the affection he displayed for me. Your watchful care to guard me from his addresses has cost me many a sigh: nay, I will own I have in secret wept his absence; and repaid with my tears the sufferings your vigilance has caused him. Even at this moment, instead of hating him for the insult he has offered to my honour, my heart against my will excuses him, and throws his fault on your severity."

"My child," said the governante, "since you give me reason to believe that his attentions are pleasing to you, I will endeavour to secure this lover." "I am very sensible," replied Leonora, "of the kindness you intend me. It is not that the Count holds the first place at court; were he but an honourable private gentleman, I should prefer him to all others upon earth, but let us not flatter ourselves: Belflor is a noble signor, destined, without doubt, for one of the richest heiresses in our kingdom. Let us not expect that he would descend to ally himself with Don Luis, who has but a moderate fortune to offer with his daughter. No, no," she added, "he entertains for me no such favourable thoughts: he thinks not of me as one worthy to bear his name, but seeks only my dishonour."

"Ah! wherefore," said the duenna, "will you insist he loves you not well enough to seek your hand? Love daily works much greater miracles. One would imagine, to hear you, that Heaven had made some infinite distinction between you and the Count. Do yourself more justice, Leonora! He would not condescend, in uniting his destiny with yours. You are of an ancient and noble family, and your alliance would never call a blush upon his cheek. However, you love him," continued she; "and I must therefore see him, and sound him on the subject; and if I find his designs as honourable as they should be, I will indulge him with some slight hopes." "Not for the world!" cried Leonora; "on no account would I have you seek him: should he but suspect my knowledge of your proceedings, he must cease even to esteem me." "Oh! I am more cunning than you think me," answered Marcella. "I shall begin by accusing him of a design to seduce you. He of course will not fail to defend himself; I shall listen to his excuses, and shall mark the event: in short, my dear child, leave it to me; I will be as careful of your honour as of my own."

Towards night, the duenna left the house, and found Belflor watching in the neighbourhood. She informed him of her conversation with his mistress, not forgetting to boast of the address with which she had elicited from Leonora the confession of her love. Nothing could more agreeably surprise the Count than this discovery; and accordingly his gratitude was displayed in the most ardent manner; that is to say, he promised to Marcella the thousand ducats on the morrow, and to himself the most complete success of his enterprise; well knowing, as he did, that a woman prepossessed is half seduced. They then separated, extremely well satisfied with each other, and the duenna returned to her home.

Leonora, who had waited for her with extreme anxiety, timidly inquired if she brought any news of the Count. "The best news you could hear," replied the governante. "I have seen him, and I can assure you of the purity of his intentions: he declared that his only object is to marry you; and this he confirmed by every oath that man holds sacred. I did not, however, as you may suppose, yield implicitly to these protestations. 'If you are sincere,' said I to him, 'why do you not at once apply to Don Luis, her father?' 'Ah! my dear Marcella,' replied he, without appearing in the least embarrassed by this question, 'could you, even, approve that, without assuring myself of Leonora's affection, and following, blindly, the dictates of a devouring passion, I should seek her of Don Luis as a slave? No! her happiness is dearer to me than my own desires; and I have too nice a sense of honour, even to endanger that happiness by an indiscreet avowal.'

"While he thus spoke," continued the duenna, "I observed him with extreme attention; and employed all my experience to discover in his eyes if he were really possessed of all the love that he expressed. What shall I say?--He appeared to me penetrated by the truest love; I felt elated with joy, which I took good care, however, to conceal: nevertheless, when I felt persuaded of his sincerity, I thought that, in order to secure for you so important a conquest, it would be but proper to give him some faint idea of your feelings towards him. 'Signor,' said I, 'Leonora has no aversion for you; I know that she esteems you; and, as far as I can judge, her heart would not be grieved by your addresses.' 'Great God,' he cried, transported with delight, 'what do I hear? Is it possible, that the charming Leonora should be disposed so favourably towards me? What do I not owe to you, kindest Marcella, for thus relieving me from such torturing suspense? I am the more rejoiced, too, that this should be announced by you;-- you, who have ever opposed my love; you, who have inflicted on me such lengthened suffering. But, my dear Marcella, complete my bliss! let me see my divine Leonora, and pledge to her my faith; let me swear, in your presence, to be hers only for ever.'

"To all these expressions of his devotion," continued the governante, "he added others still more touching. At last, my dear child, he entreated me in so pressing a manner to procure for him a secret interview, that I could not forbear promising he should see you." "Ah! why have you done so?" exclaimed Leonora, with emotion. "How often have you told me, that a virtuous girl should ever shun such secret conversations,--always wrong, and almost always dangerous?" "Certainly," replied the duenna, "I acknowledge to have said so, and a very good maxim it is; but you are not obliged to adhere to it strictly on this occasion; for you may look upon the Count as your husband." "He is not so yet," said Leonora, "and I ought not to see him until my father permits his addresses."

Marcella, at this moment, repented of having imbued the mind of her pupil with those notions of propriety which she found so much trouble to overcome. Determined, however, at any rate to effect her object, she thus recommenced her attack: "My dear Leonora! I am proud to witness so much virtuous delicacy. Happy fruit of all my cares! You have truly profited by the lessons I have taught you. I am delighted with the result of my labours. But, child, you have read rather too literally; you construe my maxims too rigidly; your susceptibility is indeed somewhat prudish. However much I pique myself on my severity, I do not quite approve of that precise chastity which arms itself indifferently against guilt or innocence. A girl ceases not to be virtuous who yields her ear only to her lover, especially when she is conscious of the purity which chastens his desires; and she is then no more wrong in responding to his love, than she is for her sensibility to the passion. Rely upon me, Leonora; I have too much experience, and am too much interested in your welfare, to suffer you to take a step that might be prejudicial to it."

"But where would you have me see the Count?" said Leonora. "In this room, to be sure," replied the duenna. "Where could you see him so safely? I will introduce him to-morrow evening." "You are not surely serious, Marcella!" exclaimed Leonora. "What! think you I would permit a man----" "To be sure you will!" interrupted the duenna; "there is nothing so wonderful in that, as you imagine. It happens daily; and would to heaven that every damsel who receives such visits, had desires as pure as those by which you are animated! Besides, what have you to fear? shall not I be with you?" "Alas!" said Leonora, "should my father surprise us!" "Do not trouble yourself about that," replied Marcella. "Your father is perfectly satisfied as to your conduct: he knows my fidelity, and would not do me so much wrong as to suspect it." Poor Leonora, thus artfully instigated by the duenna, and secretly moved by her own feelings, could withstand no longer; and at last yielded, although unwillingly, to her governante's proposal.

The Count was soon informed of Marcella's success, of which he was so well satisfied, that he at once gave her five hundred pistoles, and a ring of equal value. The duenna, finding his promises so well performed, was determined to be as scrupulously exact in the fulfilment of her own; and, accordingly, on the following night, when she felt assured that every one in the house was fast asleep, she fastened to the balcony a silken ladder, which the Count had provided, and introduced his lordship to the chamber of his mistress.

In the meanwhile, the fair Leonora was immersed in reflections of the most painfully agitating nature. Notwithstanding her affection for the Count, and despite her governante's assurances, she bitterly reproached herself for her weakness, in yielding a consent to an interview which she still felt was in violation of her duty; nor could a knowledge of the purity of her intentions bring comfort to her bosom. To receive, by night, in her apartment, a man whose love was unsanctioned by her parent, and not certainly known even by herself, now appeared to her not only criminal, but calculated to degrade her in the estimation of her lover also; and this last thought tortured her almost to madness, when that lover entered.

He threw himself on his knees before her; and, apparently penetrated by love and gratitude, thanked her for that confidence in his honour, which had permitted this visit, and assured her of his determination to merit it, by shortly espousing her. However, as he was not as explicit upon this point as Leonora desired, "Count," said she to him, "I am too anxious to believe that you have no other views than those you express to me; but whatever assurances you may offer must always appear to me suspicious, so long as my father is ignorant of your designs, and has not ratified them by his consent."

"Madam," replied Belflor, "that would have been long since demanded by me, had I not feared to have obtained it at the sacrifice of your repose." "Alas!" said Leonora, "I do not reproach you that you have not yet sought Don Luis,--I cannot but be sensible of your delicacy; but nothing now restrains you, and you must at once resolve to see my father, or never to see me more."

"What do I hear?" exclaimed the Count,--"never to see you more! Beauteous Leonora! how little sensible are you to the charms of love! Did you know how to love like me, you would delight in secret to receive my vows; and, for some time at least, to conceal them from your father as from all the world. Oh! who can paint the charms of that mysterious intercourse, in which two hearts indulge, united by a passion as intense as pure." "It may have charms for you," replied Leonora; "to me, such intercourse would bring but sorrow: this refinement of tenderness but ill becomes a virtuous maiden. Speak not to me of such impure delights! Did you esteem me, you had not dared to do so; and were your intentions such as you would persuade me, you would, from your soul, reproach me that I could listen to you with patience. But, alas!" she added, while tears filled her eyes, "my weakness alone has exposed me to this outrage: I have indeed deserved it, that I see you here."

"Adorable Leonora!" cried the Count, "you wrong my love most cruelly! Your virtue, too scrupulous, is causelessly alarmed. What! can you conceive that, because I have been so happy as to prevail on you to favour my passion, I should cease to esteem you? What injustice! No, madam, I know, too well, the value of your kindness; it can never deprive you of my esteem; and I am ready to do as you require me. I will, to-morrow, see Don Luis; and nothing shall be wanting on my part to ensure my happiness: but I cannot conceal from you, that I scarcely indulge a hope." "How!" replied; Leonora, with extreme surprise; "is it possible that my father should refuse me to the Count de Belflor?"--"Ah! it is that very title which gives me cause for alarm. But I see this surprises you: your astonishment, however, will soon cease.

"Only a few days ago," continued he, "the King was pleased to declare his will, that I should marry: you know how these matters are managed at our Court. He has not, however, named the lady for whom I am intended; but has contented himself with intimating that she is one who will do me honour, and that he has set his mind upon our union. As I was then ignorant of your disposition towards me,--for, as you well know, your rigorous severity has never until now, permitted me to divine it,--I did not let him perceive in me any aversion to the accomplishment of his desires. You may now therefore, judge, madam, whether Don Luis would hazard the King's displeasure, by accepting me as his son-in-law."

"No, doubtless," said Leonora; "I know my father well: however desirable he might esteem your alliance, he would not hesitate to renounce it, rather than expose himself to the anger of his Majesty. But, even though my father had consented to our union, we should not be less unfortunate; for, Belflor, how could you possibly bestow on me a hand which the King has destined for another?" "Madam," replied the Count, "I will not disguise that your question embarrasses me. Still, I am not without hope that, by prudent management with the King, and by availing myself of the influence which his friendship for me secures, I should find means to avoid the misfortune which threatens me; and yourself, lovely Leonora, might assist me in so doing, did you but deem me worthy of the happiness of being yours." "I assist you!" she exclaimed; "how could I possibly enable you to avert an union which the King proposes for you?" "Ah! madam," he replied, with impassioned looks, "would you deign to receive my vows of eternal fidelity to you, I should have no difficulty in preserving my faith inviolate, without offending my sovereign. Permit, charming Leonora," he continued, throwing himself at her feet, "permit me to espouse you in the presence of our friend Marcella; she is a witness who will vouch for the sanctity of our engagements. I shall thus escape the hateful bonds they would impose upon me; for, should the King still press me to accept the lady he designs for me, I will prostrate myself before him, and, on my knees, confess how long and ardently my love has been devoted to you, and that we are secretly married. However desirous he may be to unite me with another, he is too gracious to think of tearing me from the object I adore, and too just to offer so grievous an affront to your honourable family.

"What is your opinion, discreet Marcella?" added he, turning towards the governante; "what think you of this project with which love has so opportunely inspired me?" "I am charmed with it," said the duenna; "the rogue, Cupid, is never at a loss for an expedient." "And you, dearest Leonora," resumed the Count, "what do you say to it? Can your heart, always mistrustful, refuse its assent to my proposal?" "No," she replied, "provided my father consent to it; and I do not doubt that he will, when you have explained to him your reasons for secrecy." "You must be very cautious how you consult him upon the subject," interrupted the abominable duenna; "you do not know Don Luis: his notions of honour are too scrupulous to permit him to engage himself with secret amours. The proposal of a private marriage would shock him; besides which, he is too prudent not to foresee the possible consequences of one which interfered with the designs of the King. And, once proposed to him, and his suspicion aroused, his eyes will be constantly upon you; and he will take good care to prevent your marriage, by separating you for ever."

"And I should die with grief and despair," cried our courtier. "But madam," continued he, addressing himself to Marcella, with an air of profound disappointment, "do you really think, then, that there is no chance of Don Luis yielding to our prayer?" "Not the slightest!" replied the governante. "But suppose he should! Exact and scrupulous as he is, he would never consent to the omission of a single religious ceremony on the occasion; and if they are all to be observed in your marriage, the secret will be soon known in Madrid."

"Ah! my dear Leonora," said the Count, taking her hand, and tenderly pressing it within his own, "must we, then, to satisfy a vain notion of decorum, expose ourselves to the frightful danger of an eternal separation? Our happiness is in your hands; since it depends on you alone to bestow yourself on me. A father's consent might, perhaps, spare you some uneasiness; but since our kind Marcella has convinced us of the impossibility of obtaining it, yield yourself, without further scruple, to my innocent desires. Receive my heart and hand; and when the time shall have arrived, that we may inform Don Luis of our union, we shall have no difficulty in satisfying him as to our reasons for its concealment." "Well, Count," said Leonora, "I consent to your not at once speaking to my father, but that you first sound the King upon the subject. Before, however, I receive thus secretly your hand, I would have this done. See his Majesty; tell him even, if necessary, that we are married. Let us endeavour, by this show of confidence,----" "Alas! madam," interrupted Belflor, "what do you ask of me? No, my soul revolts at the thoughts of falsehood. I cannot lie; and you would despise me, could I thus dissemble with the King;--besides, how could I hope for pardon at his hands, should he discover the meanness of which I had been guilty?"

"I should never have done, Signor Don Cleophas," continued the Demon, "were I to repeat word for word all that Belflor said, in order to seduce his lovely mistress; I will only add, that he repeated, without my assistance, all those passionate phrases with which I usually inspire gallants upon similar occasions. But in vain did he swear he would publicly confirm, as soon as possible, the faith which he proposed to pledge in secret: Leonora's virtue was proof against his oaths; and the blushing day, which surprised him while he called Heaven to witness for his fidelity, compelled him to retire less triumphant than he had anticipated."

On the following morning, the duenna, conceiving that her honour, or rather her interest, engaged her not to abandon the enterprise, took an opportunity of reverting to the subject. "Leonora," said she, "I am confounded by what passed last evening; you appear to disdain the Count's affection, or to regard it as inspired by an unworthy motive. Perhaps, however, after all, you remarked something in his person or manner that displeased you?" "No, good governante," replied Leonora; "he never appeared to me more amiable; and his conversation discovered to me a thousand new charms." "If that be the case," said the duenna, "I am still more perplexed. You acknowledge to be strongly prepossessed in his favour, and yet refuse to yield in a point, the absolute necessity of which he has so clearly demonstrated."

"My dear Marcella," replied her ward, "you are wiser, and have had more experience in these matters, than myself; but have you sufficiently reflected on the consequences of a marriage contracted without my father's knowledge?" "Yes, certainly," answered the duenna, "I have maturely considered all that; and I regret to find you oppose yourself, with an obstinacy of which I deemed you incapable, to the brilliant establishment which fortune presents so uselessly. Have a care that your perverseness does not weary and repel your lover; remember that he may discover the inequality of your station and fortune, which his passion overlooks. While he offers you his faith, receive it without hesitation. His word is his bond; there is no tie more sacred with a man of honour, like Belflor: besides, I am witness that he acknowledges you as his wife; and I need not tell you that a testimony like mine would be more than sufficient to condemn a lover who should dare to perjure himself, and attempt to evade a legal contract."

By this and similar conversations, the resolution of the artless Leonora was at last shaken; and the perils which surrounded her were so adroitly concealed by her perfidious governante, that, some days afterwards, she abandoned herself, without further reflection, to the will of the Count. Belflor was introduced nightly, by the balcony, into his mistress's apartment; which he left again before daybreak, when summoned by the duenna.

One morning, the old lady overslept herself; and Aurora had already half opened the golden chambers of the east, when the Count hastily departed, as usual. Unfortunately, in his hurry to descend the ladder, his foot missed, and he fell heavily on the ground.

Don Luis de Cespedes, who slept in the room over Leonora's, had that morning risen earlier than usual to attend to some important engagements; and hearing the noise of Belflor's fall he opened his window to learn whence it proceeded. To his astonishment, he perceived a man just raising himself, with difficulty, from the earth, while Marcella was busily engaged in the balcony with the silken ladder, of which the Count had made such bad use in his descent. Scarcely believing his eyes, and rubbing them to make sure that he was awake, Don Luis stood for some time in amazement; but he was too soon convinced that what he saw was no illusion; and that the light of day, although just breaking, was bright enough to discover to him, too clearly, his disgrace.

Afflicted at this fatal sight, transported by a just wrath, he instantly sought the apartment of Leonora, holding the light by which he had been writing in one hand, and his sword in the other. With a frantic determination of sacrificing his daughter and her governante to his resentment, he struck the door of their chamber violently, and commanded them to admit him. Trembling, they obeyed his summons; when he entered with infuriated looks, and displaying his naked sword: "I come," he cried, "to wash out, in the blood of an infamous child, the stains on the wounded honour of her father; and to punish the crime of a perfidious wretch, who has betrayed his confidence."

They were in a moment on their knees before him; and, as he raised his arm, the trembling duenna exclaimed: "In mercy hold, Signor! Before you inflict on us the punishment you meditate, deign but to listen to me for a moment." "Speak, then, unhappy woman," said Don Luis; "I will retard my vengeance but for the instant you require: speak, I repeat! tell me all the circumstances of my misfortune. But what do I say,--all the circumstances? Alas! I am ignorant but of one; it is, the name of the villain who has dishonoured me." "Signor," replied Marcella, "the cavalier who has just left us is the Count de Belflor." "The Count de Belflor!" repeated Don Luis; "and where did he see my daughter? By what means has he seduced her? On your life, hide nothing from me!" "Signor," replied the governante, "I will relate the whole history to you, with all the sincerity of which I am capable."

She then related, with infinite art, all the conversations she had previously narrated to Leonora, as having passed between herself and the Count; whom she painted in the most flattering colours, as a lover tender, delicate, and sincere, beyond description. As, however, there was no escaping the event in which this heroic love most naturally terminated, she was obliged to avow the truth. But she managed this so adroitly, insisting on the weighty reasons which Belflor had for secrecy in his nuptials, and on the regret he had always expressed for its necessity, that she gradually appeased the fury of her master.

Alain René Le Sage

This she was not slow to perceive; and, to completely soften the old man, she wound up by a peroration that would have done as much honour to a wig as to a gown:--"Signor," said she, "I have thus told you the simple truth: now punish us if you will, and plunge your sword into your daughter's bosom! But what say I? No! Leonora is innocent; she has but followed the faithful counsels of her to whom you confided the guidance of her conduct. It is my heart against which your sword should be directed; it was I who first introduced the Count to her apartment; it is I who formed those ties which bind him to your daughter. I would not perceive the irregularity of his engagement, although unauthorised by you: I saw in him but a son-in-law, whom I was anxious to secure to you; but the channel through which the favours of our Court might reach you. I forgot all but the happiness of Leonora, and the advancement of your family, in the brilliant alliance of the Count. I have erred: the excess of my zeal has made me forgetful of my duty."

While the subtle Marcella was speaking thus, poor Leonora was not sparing of her tears; and her grief appeared so excessive that the good old man could not resist it. He was affected. His anger was changed into compassion; his sword fell on the ground; and, quitting the air of an irritated parent: "Ah! my daughter," he cried, while tears sprung from his aged eyes, like water from the rock of Horeb, "what a fatal passion is love! Alas! you know not yet all the causes it will bring you for affliction. The shame which a father's presence alone excites, can bring tears to your eyes at this moment; but you foresee not the woes which your lover is, perhaps even now, preparing for the future. And you, imprudent Marcella, what have you done? Into what an abyss has your indiscreet zeal for my family plunged us! I allow that an alliance with a man like Belflor might dazzle you, and it is that which alone excuses and saves you; but, miserable that you are, why were you not more cautious with a lover of his station? The greater his credit and favour at court, the more guarded should you have been against his approaches. Should he not scruple to break his faith with my daughter, how shall I avenge the insult? Shall I implore the power of our laws? A person of his rank can easily shelter himself from its severity. I will suppose that, faithful to his oaths, he would abide by his engagements with my daughter: if the King, as you say, has decreed that he shall marry with another, is it likely that our sovereign will fail to be obeyed?"

"Oh! my father," replied Leonora, "that need not alarm us. The Count has assured us that the King would never do so great a violence to his feelings--" "Of which I am convinced," interrupted the duenna; "for, besides that the monarch loves Belflor too much to exercise so great a tyranny upon his favourite, he is of too noble a character to afflict so grievously the valiant Don Luis de Cespedes, who has devoted to the service of the state the best years of his life."

"Heaven grant," exclaimed the old man, sighing, "that all my fears are vain! I will seek the Count, and demand a full explanation of his conduct: the eyes of a father, alarmed for a daughter's welfare, will pierce his very soul. If I find him what I would hope, and what you would persuade me he is, I will pardon what has passed; but," added he firmly, "if in his discourse I discern the perfidy of his heart, you go, both of you, to bewail in retirement, for the rest of your days, the imprudence of which you have been guilty." As he finished, he took up his sword, and retired to his own room, leaving his daughter and her governante to recover themselves from the fright into which this discovery had so unexpectedly thrown them.

Asmodeus was at this moment interrupted in his recital by the Student, who thus addressed him:-- "My dear Devil, interesting as is the history you are relating to me, my eyes have wandered to an object which prevents my listening to you as attentively as I could wish. I see a lady, who is rather good-looking, seated between a young man and a gentleman old enough to be his grandfather. They seem to enjoy the liqueurs which are on the table near them, but what amuses me is, that as from time to time the amorous old dotard embraces his mistress, the deceiver conveys her hand to the lips of the other, who covers it with silent kisses. He is doubtless her gallant." "On the contrary," replied the cripple, "he is her husband, and the old fool is her lover. He is a man of consequence,--no less than a commandant of the military order of Calatrava; and is ruining himself for the lady, whose complaisant husband holds some inferior place at court She bestows her caresses on the sighing knight, for the sake of his gold; and is unfaithful to him in favour of her husband, from inclination."

"That is a marvellously pretty picture," said Zambullo. "The husband of course is French?" "No, no," replied the Demon: "he is a Spaniard. Oh! the good city of Madrid can boast within its walls a fair proportion of such well-bred spouses: still, they do not swarm here as in Paris, which is, beyond contradiction, the most fruitful city of the world in such inhabitants." "I thought so," said Don Cleophas; "but pardon me, Signor Asmodeus, if I have broken the thread of the fair Leonora's story. Continue it, I pray you; it interests me exceedingly; and exhibits such variety in the art of seduction as transports me with admiration."

27

CHAPTER V

CONTINUATION OF THE STORY OF THE LOVES OF THE COUNT DE BELFLOR AND LEONORA DE CESPEDES.

Don Luis, (continued Asmodeus), on returning to his apartment, dressed himself hastily, and, while it was still early, repaired to the Count; who, not suspecting a discovery, was much surprised by this visit. On the old man's entrance, however, Belflor ran to meet him, and, embracing him cordially, exclaimed, "Ah Signor Don Luis; I am delighted to see you. To what do I owe this happiness? Am I so fortunate as to have an opportunity of serving you?" "Signor," replied Don Luis sternly, "I would speak with you alone."

Belflor desired his attendants to withdraw; and as soon as they were seated, "Signor," said Cespedes, "I come to ask of you an explanation of circumstances in which my honour and happiness are deeply interested. I saw you this morning leaving the apartment of my daughter. She has disguised nothing from me: she informed that----" "She has told you that I love her," interrupted the Count, to avoid hearing what he knew could not be very agreeable; "but she can but have feebly described all that I feel for her. I am enchanted with her; she is an adorable creature: beauty, wit, virtue,--nothing is wanting to perfect her charms. I am told you have a son, too, who is finishing his studies at Alcala: does he resemble his sister? If he have her beauty, and have at all inherited the noble bearing of his father, he must be a perfect cavalier. I die with anxiety to see him; and I assure you that I shall be proud to advance his fortunes."

"I am obliged to you for so kind an offer," gravely replied Don Luis; "but to return to the subject of----" "He must enter the service at once," again interrupted the Count: "I charge myself with the care of his interests: he shall not grow old among the crowd of subalterns; on that you may depend." "Answer me, Count!" replied the old man vehemently, "and cease these interruptions. Do you intend, or not, to fulfil the promise----?" "Yes, certainly," interrupted Belflor for the third time; "I engage faithfully to support your son with all the interest I possess: rely on me; I am a man of my word." "This is too much, Count," cried Cespedes, rising: "after having seduced my daughter, you dare thus to insult me! But I also am a noble; and the injury you have done me shall not remain unpunished." In finishing these words, he left the Count, his heart swelling with anger, and his mind tormented with a thousand projects of revenge.

On arriving at home, still greatly agitated, he immediately went to Leonora's apartment, where he found her with Marcella. "It was not without reason," said he, addressing them, "that I was suspicious of the Count: he is a traitor; but I will avenge myself. For you, you shall at once hide your shame within a convent: both of you, prepare to leave this house to-morrow; and thank Heaven that my wrath contents itself with so moderate a punishment." He then left them, to shut himself in his cabinet, that he might maturely reflect on the conduct it would be proper to observe in so delicate a conjuncture.

How poignant was the grief of Leonora, when thus informed of Belflor's perfidy! She remained for some time motionless; a death-like paleness overspread her lovely features; life itself seemed about to abandon her, and she fell senseless into the arms of her governante. The alarmed duenna at first thought that the victim of her intrigues was really dead; but, on perceiving that she still breathed, used every effort to restore her to consciousness, and at last succeeded. Existence, however, had no longer charms for Leonora; and when, somewhat recovered, she unclosed her eyelids, and perceived the officious governante busy about her person, "Cruel Marcella!" she exclaimed, sighing deeply; "wherefore have you drawn me from the happy state in which I was? Then, I felt not the horror of my destiny. Why did you not let me perish? You, who know so well that life henceforth must be but one long misery, why have you sought to preserve it?"

The duenna endeavoured to console her, but her words only added to Leonora's sufferings. "It is in vain you would comfort me," she cried, "I will not hear you: strive not to combat my despair. Rather seek to add to its profundity; you, who have plunged me into the frightful gulph in which all my hopes are swallowed;--you it was who assured me of the Count's sincerity; but for you I had never yielded to my passion for him; I should have insensibly triumphed over it, or at least, he would never have had cause to boast of my weakness. But no! I will not," she continued, "attribute to you my misfortunes; it is myself alone I should accuse. I ought not to have followed your advice, in accepting the faith of a man, without the sanction of my father. However flattering to me were the attentions of Count de Belflor, I should have despised them, rather than have endeavoured to secure them at the price of my honour: I should have mistrusted him, you! Marcella, and myself. For my folly in listening to his perfidious oaths, for the affliction I have caused to the unhappy Don Luis, and for the dishonour I have brought upon my family, I detest myself; and, far from fearing the state of seclusion with which I am menaced, I would willingly conceal my guilt and shame in the most frightful dungeon in the world."

While her grief thus vented itself in exclamations, and tears streamed from her eyes, she frantically tore her clothes, and revenged the injustice of her lover on the beautiful locks which fell around her neck. The duenna, also, to appear in keeping with her mistress's grief, was not sparing of grimaces; she managed to squeeze out some convenient tears, and directed a thousand imprecations against mankind in general, and against Belflor in particular. "Is it possible," she cried, "that the Count, who had all the semblance of amiability and rectitude, should be so great a villain as to have deceived us both? I cannot get over my surprise, or rather, I cannot even yet persuade myself that he is so."

"Indeed," said Leonora, "when I picture him myself at my feet, what maiden could but have confided to so much tenderness,--to his oaths, which he so daringly called on Heaven to witness,--to his boundless transports, which seemed so sincere? His eyes to me discovered a love far more intense than his lips could express; and the very sight of me appeared to charm him:--no, he did not deceive me; I cannot believe it. My father has not spoken to him with sufficient caution; they have quarrelled, and the Count has replied to his reproaches less as the lover than the lord. Still, may I not deceive myself? I will, however, end this horrible suspense. I will write to Belflor,--tell him I expect him here this night: I am resolved he comes to reassure my troubled heart, or to confirm, himself, his treachery."

Marcella loudly applauded this resolution; she even conceived a hope that the Count, all ambitious as he was, might yet be affected by the tears of his Leonora, which could not fail at this interview, and that he might determine on espousing her in truth.

Meanwhile, Belflor, relieved of the presence of Don Luis, was revolving in his mind the probable consequences of the reception he had given to the good old man. He felt certain that all the Cespedes, enraged at the injury he had done their family, would unite to avenge it: this, however, gave him but little trouble; the possible loss of Leonora occasioned him far greater anxiety. She would, he imagined, at once be placed in a convent, or, at least, that she would be carefully guarded from his sight; and that she was consequently lost to him for ever. This thought afflicted him; and he was occupied in devising some means to prevent so great a misfortune, when his valet entered the apartment, and presented a letter which Marcella had placed in his hands. It was from Leonora, and ran as follows:--

"MY STILL DEAREST BELFLOR,

"I shall to-morrow quit the world, to bury myself in a convent. Dishonoured, odious to my family and to myself, such is the deplorable condition to which I am reduced by listening to you. Still I will expect you to-night. In my despair, I seek new tortures: come, and avow to me that your heart disowned the protestations which your lips have made to me; or come to confirm them by your sympathy, which alone can soften the harshness of my destiny. As there may, however, be some danger in this meeting, after what has passed between you and my father, be sure you are accompanied by a friend. Although you have rendered life worthless to me, I cannot cease to interest myself in thine.

"LEONORA."

While the Count perused this letter, which he read over several times, his imagination depicted the situation of Leonora, in colours more sombre even than the reality, and he was deeply affected. He bitterly reflected on his past conduct: reason, probity, honour, all whose laws he had violated in the phrenzy of his passion, now regained their empire in his breast. The blindness which selfishness inflicts upon its victims was dissipated; and as the fevered convalescent blushes for the follies which, in the access of his disorder, he has committed, so was Belflor ashamed of the meanness and artifice of which he had been guilty to satisfy his lust.

"What have I done?" he cried; "wretch that I am, what demon has possessed me? I promised Leonora to espouse her, and called on Heaven to witness for the lie; I falsely told her that the King had designed me for another; lying, treachery, perjury,--I have hesitated at nothing to corrupt innocence itself. What madness! Oh! had I used, to control it, the efforts I have made to gratify my passion! To seduce one of whose beauty and virtue I was unworthy, to abandon her to the wrath of her relations, whom I have equally dishonoured, and to plunge her in misery as a return for the happiness she bestowed on me,--what ingratitude! Ought I not then to repair the injury I have inflicted? Yes, I ought, and I will; my hand shall at the altar fulfil the pledge I gave for it. Who shall oppose me in so righteous a determination? Should her tenderness for me at all prejudice her virtue? No, I know too well what that cost me to vanquish. She yielded less to my love than to her confidence in my integrity, and to my vows of fidelity. But, on the other hand, if I resolve on this marriage, I make a great sacrifice,--I, who may pretend to the heiresses of the richest and most noble houses in the kingdom, shall I content myself with the daughter of a respectable gentleman, of small fortune? What will they think of me at court? They will say that I have made a splendid alliance indeed!"

Belflor, thus divided between love and ambition, knew not how to resolve; but although undetermined whether he should marry Leonora or not, he had no difficulty in making up his mind to see her that evening, and at once directed his valet so to inform Marcella.

Don Luis was all this time in his cabinet, engaged in reflections on the mode he should adopt to vindicate his honour; and he was not a little embarrassed in his choice. To have recourse to the laws, was to publish his disgrace, besides which, he suspected with great reason that justice was likely to be one side, and the judges on the other. Again, he dared not to seek reparation of the King himself; as he believed that prince had views with regard to Belflor which must render such an application useless. There remained, then, but his own sword and those of his friends, and on these he concluded to rely.

In the heat of his resentment, he at first meditated a challenge to the Count; but on consideration of his great age and weakness, he feared to trust his arm; so resolved to confide the matter to his son, whose thrust he thought was likely to be surer than his own. He therefore sent one of his domestics to Alcala, with a letter commanding his son's immediate presence in Madrid, to revenge, as he stated it, an insult offered to the family of the Cespedes.

"This son, Don Pedro, is a cavalier of eighteen years of age, perfectly handsome, and so brave, that he passes at Alcala for the most valiant student of that university; but you know him," added the Devil, "and I need not enlarge on the subject." "I can answer," said Don Cleophas, "for his having all the valour and all the merit that can adorn a gentleman."

"But this young man," resumed Asmodeus, "was not then at Alcala, as his father imagined. Love had brought him also to Madrid, where the object of his passion resided; and where he had met her for the first time, on the Prado, on the occasion of his last visit to his family. Who she was, he knew not: and his fair conquest had exacted of him a pledge that he would take no steps to inform himself on this head,--and although he was as good as his word, it cost him some trouble to keep it. I need hardly add, that she was of higher rank than her lover; and that, wisely mistrusting the discretion and constancy of a student--no offence to your highness--she thought proper to test him as to these necessary qualifications for a suitor, before she disclosed to him her station or name."

His thoughts were, of course, more occupied by his lovely incognita than with the philosophy of Aristotle; and the vicinity of Alcala to Madrid occasioned the youthful Pedro to play truant to his studies as frequent as yourself; but, I must say, with a better excuse than your Donna Thomasa afforded. To conceal from his father, Don Luis, his amorous excursions, he usually lodged at a tavern at the other end of the town, where he passed under a borrowed name; and only went abroad at a certain hour in the morning, that he might repair to a house where the lady, for the love of whom he neglected his Ovid, did him the honour to wait, in company with a trusty female attendant. During the rest of the day he shut himself up in his hotel; but as soon as night was come, he wandered fearlessly throughout the city.

He happened one evening, as he was traversing a bye-street, to hear the sound of instruments and voices, which attracted his attention, and he stopped to listen. It was a serenade, and tolerably performed; but the cavalier, who was drunk, and naturally brutish, no sooner perceived our student than he hurried towards him, and, without preface,--"Friend," said he, with an insolent air, "make yourself scarce; or your curiosity may find you more than you expect." "I would have withdrawn," replied Don Pedro, proudly, "had you requested me to do so with civility; but I shall now stay, to teach you better manners." "We shall see, then," said the serenading gallant, drawing his sword, "which of us two will give place to the other."

Don Pedro also drew his sword, their weapons were crossed in a moment, and a furious combat ensued; but although the Student's adversary was not wanting in skill, he could not parry a mortal thrust of Don Pedro, and fell dead upon the pavement. The musicians, who had already quitted their instruments, or stopped their singing, and had drawn their swords to protect their patron, now came in a body to avenge his death, and attacked Don Pedro all together. He, however, gave them satisfactory proofs of what he could do upon occasion; for, besides parrying, with surprising dexterity, all the thrusts which they designed for him, he dealt furiously among them, and found work for them all to protect themselves.

Still, they were so numerous, and apparently so determined on the Student's death, that, skilful as he was with his weapon, they would have most probably accomplished their object, had not the Count de Belflor, who was accidentally passing through the street, come to his assistance. The Count was of too noble a nature to see so many armed men striving against one man to hesitate upon the part he should take. His sword was therefore instantly directed against the musicians, and with so much vigour that they were soon put to flight, some wounded, and the others for fear they should be.

The field thus cleared, the Student, with what breath remained to him, began to express his sense of the valuable service he had so seasonably received; but Belflor at once stopped him: "Not a word, my dear Sir," said he; "are you not wounded?" "No," replied Don Pedro. "Then let us leave this place at once," said the Count: "I see you have killed your man; and it will be dangerous to stay in his company, lest the officers of justice surprise you." They immediately decamped as quickly as possible, and did not stop until they had gained a street at some distance from the field of battle.

Don Pedro, filled with a natural gratitude, then begged the Count not to conceal from him the name of a person to whom he owed so great an obligation. Belflor made no difficulty in complying with this request; but when in turn he asked that of the Student, the latter, unwilling to discover himself to any person in Madrid, replied, that he was Don Juan de Maros, and that he should eternally bear in his remembrance the debt of gratitude which he owed to the Count.

"Well," said Belflor to him, "I will this night give you an opportunity of repaying it in full. I have an appointment, which is not without risk; and I was about, when I fell in with you, to seek the protection of a friend. However, I know your valour, Don Juan: will you accompany me?" "To doubt it, were to insult me," replied the Student: "I cannot better employ the life you have preserved, than in exposing it in your defence. Go! I am ready to follow you." Accordingly, Belflor conducted Don Pedro to the house of Don Luis, and they both entered, by the balcony, the apartment of Leonora.

Here Don Cleophas interrupted the Devil: "Signor Asmodeus," said he, "impossible! What! not know his own father's house? No, no, no; that will never do." "It was not possible he should know it," replied the Demon; "for it was a new one: Don Luis had lately changed his habitation, and had only taken this house a week before; which was just what Don Pedro did not know, and was what I was just going to tell you when you stopped me. You are too sharp; and have that shocking habit of displaying your intelligence by interrupting people in their stories: get rid of that fault, I pray you."

"Well," continued the Devil, "Don Pedro did not think he was in his father's house; nor did he even perceive that it was Marcella who let him into it; since she received him without a light, in an antechamber, where Belflor requested his companion to remain while he was in the next room with his mistress. To this the Student made no demur; so quietly sat himself down in a chair, with his drawn sword in his hand for fear of surprise, while his thoughts ran on the favours which he suspected love was heaping on the Count, and his wishes that he might be as happy with his incognita,--for although he had no great cause of complaint as to her kindness, still it was not exactly paid after the kind of that of Leonora for the Count."

While he was making, upon this subject, all those pleasing reflections which occur so readily to an impassioned lover, he heard some one endeavouring quietly to open a door, which was not that of The Delights, but one which discovered a light through the keyhole. He rose quickly, and advanced towards it; and, as the door opened, presented the point of his sword to his father; for he it was who entered Leonora's apartments, for the purpose of seeing that the Count was not there. The good old man did not exactly suppose, after what had passed, that his daughter and Marcella would dare to receive him again, which had prevented his assigning to them other chambers; but he had thought it probable that, as they were to go to a nunnery on the following day, they might desire to converse with him, for the last time, ere they left his roof.

"Whoever thou art," said the Student, "enter not this room, or it may cost thee thy life." At these words, Don Luis stared at Don Pedro, who also regarding the old man with attention, they soon recognised each other. "Ah! my son," cried the old man, "with what impatience have I expected you: why did you not inform me of your arrival? Did you fear to disturb my rest? Alas! that is for ever banished, in the cruel situation in which I am placed." "Ah, my father!" said Don Pedro, utterly amazed, "is it you whom I behold? Are not my eyes deceived by some fantastic vision?" "Whence this astonishment?" replied Don Luis; "are you not within your father's house? Have I not, a week ago, informed you where to find me?" "Just Heaven!" cried the Student, "what do I hear?--and this then is my sister's apartment."

As he finished these words, the Count, whom the noise had alarmed, and who expected that his escort was attacked, came out, sword in hand, from Leonora's chamber. No sooner did the old man perceive him than, with fury in his eyes, he pointed to Belflor, and exclaimed to his son,--"There is the villain who has robbed me of my happiness, and who has stained our honour with a mortal taint. Revenge! Let us hasten to punish the traitor!" As he thus vented his rage, he opened his dressing-gown, and drew from beneath it his sword, with which he was about to fall on the Count, when Don Pedro restrained him. "Stay, my father," said he; "moderate, I entreat you, the fury of your wrath: what are you about to do?" "My son," replied the old man, "you withhold my arm. You doubtless think it is too weak to revenge our wrongs. Be it so! Do you then exact full satisfaction for the injury he has done us: it was for this purpose that I summoned you to Madrid. Should you perish, I will take your place; for either shall the Count fall beneath our arms, or he shall take from both of us our lives, after having blasted our reputation."

"My father," said Don Pedro, "I cannot yield to your impatience that which it requires of me. Far from attempting the life of the Count, I am now here to defend it. For that my word is pledged,--to that my honour is assured. Let us depart, Count," continued he, addressing himself to Belflor. "Ah! wretch," interrupted Don Luis, while he surveyed his son with anger and astonishment,--"thus to oppose thyself to a vengeance, which it should be the business of thy life to accomplish! My son, my own son, is leagued, then, with the villain who has corrupted my daughter! But think not to escape my resentment: I will place a sword in the hand of every servant in my house, to punish his treachery and thy despicable meanness."

"Signor," replied Don Pedro, "be more just towards your son. Call him not despicable or mean--he merits not those odious appellations. The Count this night saved my life. He proposed to me, in ignorance of my real name, to accompany him here; and I freely consented to share the perils he might run, without knowing that my gratitude imprudently engaged my arm against the honour of my family. My word is passed, then, here to defend his life; that done, I stand acquitted of my obligation towards him: but I am not the less insensible of the wrong that he has done to you and to us all; and to-morrow you shall find that I will as readily shed his blood, as you behold me now determined to preserve it from your hands."

The Count had witnessed in silence all that passed, so much was he surprised at this extraordinary adventure; he now, however, thus addressed the Student: "It is possible that the injury I have inflicted might be but imperfectly avenged by your sword; I will, therefore, present to you a means much more certain of repairing it. I will confess to you that, until this day, I did not intend to marry Leonora; but I this morning received from her a letter which touched my heart, and her tears have finished what her letter began. The happiness of being united to your sister is now my dearest hope." "But if the King has destined you for another," said Don Luis, "how can you dispense----?" "The King has not troubled himself upon the subject," interrupted Belflor, blushing: "pardon, I beseech you, that fiction, to a man whose reason was deranged by love; it is a crime that the violence of my passion incited me to commit, and which I expiate in avowing to you my shame."

"Signor," replied the old man, "after this frankness, which belongs only to noble minds, I cannot doubt your sincerity. I see, with joy, that you are anxious to repair the injury you have done us; my anger yields to this assurance of your contrition; I will forget it for ever in your arms." He advanced towards the Count, who rushed to meet him, and they embraced each other cordially. Then, turning towards Don Pedro, "And you, false Don Juan," said Belflor,--"you, who have already gained my esteem by your valour, come, let me vow to you a brother's love." Don Pedro received the Count's embraces with a submissive and respectful air, saying, "Signor, in offering to me so valuable a friendship, you secure mine for yourself: rely on me, as one devoted to your service to the last moment of his life."

While these cavaliers were thus discoursing, Leonora was at the door of her chamber, intently listening to every syllable they uttered. She had been, at the first, tempted to discover herself, and to throw herself in the midst of their swords; but fear, and Marcella, had withheld her. But when the adroit duenna saw that matters were arranging very amicably, she guessed that the presence of her mistress, and her own, would spoil nothing. Accordingly, she appeared, her handkerchief in one hand and her ward in the other; and, with tears in their eyes, they prostrated themselves before Don Luis. Neither of them, indeed, felt perfectly assured; for they recollected the surprise of the previous night, and feared the old man's reproaches for this renewal of their disobedience. However, raising Leonora,--"My child," said he, "dry your tears; I will not upbraid you now: since your lover is disposed to keep the faith he has sworn to you, it is fitting that I should forget the past."

"Yes, Signor Don Luis," interrupted Belflor, "I will indeed keep my faith with Leonora; and as some amends for the insult I had intended, as the fullest satisfaction I can give to you, and as a pledge of that friendship I have vowed to Don Pedro, I offer him in marriage my sister Eugenia." "Signor!" cried Don Luis, "how can I express my satisfaction at the honour you confer upon my son? Was ever father happier than myself? You overpay me, in joy, for the grief you have caused me."

Though the old man was charmed with the Count's proposals, I cannot say as much for his son. Being sincerely taken with love for his incognita, he was so overcome with surprise and chagrin at Belflor's offer, that he had not a word to say for himself; when the latter, who did not observe his embarrassment, took leave, stating that he should at once order the necessary preparations for this double union, and that he was impatient to be bound to them eternally, by ties so endearing.

After his departure, Don Luis left Leonora with the duenna, taking with him his son, who, when they had reached his father's apartment, said, with all the frankness of a student: "Signor, do not insist, I pray you, on my marriage with the Count's sister; it is enough for the honour of our family, that he should espouse Leonora." "What! my son," replied the old man, "can you have any objection to an union with Eugenia de Belflor?" "Yes, my father," said Don Pedro; "I must confess to you, that union would prove to me the most cruel of punishments; and I will not disguise from you the reason. I love, or, rather, I adore another: for the last six months she has listened to my vows: and now, on her alone depends the happiness of my life."

"How miserable is the condition of a father!" exclaimed Don Luis: "how rarely does he find his children disposed to do as he desires them. But who is this lady that has made such deep impression on your heart?" "That, I do not yet know," replied Don Pedro. "She has promised to inform me of her name when I shall have satisfied her of my constancy and discretion; but I doubt not she does honour to one of the noblest houses of Spain."

Alain René Le Sage

"And you think then," said the old man, changing his tone, "that I shall be so obliging as to sanction this romantic love!--that I shall permit you to renounce an alliance, as glorious as fortune could offer to you, that you may remain faithful to an illustrious lady of whose very name you are ignorant! Do not expect so much of my kindness. No, rather strive to vanquish feelings that are inspired by an object which is most probably unworthy of them; and seek, in so doing, to merit the honour which the Count proposes for you." "You speak to me in vain, my father," replied the Student; "I feel that I can never forget her whom I have sworn to love--unknown though she be,--and that nothing can tear me from her. Were the Infanta proposed to me----" "Hold!" cried the old man angrily; "it is too much to boast thus insolently of a constancy which excites my displeasure: leave me, and let me not see you again until you are prepared to obey my will."

Don Pedro did not dare to reply to these words, for fear of hearing others more unpleasant still; so he retired to his chamber, where he passed the remainder of the night in reflections in which sorrow was not all unmixed with joy. He thought with grief that he was about to estrange himself from his family, by refusing the hand of Belflor's sister; but then he was consoled, when he reflected that his incognita would worthily esteem the greatness of the sacrifice. He even flattered himself that, after so convincing a proof of his fidelity, she would no longer conceal from him her station, which he imagined also must be equal at least to that of Eugenia.

In this hope, as soon as day appeared, he went out, and directed his steps towards the Prado, that he might pass away the time until the hour of his meeting with his mistress. With what impatience did he count the minutes as they lingered,--with what joy did he hail the happy moment when it arrived!

He found his fair unknown with Donna Juanna, the lady at whose house they met; but alas, he found her in tears, and apparently in the deepest affliction. What a sight for a lover! His own grief was forgotten: he approached her with tenderness; and throwing himself on his knees before her, "Madam," he exclaimed, "what must I think of the condition in which I see you? What dreadful misfortune do these tears, which pierce my heart, forbode?" "You dream not," she replied, "of the fatal news I bring you. Cruel fortune is about to separate us for ever;--yes! we shall meet no more."

She accompanied these words with so many and such heart-rending sighs, that I know not if Don Pedro was more affected at what she told him, than at the affliction with which she appeared oppressed in telling it. "Just Heaven!" he cried, in a transport of fury, which he could not control, "is it thy will that they prevent an union whose innocence is worthy of thy protection? But, Madam," he continued, "you are perhaps falsely alarmed! Is it certain that they would snatch you from the most faithful of lovers? Can it be possible that I should be so unhappy?" "Our misfortune is but too certain," answered the Unknown; "my brother, upon whom my hand depends, has bestowed it this very day; he has this moment announced to me his decision." "And who is the happy man?" exclaimed Don Pedro. "Tell me! In my despair I will seek him, and----" "I do not know his name," interrupted the Unknown. "I cared not to ask, nor did my brother inform me; he told me indeed that it was his wish that I should first see the cavalier."

"But, Madam," said Don Pedro, "will you then yield without resistance to your brother's will? Will you be dragged to the altar, without complaint? Will you go, a willing sacrifice, and abandon me so easily? Alas! I have not hesitated to expose myself to the anger of a father for love of you; nor could his menaces for a moment shake my fidelity. No! nor threats, nor persuasion, could move me to espouse another, although the lady he proposed for me was one to whom I had hardly dared aspire." "And who is this lady?" asked the Unknown. "She is the sister of the Count de Belflor," replied the scholar. "Ah, Don Pedro!" cried the Unknown, with extreme surprise, "surely, you are mistaken; it cannot be she whom they propose to you. What! Eugenia, the sister of Belflor? Are you sure of what you say?" "Yes, Madam," replied the Student; "the Count himself offered me her hand." "How!" cried she, "is it possible that you are the cavalier for whom my brother designs me?" "What do I hear?" cried the Student in his turn, "is it possible that my incognita is the Count de Belflor's sister?" "Yes, Don Pedro," replied Eugenia. "But I can hardly believe it myself, at this moment; so difficult do I find it to persuade myself of the happiness you assure to me."

Don Pedro now fell again at her feet, and seizing her hand, he kissed it with all the transport that lovers only can feel who pass suddenly from the depths of despair to the highest pinnacle of hope and joy. While he abandoned himself to the feelings of his heart, Eugenia for the first time forgot her reserve, and freely returned his caress--she felt that her love was sanctioned, and gave, her lips where her heart had long been engaged. "Alas!" said she, when her love could form itself into words, "what tortures had my brother spared me, had he but here named the husband of his choice! What aversion had I already conceived for my future lord! Ah, my dear Don Pedro, how I have hated you!" "Lovely Eugenia," replied he, "what charms has that hatred for me now! I will endeavour to merit it by adoring you for ever."

After the happy pair had exhausted love's vocabulary, and the tumult of their hearts was somewhat calmed, Eugenia was anxious to know by what means the Student had gained her brother's friendship. Don Pedro did not conceal from her the amours of the Count and his sister, and related all that had passed the night before. It was for Eugenia an additional pleasure to learn that Belflor was to marry the sister of her own lover. Donna Juanna was too much interested in the welfare of her friend not to partake of her joy for this happy event, and warmly congratulated her, as also Don Pedro thereon. At last the lovers separated, after having agreed that they should not appear to know each other when they met before the Count and Don Luis.

Don Pedro returned to his father, who, finding his son disposed to obey him, was the more pleased, inasmuch as he attributed this ready compliance to the firm manner in which he had spoken to him overnight. They presently received a note from Belflor, in which he informed them that he had obtained the King's consent to his marriage, as also for that of his sister with Don Pedro, on whom his Majesty had been pleased to confer a considerable appointment. He added, so diligently had his orders for the nuptials been executed, that everything was arranged for their taking place on the following day; and he came soon after they had received his letter, to confirm what he had written, and to present to them his sister Eugenia.

Don Luis received the lady with every mark of affection, and Leonora kissed her so much that her brother was almost jealous--although, whatever he might feel, he managed to constrain his love and delight, so as not to give the Count the least suspicion of their intelligence.

As Belflor remarked his sister with great attention, he thought he could discover, notwithstanding her reserve, which he attributed to modesty, that Don Pedro was by no means displeasing to her. To be certain, however, he took an opportunity of speaking to her aside, and drew from her an avowal of her entire satisfaction. He then informed her of the name and rank of her intended, which he would not before communicate, lest the inequality of the stations should prejudice her against him; all which she feigned, marvellously well, to hear as for the first time.

At last, after many compliments, which were remarkable for their sincerity, it was resolved that the weddings should take place at the house of Don Luis the next day, as Belflor had arranged. They were accordingly celebrated this evening, the rejoicing still continues, and now you know why they are so merry in that house. Every one is delighted--except the lady Marcella: she, while all else are laughing, is at this moment in tears. They are real tears too, this time! for the Count de Belflor, after the ceremony, informed Don Luis of the facts which preceded it; and the old gentleman has sent the duenna to the Monasterio de las Arrepentidas, where the thousand pistoles she received for seducing Leonora will enable her to repent having done so for the rest of her days.

CHAPTER VI

NEW OBJECTS DISPLAYED TO DON CLEOPHAS; AND HIS REVENGE ON DONNA THOMASA.

The Demon now directed the Student's attention to another part of the city. "You see," he continued, "that house which is directly under us: it contains something curious enough,--a man loaded with debt and sleeping profoundly." "Of course then," said Leandro, "he is a person of distinction?" "Precisely so," answered Asmodeus: "he is a marquis, possessed of a hundred thousand ducats per annum, but whose expenses, nevertheless, exceed his income. His table and his mistresses require that he should support them with credit, but that causes him no anxiety; on the contrary, when he opens an account with a tradesman, he thinks that the latter is indebted to him. 'It is you,' said he the other day to a draper, 'it is you, that I shall henceforth trust with the execution of my orders; it is a preference which you owe to my esteem.'

"While the marquis enjoys so tranquilly the sweet repose of which he deprives his creditors, look at a man who----" "Stay, Signor Asmodeus," interrupted Don Cleophas hastily; "I perceive a carriage in the street, and cannot let it pass without asking what it contains." "Hush," said the Cripple, lowering his voice, as though he feared he should be heard:--"learn that that vehicle conceals one of the most dignified personages in this kingdom, a president, who is going to amuse himself with an elderly lady of Asturia, who is devoted to his pleasures. That he may not be known, he has taken the precaution of imitating Caligula, who on a similar occasion disguised himself in a wig.

"But,--to return to the picture I was about to present to your sight when you interrupted me,--observe, in the very highest part of the mansion, where sleeps the marquis, a man who is writing in a chamber filled with books and manuscripts." "He is probably," said Zambullo, "the steward, labouring to devise some means for discharging his master's obligations." "Excellent," exclaimed the Devil; "that, indeed, forms a great part of the amusement of such gentry in the service of noblemen! They seek rather to profit from derangement of their masters' affairs than to put them in order. He is not, then, the steward whom you see; he is an author: the marquis keeps him in his house, to obtain the reputation of a patron of literature." "This author," replied Don Cleophas, "is apparently a man of eminence." "Judge for yourself!" replied the Demon. "He is surrounded by a thousand volumes, and is composing one, on Natural History, in which there will not be a line of his own. He pillages these books and manuscripts without mercy; and, although he does nothing but arrange and connect his larcenies, he has more vanity than the most original writer upon earth.

"You are not aware," continued the Spirit, "who lives three doors from this mansion: it is La Chichona, the very lady who acted so honourable a part in the story of the Count de Belflor." "Ah!" said Leandro, "I am delighted to behold her. The dear creature, so considerate for youth, is doubtless one of the two old ladies whom I perceive in that room. One of them is leaning with both her elbows on the table, looking attentively at the other, who is counting out some money. Which of them is La Chichona?" "Not the one who is counting," said the Demon; "her name is La Pebrada, and she is a distinguished member of the same profession: they are, indeed, partners; and are at this moment dividing the profits of an adventure which, by their assistance, has terminated favourably.

"La Pebrada is the more successful of the two: she has among her clients several rich widows, who subscribe to her daily register." "What do you mean by her register?" interrupted the Student. "Why," replied Asmodeus, "it contains the names of all handsome foreigners, and particularly Frenchmen, who come to Madrid. The instant La Pebrada hears of an arrival, away she posts to the hotel of the new comer, to learn every particular as to his country, birth, parentage, and education,--his age, form, and appearance, all which are duly reported to her subscribers; and if, on reflection, the heart of any of her widows is inclined to an acquaintance, she adroitly manages a speedy interview with the stranger."

"That is extremely convenient," replied Zambullo, smiling, "and in some sort very proper; for, in truth, without these kind ladies and their agents, the youthful foreigner, who comes without introductions to Madrid, would lose an immense deal of time in gaining them. But, tell me, are there in other countries widows as generous and women as intriguing?" "Capital!" exclaimed the Devil--"if there are? Why! can you doubt it? I should be unworthy of my demonship if I neglected to provide all large towns with them in plenty."

"Cast your eyes upon Chichona's neighbour,--yon printer, who is working at his press, alone. He has dismissed the devils in his employ these three hours; and he is now engaged, for the night, on a work which he is printing privately." "Ah! what may it be?" said Leandro. "It treats of insults," replied the Demon; "and endeavours to prove that Religion is preferable to Honour; and that it is better to pardon than to avenge an affront." "Oh! the scoundrel!" exclaimed the Student "Well may he print in secret his infamous book. Its author had better not acknowledge his production: I would be one of the first to answer it with a horsewhip. What! can Religion forbid the preservation of one's honour?"

"Let us not discuss that point," interrupted Asmodeus, with a malicious smile. "It appears that you have made the most of the lectures on morality you listened to at Alcala; and I give you joy of the result." "You may say what you please," interrupted Cleophas in his turn, "and so may the writer of this wretched absurdity: but though his reasonings were clear as the noon-day sun, I should despise him and them. I am a Spaniard, and nothing is to me so delightful as revenge; and, by the by, since you have pledged yourself to satisfy me for the perfidy of my mistress, I call on you at once to keep your promise."

"I yield with pleasure," replied the Demon, "to the wrath which agitates your breast. Oh! how I love those noble spirits who follow without scruple the dictates of their passions! I will obey your will at once; and indeed, the hour to avenge your wrongs is come: but first I wish to show you something which will amuse you vastly. Look beyond the printing-office, and observe with attention what is passing in an apartment, hung with drab cloth." "I perceive," said Leandro, "five or six women, who are with eagerness offering phials of something to a sort of valet, and they appear desperately agitated."

"They are," replied Asmodeus, "devotees, who have great reason to be agitated. There is in the next room a sick inquisitor. This venerable personage, who is about thirty-five years old, is attended by two of his dearest penitents, with untiring watchfulness. One is concocting his gruel, while the other at his pillow is employed in keeping his head warm, and is covering his stomach with a kind of blanket made of at least fifty lamb-skins." "What on earth is the matter with him, then?" asked Zambullo. "He has a cold in his head," answered the Devil; "and there is danger lest the disorder should extend to his lungs."

"The ladies whom you see in his antechamber have hastened, on the alarm of his indisposition, with all sorts of remedies. One brings, to allay his apprehended cough, syrups of jujubes, mallows, coral, and coltsfoot; another, to preserve the said lungs of his reverence, syrups of long-life, speedwell, amaranth, and the elixir vitæ; this one, to fortify his brain and stomach, has brought balm, cinnamon, and treacle waters, besides gutta vitæ, and the essences of nutmegs and ambergris; that offers anacardine and bezoardic confections; while a fifth carries tinctures of cloves, gilly-flowers, sunflowers, and of coral and emeralds. All these zealous penitents are boasting to the valet of the virtues of the medicines they offer; and each by turns, drawing him aside, and slipping a ducat in his hand, whispers in his ear: 'Laurence, my dear Laurence, manage so, I beg of you, that what I bring for the dear man may have the preference.'"

"By Jupiter!" cried Don Cleophas, "it must be allowed that inquisitors--even sick inquisitors--are happy mortals." "I can answer for that," replied Asmodeus; "I almost envy them their lot, myself; and, like the son of Philip of Macedon, who once said that he would have been Diogenes, if he had not been Alexander, I can unhesitatingly say, that, if I were not a devil I would be an inquisitor."

"But, Signor Student," continued he, "let us go! Let us away, to punish the ingrate who so ill-requited your tenderness." Zambullo instantly seized the end of the Demon's cloak, and a second time was whirled with him through the air, until they alighted on the house of Donna Thomasa.

This frail damsel was seated at table, with the four gentlemen who, a few hours before, had so eagerly sought the acquaintance of Don Cleophas on the roof of her house. He trembled with rage, as he beheld them feasting on a brace of partridges and a rabbit, which, with some choice wine, he had sent to the traitress for his own supper; and, to add to his mortification, he perceived that joy reigned in the repast; and that it was evident, by the deportment of the lady, that the company of these scoundrels was much more agreeable to her than that of himself. "Oh! the wretches!" he cried, in a perfect fury, "to see them enjoying themselves at my expense! Vastly pleasant, is it not?"

"Why, I must confess," replied the Demon, "that you have witnessed spectacles more pleasing; but he who rejoices in the favours of such fair ones must expect to share them. This sort of thing has happened a thousand times; especially in France, among the abbés, the gentlemen of the long robe, and the financiers." "If I had a sword, though," said Leandro, "I would fall upon the villains, and spoil their sport for them." "You would be hardly matched," replied the Demon;--"what were one among so many? Leave your revenge to me! I will manage it better than you could. I will soon set them together by the ears, in inspiring each of them with a fit of tenderness for your mistress: their swords will be out in no time, and you will be delighted with the uproar."

Asmodeus had no sooner spoken than he breathed forcibly, and from his mouth issued a violet-coloured vapour which descended tortuously, like a fiery serpent, and spread itself round the table of Donna Thomasa. In an instant, one of her guests, more inflammable than his companions, rose from his seat, and, approaching the lady, embraced her amorously; when the others, in whom the spirit had begun

Alain René Le Sage

to work, hastened together to snatch from him the dainty prize. Each claimed a preference: words ensued; a jealous rage possessed them; blows succeeded, and, as the Devil had foretold, they drew their weapons and commenced a furious combat. In the meanwhile Donna Thomasa exerted her lungs, and the neighbourhood was speedily alarmed by her cries. They call for the police; the police arrive: they break open the door, and find two of the Hectors extended on the floor. They seize upon the others, and take them with the Helen of the party to prison. In vain did she weep; in vain did she tear her locks, and exclaim in despair:--the tears of unfortunate beauty had no more effect on the cavaliers who conducted her, than they had on her former knight Zambullo, who almost died with laughter, in which the god of love most unnaturally joined him.

"Well!" said the Demon to the Student, "are you content?" "No, no!" replied Don Cleophas; "to satisfy me in full, place me upon the prison, that I may have the pleasure of beholding in her dungeon, the miserable who trifled with my love. I feel for her, now, a hatred which exceeds even the affection with which she formerly inspired me." "Be it so!" said the Devil; "you shall ever find me a slave to your will, though it interfered with mine and my interests,--provided always, that it is safe to indulge you."

They flew through the air, and were on the prison before the officers arrived with their captives. The two assassins were at once consigned to one of its lowest deeps, while Thomasa was led to a bed of straw, which she was to share with three or four other abandoned women, who had fallen into the hands of justice the same day; and with whom she was destined to be transported to the colonies, which a grateful mother country generally endows with this description of female inhabitants.

"I am satisfied," said Zambullo; "I have tasted a delicious revenge: my dear Thomasa will not pass the night quite so pleasantly as she had anticipated. So, now, if you please, we will continue our observations." "We could not be in a better place, then," replied the Spirit. "Within these walls is much to interest you. Innocent and guilty, in somewhat equal numbers, are here enclosed: it is the hell in which commences the punishment of the one, and the purgatory in which the virtue of the others may be purified,--you see I'm a good Catholic, Signor Student! Of both of these species of prisoners I will show you examples, and I will inform you why they are here enfettered."

CHAPTER VII

THE PRISON, AND THE PRISONERS.

"And before I commence my memoirs, just observe the gaolers at the entrance of this horrible place. The poets of antiquity placed but one Cerberus at the gate of their hell: there are many more here, however, as you perceive. They are creatures who have lost all the feelings of humanity, if they ever possessed any;--the most malicious of my brethren could hardly replace one of them. But I observe that you are looking with horror on those cells whose only furniture consists of a wretched bed,--those fearful dungeons appear to you so many tombs. You are reasonably astonished at the misery you behold; and you deplore the fate of those unhappy persons whom the law restrains; still, they are not all equally to be pitied; and I will enable you to distinguish between them.

"To begin, in that large cell to the right are four men sleeping in two beds; one of them is an innkeeper, accused of having poisoned a foreigner who died suddenly the other day in his house. They assert that the deceased owed his death to the quality of the wine he partook of; the host maintains, that the quantity, alone, killed him: and the accused will be believed, for the stranger was a German." "Well! who is in the right, the innkeeper or his accusers?" said Don Cleophas. "It is difficult to decide," replied the Devil "The wine was certainly drugged; but, i' faith, the Baron drank so largely, that the judges may for the nonce most conscientiously acquit a tavern-keeper of poisoning his customer."

"His bedfellow is an assassin by profession;--not a soldier, but one of those scoundrels who are called Valientes, and who for four or five pistoles obligingly minister to all who will go to so great an expense for the purpose of secretly ridding themselves of some one to whom they owe an obligation. The third prisoner is a dancing-master, who has been teaching one of his female pupils a step not usually practised in genteel society; and the fourth is an unlucky gallant caught by the patrole in the act of entering, by the balcony, the apartment of a lady, whom he was about to console for the absence of her husband. He has only to declare the charitable object of his visit, to withdraw himself from the hands of justice; but he nobly prefers to suffer as a robber, rather than endanger the reputation of his mistress."

"He is a model of discretion, indeed," said the Student; "but it must be allowed that the cavaliers of Spain excel those of all other nations in affairs of gallantry; I would bet anything that a Frenchman, for example, would never permit himself to be hanged under similar circumstances." "And I would back you for that," answered the Devil; "he would rather scale the balcony of a lady, of whose favours he could boast, in broad day-light, for the express purpose of proclaiming her disgrace."

"In a cell near that of the four men I have just spoken of," continued Asmodeus, "is a celebrated witch, who enjoys the reputation of doing all impossible things. By the power of her magic, old dowagers can find, they say, youthful admirers who will love them for their bloom; husbands are rendered faithful to their wives; and coquettes sincerely devoted to the rich fools who keep them: all which is, I need not tell you, absurd enough. Her only secret is in persuading people that she has one, and in making the most of that opinion. The Holy Office is jealous of the poor creature, so have called her to account; and she is likely to be burnt at the first aúto de fé."

"Under this cell, in a dark dungeon, lodges a young tavern keeper."--"What! another?" cried Leandro,--"surely these people are going to poison all the world." "Mine host, in this case," replied Asmodeus, "will not suffer for his wine; it is for an illegal traffic in spirits that he was arrested yesterday, at the instance of the Holy Office also. I will explain the matter to you in a few words.

"An old soldier, having risen by his courage, or rather by his patience, to the rank of serjeant, came to Madrid in search of recruits, and demanded a lodging in a tavern to which he was directed by his billet. The host told the serjeant that he certainly had spare rooms in his house, but that he could not think of putting him into any one of them, as they were haunted by a ghost who visited them nightly, and most shockingly ill-treated those who had the temerity to occupy them. The serjeant was not however to be daunted: 'Place me,' said he, 'in any room you please; give me a light, some wine, a pipe and tobacco, and never trouble yourself for my safety; ghosts, depend upon it, have the highest respect for an old campaigner, whose hairs have whitened under arms.'

"As he appeared so resolute, they showed the old soldier to a chamber, gave him all he had required; and he began to smoke and drink at his ease. The hour of midnight sounded, but no ghost appeared to disturb the profound silence that reigned throughout the house; it seemed as though the

Alain René Le Sage

spirit did indeed respect the valiant bearing of his new guest: but, between one and two o'clock, the wakeful sentinel was alarmed by a horrible din, as of rattling chains, and beheld, entering his apartment, a fearful spectre, clothed in black, and enveloped with iron chains. Our old smoker, not in the least alarmed at this spectacle, rose calmly from his chair, advanced towards the spirit, drew his sword, and gave him with the flat side of it, a terrible blow on the head.

"The phantom, unaccustomed to find such courageous tenants in his domain, and perceiving that the soldier was preparing to repeat the blow, fell upon his knees before him, crying out,--'Pardon, signor serjeant; for the love of Heaven, do not kill me: have pity upon a poor devil, who throws himself at your feet to implore your clemency. I conjure you by St James, who, like yourself, was a valiant soldier----' 'If you would preserve your life,' interrupted the serjeant, 'tell me who you are, and what you do here. Speak the truth,--or, by our Lady, I will cut you in two, as the knights of old split the giants they encountered.' At these words, the spirit, finding with whom he had to do, saw that he had better lose no time in his explanation.

"'I am,' said he, 'the head-waiter of this inn; my name is William; and I love Juanilla, the only daughter of the landlord, and I do not love without return; but as her parents have a better match in view, my sweetheart and myself have arranged that, in order to compel them to choose me for their son-in-law, I shall nightly disguise myself in this manner. I clothe myself in a long black cloak, and put the jack-chain round my neck; and, thus equipped, I go about the house, from the cellar to the garret, making all the noise I can, of which you have heard a specimen. When I arrive at the door of my master and mistress's bed-room, I rattle my chains, and cry loud enough for them to hear,--"Hope not to rest in peace, until you have married Juanilla to your head-waiter, William!"'

"'After having pronounced these words in a hoarse and broken voice, I continue my clatter, and vanish by a window into the chamber where Juanilla sleeps alone, to inform her of what I have done. And now, signor serjeant, you may be assured that I have told you the whole truth. I know that after this confession you may ruin me, by informing my master of the affair; but if, instead of thus injuring me, you are inclined to serve me, I swear that my gratitude----' 'Ah!' interrupted the soldier, 'what service can you hope from me?' 'You have only in the morning,' replied the young man, 'to say that you have seen the ghost, and that it has so terribly frightened you,----' 'What, the deuce! frightened me!' again interrupted the old warrior; 'do you expect that Serjeant Hannibal Antonio Quebrantador is going to say that he was frightened? I would rather say that a hundred thousand devils had me----' 'That is not absolutely necessary,' in his turn interrupted William; 'and after all, it is of no great consequence what you say, provided that you but assist me in my design: only let me marry Juanilla, and see myself established by the assistance of her father, and I promise to keep open house for you and all your friends.'

"'You are a regular seducer, master William,' cried the soldier; 'you want to join me in a downright cheat: the matter may be serious, and you take it so lightly, as to make me, even, tremble for the consequences. But away with you! continue your infernal noise, and go to Juanilla to render your account: I will manage the rest.'

"Accordingly, on the following morning, the serjeant said to his host and hostess: 'Well! I have seen the ghost, conversed with it, and found it very civil and reasonable.' "I am," said he to me, "the great-great-grandfather of the master of this house. I had a daughter, whom I solemnly promised to the father of master William's grandfather: nevertheless, despite my pledge, I gave her hand to another, and died shortly afterwards. Ever since then, I have remained in purgatory, suffering for this perjury; and I shall continue in torment until some one of my descendants has married into the family of the head waiter. To accomplish this, I come here nightly; but it is in vain that I command them to unite Juanilla and young William,--the son of my grandchild turns a deaf ear to my entreaties, as well as his wife; but tell them, if you please, signor serjeant, that if they do not as I desire of them soon, I shall come to extremities with them, and will plague them both in a way they little dream of."'

"The host, who is simple enough, was somewhat shaken by this discourse; but the hostess, still more silly than her husband, was so much affected by it, that she fancied she already saw the ghost at her heels, and at once consented to the match, which took place on the following day. William shortly afterwards took an inn in another part of the town, and serjeant Quebrantador failed not to visit him frequently. The new tavern-keeper at first, out of gratitude, filled him with wine at discretion; which so pleased the old moustache, that he took all his friends to the house: he even there enrolled his recruits, and made them drunk at the host's expense.

"At last, therefore, master William became tired of constantly wetting so many parching throats; but, on communicating his ideas upon the subject to the serjeant, the latter, with a disregard of his own infraction of their treaty which would have fitted him to command an army, was unjust enough to accuse mine host of ingratitude. William replied, the other rejoined, and the conversation ended, as their first had begun, with a blow of the serjeant's long sword on the thick head of the unfortunate tavern-keeper. Some passers-by naturally sided with the civilian: of these Quebrantador wounded three or four; and his wrath was yet unsatisfied, when he was suddenly assailed by a host of archers, who arrested him as a disturber of the peace. They conducted him to prison, where he declared all that I have told you; and upon his deposition the ex-head-waiter was encaged also. His father-in-law demands a divorce; and the Holy Office, hearing that William has acquired some considerable property, has kindly undertaken to investigate the matter."

"Egad!" cried Don Cleophas, "our holy inquisition is ever alive to its interests. No sooner do they light upon a profitable----" "Softly!" interrupted the devil, "have a care how you launch out against that tribunal:--for it, the very walls have ears. They echo even words that the mouth has never spoken; and for myself, I hardly dare to mention it without trembling."

"Over the unfortunate William, in the first chamber to the left, are two men worthy of your pity; one of them is a youthful valet, whom his master's wife privately indulged with the use of more than her husband's clothes. One day, however, the husband surprised them together; when the lady immediately began crying out for help, and accused the valet of having violated her person. The poor fellow was arrested, of course; and, according to appearances, will be sacrificed to his mistress's reputation. His companion, still less guilty than the valet, is also about to pay the forfeit of his life. He was footman to a duchess who has been robbed of a valuable diamond, which they accuse him of having taken. He will be to-morrow put to the torture, until the rack wrings from him a confession of the theft; and in the meanwhile the lady's maid, who is the real culprit, and whom no one dares to suspect, will moralise with the duchess on the depravity of modern servants."

"Ah! Signor Asmodeus," said Leandro, "let not the wretched footman perish, I entreat you! His innocence interests me for his life. Save him, by your power, from the unjust and cruel torture they would inflict: he deserves----" "You cannot expect it, Signor Student!" interrupted the demon. "What! do you suppose that I would prevent injustice?--that I would snatch the guiltless from destruction? As well might you pray an attorney to desist from the ruin of the widow or the orphan!"

"Oh! and it please you," added the Devil, "expect not of me that which is contrary to my interest, unless indeed it be of great advantage to yourself. Besides, were I willing to deliver yonder prisoner from bondage, how could I effect it?" "How!" repeated Zambullo, "do you mean to say that you have not the power so to do?" "Certainly," replied the Cripple. "Had you read the Enchiridion, or Albertus Magnus, you would know that neither I, nor any of my brethren, can liberate a prisoner from his cell: even I, were I so unfortunate as to be within the talons of the law, could only hope to escape by bribing my jailer, or my judges.

"In the next room, on the same side, lodges a surgeon convicted of having, in a fit of jealousy, drained the warm blood which wantoned in the veins of his handsome wife, after the model of the death of Seneca. He was yesterday tenderly questioned on the rack; and having confessed the crime of which he was accused, he let out the secrets of his profession, by detailing a very novel and interesting mode which he had especially adopted for increasing his practice. He stated that he had been in the habit of wounding persons in the street with a bayonet, and of then lancing himself into his house by a back-door. Of course the patient used to call out lustily at this unexpected operation; and as the neighbours flocked around at his cries, the surgeon, mingling with the crowd, and finding a man bathed in his blood, very charitably had him carried to his shop, and dressed the wound with the same hand that had given it.

"Although the rascally practitioner has confessed to this atrocity, for which a thousand deaths were not one too many, he still hopes that his life will be spared; and it is not improbable that it may be so, seeing that he is related to the lady who has the honour of clouting the little princes of Spain: besides which, he is the inventor of a marvellous wash, of which the secret would die with him, and which has the virtues of whitening the skin, and of giving to the wrinkled front the juvenile appearance of fifteen. Now, as this incomparable water serves as the fountain of youth to three ladies of the palace, who have united their efforts to save him, he relies so confidently on their credit at court, or rather on that of his wash, that he sleeps tranquilly in the soothing hope that he will awaken to the agreeable intelligence of his pardon."

"I perceive, upon a bed in the same room," said the Student, "another man, who appears to me to be sleeping peaceably enough; his business is not a very bad one, I expect." "It is a very ticklish affair, though," replied the Demon. "That cavalier is a gentleman of Biscay, who has enriched himself by the fire of a carbine: I will tell you how. About a fortnight ago, shooting in a forest with his elder and only brother, who was in possession of a large estate, he killed him, by mistake, instead of a partridge." "A very lucky mistake, that," cried Don Cleophas, laughing, "for a younger son." "Yes," replied Asmodeus: "but a collateral branch of the family, the members of which would have no objection to see the deceased's estate fall within their line, have disinterestedly prosecuted his murderer on the charge of having designedly shot him, that he might succeed to his property. The accused, however, immediately rendered himself into the hands of justice; and he appears to be so deeply afflicted by the death of his brother, that they can scarcely imagine him guilty of deliberately taking his life." "And has he really nothing with which to reproach himself, beyond his fatal awkwardness?" asked Leandro. "No," replied Asmodeus; "his design was innocent enough; but when an elder son is in possession of all the wealth of

Alain René Le Sage

his family, I should certainly not advise him to make a shooting-party in company with his younger brother.

"Observe attentively those two youths who, in a retreat near to that of the fatal shot, are conversing as merrily as though they were at liberty. They are a pair of veritable picaros; and there is one, especially, who may some day amuse the public with one of those details of roguery which never fail to delight it. He is a modern Guzman d'Alfarache: it is he who wears the brown velvet vest, and has a plume of feathers in his hat.

"Not three months since, in this very town, he was page to the Count d'Onato; and he would still have been in the suite of that nobleman but for a little piece of rascality, which gained for him his present lodging, and which I will narrate to you.

"One day, this youth, whose name is Domingo, received a hundred lashes, which the Count's intendant, otherwise governor of the pages, directed to be bestowed on him as a reward for some trick which appeared to deserve it. Domingo was, however, impatient under such a load of obligation; and so, proudly resolved to return it on the first opportunity. He had remarked more than once that the Signor Don Como, as the intendant styled himself, delighted to wash his hands with orange-flower water, and to anoint himself with pastes redolent of the pink or jessamine; that he was more careful of his person than an old coquette, and that, in short, he was one of those coxcombs who imagine that no woman of taste can behold them without loving them. These observations inspired Domingo with a scheme for revenge, which he communicated to a young waiting-woman who resided in the neighbourhood, whose assistance he required for the execution of his project, and in whose favour he stood so high that she had none left to grant him.

"This damsel, called Floretta, in order to have the pleasure of an unrestrained intercourse with the page, introduced him as her cousin into the house of Donna Luziana, her mistress, whose father was at that time absent from Madrid. The cunning Domingo, after having informed his pretended relative of her part in his design, going one morning into the apartment of Don Como, found my gentleman trying on a new dress, looking with complacency at his figure in a mirror, and evidently by no means displeased with its reflection. The page affected to be struck with admiration of this Narcissus, and exclaimed, in well-feigned transport: 'Upon my honour, Signor Don Como, you have the air of royalty itself. I see, daily, nobles richly clad; but notwithstanding the elegance and splendour of their vestments, I discern in none that dignity of mien which distinguishes you. I will not assert,' added he, 'that with the respect I have for you, I may not regard you with eyes somewhat prepossessed in your favour; but this I can say, that I know of no cavalier at court whom you would not totally eclipse.'

"The intendant smiled at this discourse, which offered so agreeable a tribute to his vanity, and graciously replied:--'You flatter me, my friend; or rather, as you say, you esteem me so highly, that your friendship endows me with graces that nature has refused.' 'I cannot think so,' replied the parasite; 'for there is no one who does not speak of you in terms which I dare not repeat, lest you should think I flattered you indeed. I wish you had heard what was said to me yesterday by one of my cousins, who is in the service of a lady of quality.'

"Don Como failed not to ask what it was that Domingo's cousin had said of him. 'Why,' replied the page, 'I ought hardly to tell you; but she enlarged on the majesty of your figure,--on the charms which are everywhere visible in your person; and, what is better, she told me, in confidence, that the greatest delight of Donna Luziana, her mistress, is to watch for your passing her house, and to feast her eyes with beholding you.'

"'And who is this lady?' said the intendant,--'where does she live?' 'What!' replied Domingo; 'do you not know the only daughter of general Don Fernando, our neighbour?' 'Ah! to be sure I do,' replied Don Como: 'I remember to have frequently heard of the wealth and surpassing beauty of this Luziana; she is not to be despised. But is it possible that I can have attracted her attention?' 'Can you doubt it?' exclaimed the page. 'Besides, my own cousin told me of the fact; and, though in a humble situation, she is incapable of falsehood, and I would answer for her word with my life.' 'In that case,' said the intendant, 'I should be glad to have a little private conversation with your relative, to engage her in my interest by the customary trifling presents to which her situation entitles her; and if she should advise me to pay court to her mistress, egad! I'll try my fortune. And why not? It is true that there is some difference between my rank and that of Don Fernando; but still I am a gentleman, and have a good four hundred ducats per annum. There are more extraordinary matches than this made every day.'

"The page fortified his governor in his resolution, and procured for him an interview with his cousin; who, finding the intendant disposed to swallow anything, assured him of her mistress's inclination in his favour. 'You have no idea,' said she, 'how often Luziana has questioned me as to the handsome cavalier who had made such an impression on her heart; and you may be sure that my replies were neither unpleasing to her, nor unfavourable to you: in short, Signor, she loves you; and you have everything to hope from her affection. Seek then her hand, openly and without hesitation; justify her secret passion, by showing that she loves a cavalier, not only the most charming and well-made, but the most gallant, of all Madrid. Give her, in serenades, the delightful assurance that your heart responds to

41

hers; and rely on me to picture your devotion in the most pleasing colours,--an office as agreeable to myself as I hope it will be useful to you.' Don Como, transported with joy at finding the maid so warmly disposed to serve him, almost stifled her with his caresses; and, placing a worthless ring upon her finger, which he had liberally purchased of a Jew, and which had served the same purpose fifty times, he exclaimed,--'Dearest Floretta! accept this ring as an earnest of my gratitude, until I have an opportunity of more worthily recompensing the favours you are about to shower on me.'

"Never was lover in greater ecstacy than was our intendant at the result of his conversation with Floretta; and as he was indebted to Domingo for this happiness, the page not only received his thanks, but was rewarded by the magnificent present of a pair of silk stockings, some shirts trimmed with lace, and a promise of the Signor's losing no opportunity which might offer for promoting his interests. 'My dear friend,' said he, on leaving Floretta, 'what is your opinion of the steps I should take in this matter? Do you think I should commence with an impassioned and sublime epistle to my Luziana?' 'Decidedly,' replied the page. 'Make her a declaration of your love in fitting terms: I have a presentiment that it will not be badly received.' 'Well! I think so too,' replied the intendant; 'at all events, I will try the experiment.' Accordingly, down he sat to compose the missive; and after having torn in pieces at least fifty scrawls, which would have made the fortune of a German romancist, he at last succeeded in composing a billet-doux which satisfied his scruples. It was conceived in the following grandiloquent and affecting terms:--

"'Months have rolled like centuries, oh! lovely Luziana, since, inspired by the renown which everywhere proclaims your perfections, my too-sensible soul has yielded to the flames of love, to burn for you alone! My heart consumed in secret, a willing prey to the fires that devoured me; and I never dared proclaim my sufferings to you, much less to seek for consolation. But a happy chance has recently revealed the soothing secret that, from behind the jealous screen which conceals your celestial charms from the eyes of men, you sometimes deign to look with pity on me as I pass;--that, directed by the divinity who guards you, and the destiny of your star,--oh, happy star for me!--you even think of me with kindness. I hasten then in all humility to consecrate my life unto your service; and should I be so fortunate as to obtain permission so to do, to renounce in your favour all ladies past, or present, or to come.

"'DON COMO DE LA HIGUERA.'

"Domingo and Floretta were not a little amused, on the receipt of this letter, at the expense of the poor intendant. But, not contented with the folly they had already induced him to commit, they set their wits to work to compose an answer to the billet which should be sufficiently tender. This done, it was copied by Floretta, and delivered by the page on the following day to Don Como. It was in these words:--

"'I know not who can have so well informed you of my secret sentiments. Some one has however betrayed me. Still, I pardon the treachery, since, to it I owe an avowal of your love. I see many pass before my window, but I look with pleasure upon you alone; and I am too happy to find that I am dear to you. Perhaps I am wrong to feel this delight, and still more wrong to dare to tell you so. If it be a fault in me, your virtues have caused, and must excuse it.
"'DONNA LUZIANA.'

"Although this letter was rather too warm for the daughter of a Spanish general, as its authors had not thought much about ceremony, the presumptuous Don Como received it without suspicion. He thought sufficiently well of himself to imagine that for him a lady might well forget somewhat of the usages of society. 'Ah! Domingo,' he cried, with an air of triumph, after having read the letter aloud, 'you see, my friend, that the fish bites. Congratulate me! I shall soon be son-in-law to Don Fernando, or my name's not Don Como de la Higuera.'

"'It is beyond a doubt,' said the rascally confidant; 'you seem to have made a tremendous impression on the girl. But, à-propos,' added he, 'I must not forget to tell you that my cousin particularly desired me to say, that to-morrow, at latest, you should serenade your mistress, in order to complete her infatuation.' 'I will on no account omit it,' replied the intendant. 'You may assure your cousin that I will in all things follow her advice; and that to-morrow, without fail, in the middle of the night, the street shall resound with one of the most gallant concerts that was ever heard in Madrid.' And away went the intendant to secure the assistance of a celebrated musician, to whom he communicated his project, and whom he charged with the care of its execution.

"In the meanwhile, Floretta, informed of the intended serenade, and finding her mistress in a desirable mood, said to her,--'Madam, I am preparing for you an agreeable diversion.' 'What may that be?' asked Luziana. 'Why,' replied the waiting-maid, laughing until the tears ran from her eyes, 'there is much to amuse you. An original, one Don Como, governor of the pages of the Count d'Onato, has taken it into his head to choose you as the sovereign lady of his thoughts; and he intends, to-morrow, in order that you may no longer remain ignorant of his devotion, to gratify you with the sound of music and sweet voices, in an evening serenade.' Donna Luziana, whose composition was none of the most grave, and who was far from foreseeing an unpleasant consequence to her in the gallantries of the intendant, instead of regarding the matter seriously, was delighted at the anticipated tribute to her charms; and thus, without knowing what she did, assisted in confirming the amorous Don Como in an illusion, of which it would have shocked her greatly to have been supposed designedly the author.

"The night came, and with it appeared, before the balcony of the lady, two carriages, from which descended the gallant Como and his confidant, accompanied by six musicians, vocal and instrumental, who commenced a very decent concert, which lasted for a considerable time. They performed many of the newest airs, and sang all the songs in vogue whose verses told the power of love in uniting hearts despite the obstacles of fortune, and the inequality of rank; while at every couplet, which the general's daughter perceived to be directed to herself, her merriment knew no bounds.

"When the serenade was over, and the performers had departed in the carriages which brought them, the crowd which the music had attracted dispersed, and our lover remained in the street with Domingo alone. He approached the balcony, whence, in a few minutes, the servant-girl, with her mistress's permission, said to him in a feigned voice: 'Is that you, Signor Don Como?' 'Who asks me that question?' replied the Don in a languishing tone. 'It is,' rejoined the girl, 'Donna Luziana, who would know if the concert she has heard but now, is an offering of your gallantry to her.' 'It is,' exclaimed the intendant, 'but a shadow of those festivals my love prepares for her who is the marvel of our days, if she will deign receive them from a lover who is sacrificed on the altar of her beauty.'

"At this brilliant metaphor, Luziana with difficulty restrained her laughter; but, coming forward and putting her head partially out of the little window from which her maid had addressed him, she said to the intendant, as seriously as possible: 'Signor Don Como, you are, I perceive, no novice in the art of love; in you, each gallant cavalier who would gain his lady's heart, may find a model for his conduct. I thank you for your serenade, and feel flattered by your attention; but,' added she, 'retire now, lest we should be observed; another time we may, unrestrained, indulge in further conversation.' As she finished these words, she closed the window, leaving the intendant in the street, highly delighted at the kindness she had displayed for him, and the page greatly astonished that the lady had herself undertaken a part in the comedy.

"This little fête, including the carriages and the enormous quantity of wine which its bibulous performers had consumed, cost Don Como upwards of a hundred ducats; and, two days afterwards, his confidant engaged him in a further outlay, in the following manner. Having learned that, on the night of St. John,--a night so celebrated in this city,--Floretta was about to join the damsels of her class at the fiesta del sotillo, Domingo undertook to enliven this dance by a magnificent breakfast at the intendant's expense.

"'Accordingly, Signor Don Como,' said he, on the eve of this festival, 'you are aware of what takes place to-morrow. I thought, however, you would like to be informed that Donna Luziana intends to repair at break of day to the banks of the Mançanarez, to witness the sotillo. I need say no more to the Corypheus of gallant cavaliers;--you are not the man to neglect so favourable an opportunity, and I am certain that your mistress and her companions will not fare badly to-morrow.' 'Of that you may be sure,' replied the governor, 'and I am obliged to you for informing me of her intention: you shall see if I know how to kick the ball as it bounds.' In effect, very early on the following day, four of the Count's servants, conducted by Domingo, and loaded with every description of cold meat, cooked in all fashions, with an infinite number of small loaves and bottles of delicious wines, arrived on the bank of the river, where Floretta and her companions were dancing, like nymphs before the golden throne of Aurora.

"Had that goddess herself appeared, she would hardly have been more cordially greeted than were the wines and cold collation which the page brought on the part of Don Como; offering, as they did, so agreeable a repast after the delightful fatigues of the dance, which they so agreeably interrupted. The damsels seated themselves on the velvet turf of the meadow, and lost no time in paying due honour to the feast, the while laughing immoderately at the dupe who gave it; for Domingo's kind cousin had not omitted to inform them of their benefactor, and his amorous adventure.

"While they were in the midst of their rejoicing and their breakfast, they perceived the squire, richly dressed, and mounted on one of the Count's steeds, which was ambling towards them. He rode up to his confidant, and gaily saluted the ladies, who rose at his approach, and politely thanked him for his generosity. His eyes wandered among the company in search of Donna Luziana, as he was anxious to deliver himself of a speech, glittering with compliments as the sward beneath his horse's feet with flowers, and which he had composed during his ride in honour of his mistress. Great therefore was his grief, when Floretta, taking him aside, informed him that a slight indisposition had prevented her lady from joining in the festival. The Don, with a proper display of sensibility on the occasion, was particular in his inquiries as to the ailment; but when the girl informed him that Luziana suffered from a cold, caught on the previous night from exposure in the balcony without her veil, talking of him and of his serenade, he was not without consolation to find so sad an accident proceeded from a cause so good. He therefore contented himself with the usual expressions of condolence; and, after praying Floretta to continue to interest herself in his behalf with his mistress, took the road to his dwelling, rejoicing more and more at his great good fortune.

"About this time, the intendant received a bill of exchange for a thousand crowns from Andalusia, as his portion of the effects of one of his uncles, who had died at Seville. On turning this bill into cash, he happened to count it over and place it in a coffer in the presence of Domingo, who took so lively an interest in the operation, that, in order to repeat it, he was tempted to appropriate, if possible, the shining gold; and resolved, if successful in so doing, to escape with it into Portugal. He related his project in confidence to Floretta, and even proposed to her that she should accompany him. Now this proposition was undoubtedly one which most people would think worthy of reflection; but the girl, as interested in the matter as the page, accepted it without a moment's hesitation. Consequently, one night, while the intendant was labouring in his cabinet to compose a touching letter to his mistress, Domingo found means to open the coffer in which the money was confined, to release it from its captivity, and to hasten with the enfranchised crowns into the street. He instantly repaired to the balcony of Luziana, and, as a signal which had been agreed upon between him and his confederate, commenced a caterwauling, which disturbed the gravity of all the tabbies in the neighbourhood. The girl, ready to wander with him through the world, promptly responded to the amatory call; and in a few minutes they were on the high road from Madrid, together.

"They reckoned that, in the event of pursuit, they would have plenty of time to gain the frontiers of Portugal before they could be overtaken; but, unfortunately for them, Don Como discovered the theft, and the flight of his confidant that very night. He gave immediate information to the police, whose officers were without loss of time dispersed on all sides in pursuit of the fugitives, and Domingo was taken, near Zebreros, in company with his lady. They were quickly brought back to Madrid: the girl has been sent to join our friend Marcella in las Arrepentidas, and Domingo is, as you perceive, as gay as ever within the walls of this prison."

"And the intendant," added Don Cleophas, "has saved his golden crowns; as of course they have been restored to him." "Of course they have not," replied the Devil: "the thousand pieces are the proof of the robbery, and the officers of justice understand their business too well to give them up; so that Don Como, whose loving history is spread throughout Madrid, has lost his money and his mistress, and is laughed at by everybody into the bargain."

"Domingo and his fellow-prisoner have for a neighbour," continued the Cripple, "a young Castilian who has been arrested for having, in the presence of too many witnesses, struck his father." "Oh heaven!" cried Leandro, "is it possible? Lives there a child, however lost to shame, who can raise his impious hand against a father?" "Oh yes," said the Demon: "yon Castilian is not without example; and I will cite you one whose history is rather remarkable. Under the reign of Don Pedro I., surnamed the Just and the Cruel, the eighth king of Portugal, a youth of twenty fell into the hands of justice for the same crime. Don Pedro, as much surprised as yourself at the novelty of the case, was curious to interrogate the mother of the criminal, and he examined her so adroitly as to obtain from her a confession, that the real father of this child was a certain reverend prelate. If the Castilian's judges were discreet enough to interrogate his mother with equal address, it is probable that it would be attended with a similar avowal.

"Cast your eyes into a large dungeon beneath the prisoners I have just pointed out to you, and observe what is passing there. Do you see those three ill-looking rascals? They are highwaymen. See! they are effecting their escape. Some one has furnished them with a dumb-file in a loaf of bread; and they have already cut through one of the thick bars of a window, by which they may gain the court-yard, and from thence the street. They have been more than ten months in prison, and it is upwards of eight since they should have received the public recompense due to their exploits; but, thanks to the tardiness of justice, they are about to begin again their career of robbery and murder.

"And now look into that low roofed cell where you perceive twenty or thirty men, some of them stretched upon straw. They are mostly pickpockets, shop-lifters, or professors of other branches of the Spartan craft. Do you observe five or six of them worrying a sort of labourer, who was introduced to their society this morning for having wounded an alguazil with a stone?" "And what are they thrashing him for?" asked Zambullo. "Why," replied Asmodeus, "because he has not paid his entrance-fees. But," added he, "let us leave this horrible place, and the miserable wretches it contains; they are not in my vocation: we will go elsewhere, in search of objects less disgusting."

CHAPTER VIII

OF VARIOUS PERSONS EXHIBITED TO DON CLEOPHAS BY ASMODEUS, WHO REVEALS TO THE STUDENT WHAT EACH HAS DONE IN HIS DAY.

In a few moments, the Demon and his pupil were on the roof of a large mansion, at a considerable distance from that part of the city in which they had left the prisoners. "I have brought you here," said Asmodeus, "because I am desirous of informing you what the mass of people who reside in the neighbourhood of the house we are on, have been doing in the course of to-day;--it will amuse you." "Doubtless!" replied Leandro. "Begin, I beseech you: and first for yonder cavalier who is booting in such haste: what weighty matters call him from his home in such a night as this, my Mentor?" "He is a captain," replied the Cripple, "whose steeds are waiting in the street to carry him to Catalonia, where his regiment is stationed.

"Well! yesterday, our hero, being without cash, applied to one of those gentry who, instead of giving to the poor, wisely lend unto the lords, or captains. 'Signor Sanguisuela,' said he, 'can you not oblige me with the loan of a thousand ducats?' 'Signor Captain,' replied the usurer, 'I have them not; but I think I know a friend who has, and will lend them to you:--that is to say, if you will give him your note of hand for a thousand ducats, he will give you four hundred; out of which I shall be content to receive sixty only, as my commission. Money is so extremely scarce, that----' 'What usury!' interrupted the officer, hastily. 'What! ask six hundred and sixty ducats for the loan of three hundred and forty? Infamous extortion! Such hard-hearted scoundrels deserve to be hanged.'

"'Keep your temper, at all events, Signor Captain, and go elsewhere for your money,' replied the usurer, with the greatest coolness. 'Of what do you complain? Do I force you to take the three hundred and forty ducats? Heaven forbid! you are free to take them or to leave them.' To this the Captain had no reply to make, and went his way; but, on reflecting that he must set out for the camp on the morrow, and that he had no time to lose, he resolved to lose his money; so he returned this morning to the usurer, whom he met at his door, dressed in a short black mantle, a plain collar round his neck, his hair closely trimmed, and with a rosary in his hand, garnished with saintly medals. 'Here I am again, Signor Sanguisuela,' said he; 'I will take the three hundred and forty ducats,--necessity compels me to accept your terms.' 'I am going to mass,' gravely replied the usurer; 'on my return, I will give you that amount.' 'Ah! no,' exclaimed the Captain; 'I pray you give it me at once: it will but delay you for an instant. I would not entreat you, but my haste is great as is my need.' 'I cannot,' replied Sanguisuela: 'I hear mass daily, before I think of following my worldly avocations; it is a rule I have prescribed for my conduct, and I will endeavour religiously to observe it while I live.'

"However impatient might be our captain to lay his hands upon the money, he was obliged to comport himself with the rule of the pious Sanguisuela: he therefore armed himself with patience, and even, as though he feared that the ducats would escape him, followed the usurer to church. Mass performed, he was preparing to leave; when Sanguisuela inclined his head towards him, and whispered in his ear: 'Stay! one of the most talented men in Madrid preaches here this morning, and I would not lose his sermon for the world.'

"The Captain, to whom the mass had appeared over-long, was in despair at this further call on his endurance: however, needs must--and he remained where he had been driven. The preacher mounted the pulpit, and happened to discourse against usury. The officer was delighted; and observing Sanguisuela's countenance, he said within himself: 'If this Jew is capable of being touched, now,--if he will but give me six hundred ducats, I shall really think he is not too bad, after all.' The sermon ended, they left the church together, when the Captain, addressing his companion, said: 'Well, what think you of the preacher? Did you not find his sermon extremely forcible? For myself, I was quite affected by it.' 'I am quite of your opinion,' replied the usurer; 'he treated his subject admirably. He is a learned man, and deeply skilled in his profession; and now, let us go, and show that we understand ours as well.'"

"Hollo!" cried Don Cleophas, "who are those two women in bed together, and laughing so loudly? Egad! they seem merry enough." "They are sisters," replied the Devil, "who this morning buried their father. He was an old curmudgeon, who had so great a distaste for matrimony, or rather to portioning his daughters, that he would never listen to a word about their marrying, however advantageous might be the offers made to them. They are at this moment discussing the virtues of the dear deceased. 'He is dead at last,' exclaimed the elder; 'he is dead,--the unnatural father, who so cruelly delighted still to keep us maids: he will, however, no longer oppose our innocent desires.' 'Well, sister,' said the younger, 'for myself, I love the substantial; I shall look out for a good rich husband,--stupid, if you please; and the fat Don Blanco is just the man for my money.' 'Softly, sister,' replied the elder; 'we shall have for husbands those to whom we are destined; for marriages, they say, are written in heaven.' 'So much the worse for us,' replied the younger; 'for if dear papa has the luck to be there, he will assuredly tear out our leaf.' The eldest could not help laughing at this sally, and it is that which still amuses them both.

"In the next house to that of these ladies, in a furnished apartment, lodges an Aragonese adventuress. You may see her, while others sleep, admiring in a glass those charms on which she relies, and which have gained for her to-day a conquest to be proud of: like a good general, she studies her positions for attack; and she has just discovered a new one, which will finish her campaign with her lover to-morrow. He is well worth all the pains she can take to secure him, and she is well aware of his promising qualities. To-day, for instance, one of her creditors calling to remind her of an account, which he insists on having settled in cash: 'Wait, my good friend,' said she; 'wait but for a few days longer: I am on the point of concluding a most advantageous arrangement with one of the principal persons in the Customs.'"

"I need not ask you," said Leandro, "how a certain cavalier, whom I perceive at this moment, has been passing his day: he appears to be a complete letter-writer. What enormous quantities I behold on his table!" "Yes," replied the Demon; "and, what is most amusing, all these letters are alike in their contents. He is writing to all his absent friends an account of an adventure which befel him this afternoon. He is in love with a widow of thirty, charming and discreet; he pays to her devotions which she does not despise; he proposes for her hand, and she consents to yield it without hesitation. While preparations are making for their nuptials, he has permission to visit her without ceremony. He went to her house to-day after dinner, and as he chanced to meet with no one to announce his coming, he entered the lady's apartment, where he found her stretched on a couch, en déshabillé, or, to speak more correctly, almost naked. She was sleeping profoundly. What lover could resist the temptation thus offered to his eyes? He approaches her softly, and steals a gentle kiss. She starts, exclaiming as she wakes, 'What, again! I beseech you, Ambrose, leave me to repose.'

"The cavalier, as an honourable man, made up his mind on the instant to renounce all pretensions to the widow. He therefore immediately left the apartment; and meeting the servant at the door: 'Ambrose,' said he, 'stay! your mistress prays you to indulge her with a brief repose.'

"Two doors beyond the house of this cavalier, I perceive an original of a husband, who is sleeping tranquilly,--lulled to rest by reproaches with which his wife is upbraiding him for having passed the entire day from home. She would be still more bitter against her spouse, did she know how he had spent his day." "It has been most probably occupied in some amorous adventure?" said Zambullo. "You have guessed it," replied Asmodeus; "and shall hear the detail.

"The man is a tradesman, named Patricio: he is one of those wedded libertines who live without care, as though they had neither wife nor children: the partner of this fellow, nevertheless, is pretty, amiable, and virtuous; and he has two daughters and one son, all three still in their infancy. He left his family this morning, careless if they had bread to eat, which is not unfrequently the case, and directed his steps toward the great square, attracted thither by the preparations which Were making for the bull-fight of to-day. The scaffolds were already erected around the place, and already the more curious in these matters began to take their places.

"While gazing at the company, examining first one and then another, he observed a lady finely made and very neatly dressed, who discovered, as she descended from the scaffold, a well-turned leg and foot; and their effect was heightened by rose-tinted silken stockings, and garters of silver lace, the ends of which hung down to her ankles: it was enough to have tempted a saint, and our excitable citizen was almost out of his wits at the sight. He advanced towards the lady, who was accompanied by another whose air sufficiently disclosed that they were both damsels of easy virtue. 'Ladies,' said he, accosting them, 'can I be of service to you? you have only to command me, and it will be my happiness to obey.' 'Signor cavalier,' replied the nymph with the rose-coloured stockings, 'you appear so obliging, that we will take advantage of your kindness: we have already taken our places, but are leaving them to go to breakfast, as we were unwise enough to leave home this morning without first taking our chocolate. Since you are so gallant as to offer your services, may we trouble you to escort us to some hotel, where we may eat a morsel of something? but we must beg you will select as retired a place as possible, for ladies, as you know, cannot be too careful of their reputation.'

"At these words, Patricio, becoming even more civil and polite than the occasion demanded, took the princesses to a tavern in the neighbourhood, and ordered breakfast. 'What would you like to have, sir?' inquired the host. 'I have the remains of a magnificent dinner, which took place here yesterday: there are larded fowls, partridges from Léon, pigeons from Old Castile, and the best part of a ham from Estremadura.' 'More than enough, mine host!' exclaimed the conductor of the two vestals. 'Ladies, it is for you to choose;--what would you prefer?' 'Whatever you please,' replied they: 'your choice shall be ours.' Thereupon the citizen ordered a brace of partridges and a couple of cold fowls, to be served in a

Alain René Le Sage

private room, as the ladies were too modest to think of eating in public.

"They were immediately conducted to a small chamber, and in a few minutes the host appeared with the chosen dishes, some bread, and some wine. Our Lucretias fell to eating with most unfashionable appetites, and the fowls rapidly disappeared; while the simpleton, who was to pay, was occupied in ogling his Luisita,--the name of the lady who had taken his fancy,--in admiring the whiteness of her hand, upon which glittered an enormous ring she had gained by her profession,--and, unable to eat for joy of his good fortune, in lavishing upon the lady all the tender epithets, such as his star or his sun, that his imagination could invent. On inquiring of his goddess if she were married, she told him she was not, but was living under the protection of her brother;--had she added,--by descent from our father Adam, she would not have been far from the truth.

"Good eating is nothing without good drinking; so the two harpies, having each demolished a fowl, washed them down with a proportionate quantity of wine; and, consequently, the two flagons which had been placed upon the table were soon exhausted. That they might be more speedily replenished, our gallant left the room with the empty vessels; and he had no sooner closed the door than Jacintha, Luisita's companion, clawed hold of the two partridges, which were yet untouched, and put them in a spacious pocket which her gown conveniently afforded. Our Adonis, on returning from his chase of the wine, and remarking that the eatables had vanished, was anxious to know if his Venus had eaten enough. 'Why,' said she, 'if the pigeons of which the host has spoken be very good, perhaps I might be tempted to taste them; or else a morsel of the ham of Estremadura will do.' These words were no sooner uttered than away went Patricio again in search of provender, and quickly returned, followed by three of the loving birds and a substantial dish of the ham. The two vultures pounced on their prey like lightning; and as the witless citizen was obliged a third time to leave the room for bread, they sent a pair of the pigeons to keep company with the imprisoned partridges.

"After the repast, which ended with a dessert composed of all the fruits the season afforded, the amorous Patricio began to press Luisita for that payment in kind which he expected from her gratitude. The lady, however, was resolved to look upon it as a treat; but at the same time indulged him with the hopes of a return, telling him there was a time for all things, and that a tavern was not a fitting place in which to testify, without reserve, her satisfaction for all his kindness. Then, hearing the clock strike one, she assumed an uneasy air, and said to her companion: 'Ah! my dear Jacintha, how unfortunate! We shall be too late to find a place to see the bull-fight.' 'Excuse me,' replied Jacintha; 'this gentleman has only to conduct us where he so politely accosted us, and never fear for our finding a place.'

"Before leaving the tavern, however, it was necessary to settle with the host, who presented an account amounting to fifty reals. The citizen pulled out his purse; but, as it contained but thirty of the requisite pieces, he was obliged to leave, in pawn, his rosary adorned with numerous medals of silver. This done he esquired the frail ones to the place from whence they came, and obtained for them convenient seats upon one of the scaffolds, the proprietor of which, being known to him, gave him credit for their price.

"They were no sooner seated, then they demanded further refreshment, 'I am dying with thirst,' cried one,--'that ham was terribly salt.' 'And so am I', replied the other; 'I could drink an ocean of lemonade.' Patricio, who understood but too well what all this meant, left them, in search of what they wanted; but suddenly stopping on his way, he exclaimed to himself: 'Madman! where art thou going? Would one not think thou hadst a hundred pistoles in thy purse, or in thy house? And thou halt not a single maravedi! What shall I do?' added he. 'To return to the lady without that which she requires is impossible;--and must I, then, abandon so promising an adventure? I cannot resolve on that either.'

"While thus embarrassed, he perceived among the spectators one of his friends who had frequently tendered him services, which his pride had always prevented him accepting. But now, lost to shame, he hastened towards him, and without hesitation, begged the loan of a double pistole; possessed of which his courage returned, and hurrying to a confectioner's, he ordered them to carry to his princesses so many iced liqueurs, so many biscuits and sweetmeats, that the doubloon hardly sufficed to meet this new expense.

"At length the day ended, and with it the festival; when our citizen conducted his lady to her house, in the pleasing hope of at last reaping the reward of all his thoughtless extravagance. But as they arrived near the door of a house which Luisita indicated, as her dwelling, a servant-girl came to meet her, saying with much apparent agitation: 'Ah! Where have you been until now? Your brother, Don Gaspard Heridor, has been waiting for you these two hours, swearing like a trooper.' Upon this the sister, in well-feigned alarm, turned towards her gallant, and pressing his hand, said to him in a whisper: 'My brother is a man of most violent temper, but his anger is soon appeased. Wait here awhile with patience: I will soon set all to rights; and as he sups from home every night, as soon as he has left the house, Jacintha shall inform you, and bring you to me.'

"Patricio, consoled by this promise, kissed with transport the hand of Luisita, who returned his caresses, in order to keep up his spirits, and then entered the house with Jacintha and the girl. The poor dupe took patience, as directed, and sat himself down on a stone, a few yards from the door, where he waited for a considerable time, never dreaming of the possibility of their playing him a trick. He only wondered at the stay of Don Gaspard, and began to fear that this cursed brother had lost his appetite with his passion.

"Ten o'clock, eleven o'clock, the hour of midnight, sounded; and not until then did his confidence begin to evaporate, and some slight doubts of the good faith of his lady to infuse themselves into his mind. All was darkness around him; when, approaching the door, he entered on tip-toe, and found himself in a narrow passage, in the middle of which his hand encountered a staircase. He dared not ascend it; but, listening attentively, his ears were greeted with the discordant concert which might be expected to proceed from a barking dog, a mewing cat, and a crying child, all performing their parts to admiration. He felt that he was deceived; and he was convinced of the fact when, having explored the passage to its termination, he found himself in another street, parallel with that in which he had, so long, waited for his love.

"The ghost of his money rose in judgment against him; and he returned to his own house, moralising on the deceptive influences of rose-coloured stockings. He knocked at the door; it was opened by his wife, a chaplet in her hand, and tears in her eyes. 'Ah! Patricio,' she said, in a voice which told her affliction; 'how can you thus abandon your home? how can you thus neglect your wife--your children? Where have you been from six this morning, when you left us?' The husband, whom this question would have puzzled to answer satisfactorily, and who was, besides, somewhat ashamed of himself, had not a word to say; so he undressed, and got into bed in silence. His wife, however, was not in want of a text; and she read him a lecture, the continuous hum of which, as you perceive, has soothed him to sleep."

"And now," continued Asmodeus, "cast your eyes upon the large house by the side of that in which the cavalier is writing to his friends the story of his rupture with the mistress of Ambrose. Do you not remark a young lady sleeping in a bed of crimson satin, embroidered with gold?" "Wait!--oh, yes!--I see a lady sleeping; and I fancy I see a book, open, on her pillow." "Precisely so," answered the Demon. "That lady is a talented young countess, full of life and spirit: she has recently suffered extremely from sleepless nights, and having sent for a physician, one of the most dignified of his class, he has prescribed for her a remedy, derived, he says, from Hippocrates himself. The lady, nevertheless, ridiculed his prescription; at which the physician, a crabbed sort of animal, who does not understand joking, said to her, with a proper professional gravity: 'Madam, Hippocrates is not a man to be laughed at.' 'Certainly not, signor doctor,' replied the Countess, with the most serious air imaginable; 'far from laughing at so celebrated and learned an author, I think so highly of him, that I feel assured the mere opening of his work will cure me of my sleeplessness. I have in my library a new translation from the pen of Azero; it is, I believe, the best: here! find it for me,' added she, turning to her attendant. You behold the magic power of Hippocrates! She had not read three pages before she sank into profound repose.

"In the Countess's stables there is a poor, one-armed soldier, whom the grooms, out of charity, permit, by night, to sleep upon the straw. During the day he begs about the city; and a few hours ago, he had an amusing conversation with another mendicant, who lives near Buen-Retiro, on the road to the palace. The latter has an excellent business, which he manages so well, that his daughter, who is of a marriageable age, passes among the beggars for a rich heiress. This morning, the soldier accosting the father, said to him: 'Signor Mendigo, I have lost my right arm; I can no longer serve the king; and, like yourself, I am obliged to gain a livelihood by doing the civil to the passers-by. I know well that of all trades there is not one which does more for those who follow it; and that all that is wanting to it is, that it should be a little more highly esteemed.' 'If it were a bit more honourable,' replied the old man, 'it would not be worth following at all, as we should have too much competition;--all the world would beg if it were not for shame.'

"'Very true!' replied he of the one arm. 'Well, now! I am a brother beggar; and I should be happy to ally myself with so distinguished a member of our profession: you shall give me your daughter.' 'Hold! my dear sir,' replied the warm old gentleman; 'you cannot think of such a thing. She must have a better match than you will make. You are not half lame enough. My son-in-law must be a miserable-looking object, who would draw blood out of a stone.' 'Do you think, then, that you will find one worse off than I am?' 'To be sure! Why, you have only lost an arm; and ought to be absolutely ashamed of yourself, to expect that I will give you my daughter. I'd have you to know that I have already refused a fellow without legs, and who goes about the city in a bowl.'

"I must on no account," continued the Devil, "omit to call your attention to the house which joins that of the sleeping countess, and which contains a drunken old painter and a satirical poet. The artist left home at seven o'clock this morning in search of a confessor, as his wife was at the point of death; but happening to meet with a boon companion, he went with him to a tavern, and forgot his wife until ten this evening, when he returned to find she had died unshriven. The poet, who enjoys the reputation of having frequently received most striking proofs of the merits of his caustic verses, was swaggering in a café this morning; and in speaking of a person who was absent, exclaimed: 'He is a scoundrel, to whom, some of these days, I must give a good drubbing.' 'That is kind of you,' replied a wag who heard him; 'though I believe, by the bye, that you owe him a good many.'

"I had nearly forgotten a scene which took place this morning at a banker's in this street. He is only recently established in Madrid, having returned with immense riches about three months ago from Peru. His father is an honest cobbler of Mediana,[3] a large village of Old Castile, near the Sierra d'Avila, where he lives, contented with his lot, and with his wife, who, like himself, is about sixty years of age.

"It is upwards of twenty years since the banker left his father's house, for the Indies, in search of a better fortune than he could expect from his parents. During all this time, though lost to sight, he was ever present in their thoughts, and every night and morning saw the poor couple on their knees, praying Heaven to shield him with its protection; nor did they fail, on each succeeding Sabbath, to entreat their friend the curate to recommend their child to the prayers of his humble flock. As soon as the banker had returned to Spain, having hastily established his house of business, he resolved to ascertain, in person, the condition of his parents, whom, in his prosperity, he had never forgotten. With this view, having told his domestics he should be absent for a few days, he set out alone, about a fortnight ago, and journeyed on horseback towards the place of his birth.

"It was about ten o'clock at night, and the good old cobbler was sleeping peaceably beside his spouse, when they were suddenly awakened by the noise which the banker made, as he knocked violently at the door of their little house. 'Who's there?' cried the startled pair, together. 'Open--open the door!' replied a voice; 'it is your son Francillo.' 'Tell that to the marines!' replied the ancient son of Crispin;--'be off with you, scoundrels! there is nothing here worth stealing. Francillo is at this moment in the Indies, if he be not dead.' 'Your son is not now in the Indies,' replied the banker; 'he is returned from Peru; it is he who speaks to you: will you refuse to receive him in your arms?' 'Let us go down, Jacobo,' said the wife; 'I think it is indeed Francillo; I seem to recollect his voice.'

"They immediately dressed themselves hurriedly; and, as soon as the cobbler had struck a light, they descended, and opened the door. The old woman looked at Francillo but for an instant, and, with a mother's instinct, recognised her son: she fell upon his neck, and pressed him to her bosom; while master Jacobo, as much transported as his wife, threw his arms around them, and kissed them both by turns. It was some time before the happy family, reunited after so long a separation, could tear themselves apart, or cease those expressions of delight which filled their throbbing hearts.

"At length, however, the banker was able to think of his horse, which he unsaddled and led to a stable, already occupied by a cow, whose teeming udders daily yielded their sweet food for his parents. On his return to the house, he related the adventures of his life in Peru, and told them of the wealth which he had brought with him to Spain. The story was somewhat long, and might have appeared annoying to uninterested listeners; but a son who unbosoms himself after a twenty years' absence, rarely fails to fix the attention of a father and mother. To them nothing was indifferent; they greedily devoured every syllable he uttered, and the most trifling details of his life made upon them the most lively impressions of sorrow or of joy.

"He finished his history, by telling them that his wealth would lose all its value unless shared by them, and entreated his father to think no longer of working at his stall. 'No, no, my son,' said master Jacobo to him: 'no, no! I love my trade, and I will stick to my last.' 'What,' exclaimed Francillo, 'is it not time you lived in peace? I do not ask you to go with me to Madrid; I know well that a city life would have no charms for you: I do not propose, then, that you should leave the peaceful village where your days have passed; but, at least, spare yourself a painful toil, and live here at your ease, since it is in your power to do so.'

"The mother joined her son in besieging the old cobbler with entreaties; and, at last, master Jacobo capitulated. 'Well! Francillo,' said he, 'to satisfy you I will be a gentleman; that is, I will not work any longer for all the village; I will only mend my own shoes, and those of our good friend the curate.' On this convention, the banker, having swallowed a couple of eggs that they had fried for his supper, went to bed beneath his father's roof, the first time for many years, and slept with a calmness of delight that the good alone are capable of enjoying.

"The following day, Francillo returned to Madrid, after leaving with his father a purse of three hundred pistoles. But, this morning, he was not a little astonished at beholding master Jacobo suddenly enter his room. 'Ah! my father what brings you here!' 'Why, my son,' replied the old man, 'I bring you back your purse. There, take your money; I am determined to live by my trade: I have been miserable ever since I left off work.' 'Ah, well! my father,' said Francillo, 'return to the village, and continue to work as you will: but, at all events, let it be only to amuse you. Take back your purse, too, and do not spare mine.' 'And what, then, do you think I can do with so much money?' asked master Jacobo. 'It will enable you to relieve the poor,' replied the banker: 'do with it as the curate and your own conscience shall dictate.' The cobbler, satisfied to accept it on these terms, immediately departed for Mediana."

Don Cleophas had listened, with pleasure, to the history of Francillo; and he was about to express his admiration of the good-hearted banker's filial affection, when, at the very moment, his attention was distracted by the most piercing shrieks. "Signor Asmodeus!" he exclaimed, "what frightful noises do I hear?" "Those cries, which rend the air," replied the Devil, "proceed from a receptacle for madmen, who tear their throats with shouting, or with singing." "We are not far from the place of their confinement, then," said Leandro; "so let us look at them at once." "By all means," replied the Demon: "I will afford you that amusement and inform you of the causes of their madness." It was no sooner said than done; and, in a moment, the Student found himself on the Casa de los locos.

Footnote:
    3. It is curious, that in the original of the latest Paris edition, as also in the third edition, of 1707, the earliest I have been able to consult, and which was published under the superintendence of Le Sage, this passage stands, "un honnête capareto de Viejo et de Mediana." There is a note to the word "capareto" giving its translation into French as savetier. Being puzzled by the double name of the village,--"de Viejo et de Mediana," I sought the assistance of a talented Spaniard, Signor Lazeu, and was surprised to find the Spanish for cobbler is "zapatero de viejo," or, "shoemaker of old (things)," and that it should consequently have stood in the original "zapatero de viejo de Mediana." It has been doubted by many, among others the late H. D. Inglis, whether Le Sage were really the author of Le Diable Boiteux and Gil Blas; and it has been asserted that he merely translated these works from the unpublished manuscripts of some Spanish author. If the error in question were really that of Le Sage, it would certainly go far to confirm this assertion.--Trans.

CHAPTER IX

THE MADHOUSE, AND ITS INMATES.

Zambullo surveyed, by turns, with much curiosity, the several rooms and the unfortunate creatures they contained; and while he was reflecting on the scene thus presented to his eyes, the Devil said to him: "There they are, my master! You see insanity in every form there;--men and women, laughing idiots and raging maniacs, locks grey with age, and cheeks which still retain their bloom. Well! now I will tell you what has turned their heads: we will go from room to room, but will begin with the men.

"The first whom you observe, and who appears so violent, is a political fanatic of Castile. He is a proud citizen of Madrid, in the heart of which he was born; and he is more jealous of the honour of his country than was ever citizen of ancient Rome. He went mad with chagrin at reading in the gazette, that twenty-five Spaniards had suffered themselves to be beaten by a party of fifty Portuguese.

"His neighbour is a licentiate, who was so anxious to obtain a benefice, that he played the hypocrite at court during ten long years; and whose brain was turned by despair at finding himself constantly

overlooked among the promotions: his madness, however, is not without its advantage; seeing that he at present imagines himself to be Archbishop of Toledo. And what if he deceive himself? His pleasure is none the less: indeed, I think, that he is so much the more to be envied; since his error is a golden dream, which will only end with his life, and he will not be called to account in the other world for the application of his revenues in this.

"The next in rotation is a ward, whom his guardian declared to be insane, that he might have the uncontrolled use of his property: the poor youth has become really mad from rage at his unjust confinement. After the minor, comes a schoolmaster, who lost his wits in search of the paulo post futurum of the Greek verb; and, then again, we have a merchant, whose reason was shipwrecked with a vessel that belonged to him, although it had stood the shock of two bankruptcies which had before threatened to engulph him.

"The person who is lodged in the next room is the ancient captain Zanubio, a Neapolitan cavalier, who came to establish himself in Madrid, and whom jealousy has settled where he is: you shall hear his history.

"He delighted in a youthful spouse, the lady Aurora, whom he guarded as the apple of his eye. His house was absolutely inaccessible to all mankind; and Aurora never left it but for mass, always accompanied by her aged Tithon, or to breathe with him the pure air of the pleasant fields, at an estate near Alcantara, whither he sometimes led her. Despite his vigilance, however, she had been perceived at church by the cavalier Don Garcia Pacheco, who loved her from the instant that he saw her: he was an enterprising youth, and not unworthy the attention of a pretty woman whom Fortune had badly matched.

"The difficulty of introducing himself into the house of Zanubio was not sufficient to deprive Don Garcia of hope. As his chin was yet unreaped, and he was fair to behold, he disguised himself as a virgin, took with him a hundred pistoles, and betook himself to the captain's seat, where, he had learned, that gentleman and his lady were shortly expected. Watching his opportunity to accost the female who acted as gardener in Zanubio's establishment, he addressed her in the style of the heroines of chivalry, who fly from some giant's towers: 'Kind lady,' said he, 'I come to throw myself within your arms, and to entreat your pity. I am a maiden of Toledo, of wealth and name, but my parents would compel me to give my hand to one whom my heart disowns. To escape this tyranny, I have fled by night; and I now seek shelter from a cruel world. Here I shall be safe from pursuit. Do not deny me, then, to dwell with you until my friends shall be inspired with more kindly sentiments. There is my purse: do not hesitate to receive it, it is all that I can give you now: but I trust the day will come when I may more properly acknowledge the service which you will render me by your protection.'

"The gentle gardener, especially affected by the conclusion of this touching address, replied: 'Dear lady, I will receive you with pleasure. I know that there are too many youthful maidens who are sacrificed to aged men; and I know, too, that they are not usually reconciled to their lot. I sympathize with your afflictions: you could not have more fortunately addressed yourself than to me. Come! I will place you in a little room, where you may live in confidence of security.'

"Don Garcia passed four days, shut up in the gardener's cottage, anxiously awaiting the arrival of

Aurora. At last she came, guarded as ever by her jealous spouse, who immediately, according to his usual custom, searched every chamber, from the cellar to the garret, to make sure that he was free from the hated form of man, which might endanger his honour. The gardener, who expected this visitation, anticipated it by informing her master of the manner in which a refuge had been sought with her by a youthful female. Zanubio, although extremely mistrustful, had not the slightest suspicion of the deceit now practised on him; he was, however, curious to see the unknown. At the interview which followed, the lady begged him to excuse her concealing her name, stating that it was a reserve which she owed to her family, which she in some sort dishonoured by her flight. She then related to him so pathetic a tale, and in a style so romantic, that the captain was charmed; and while he listened to her narration, he felt a rising inclination for this amiable damsel, which ended in an offer of his services and protection; after which he led her to his wife, flattering himself that this adventure would not end disagreeably to himself.

"As soon as Aurora beheld Don Garcia, she blushed and trembled, without knowing why. The cavalier, who perceived her uneasiness, shrewdly guessed that she had observed the attention with which he had regarded her at church. To ascertain this fact, as soon as they were alone, he said to her: 'Madam, I have a brother who has often spoken to me of you. He saw you for a moment at your devotions, and from that moment, which he delights to recall a thousand times each day, you have been the idol of his heart;--he loves you to madness.'

"As he spoke, Aurora scrutinized the features of Don Garcia, and when he had finished she replied to him: 'You resemble your brother too closely to permit me to remain for an instant the dupe of your stratagem: I see too clearly you are that brother in disguise. I remember, one day while at mass, my mantilla fell back from my face; it was but for an instant, but I saw that you perceived me: I afterwards watched you from curiosity, and your eyes remained fixed on my person. When I left the church, I believe that you failed not to follow me, that you might learn who I was, and the house where I dwelt. I say--I believe you did this, for my head dared not turn to observe you; as my husband was with me, jealous of my slightest motions, and would have made, of one glance, a deep crime. On the morrow and following days, when I went to the church, I always saw you; and your features have become so familiar that I know you despite your disguise.'

"'Well, Madam,' replied the lover, 'I must then unmask:--yes, I am a man, the victim of your charms:--it is indeed Don Garcia Pacheco whom Love brings here in the guise of the gentler sex----' 'And you doubtless anticipate,' interrupted Aurora, 'that I, sharing your foolish passion, shall lend myself to your design, and assist in confirming my husband in his error. You are, however, deceived: I shall at once expose the deception; my honour and my peace demand it of me. Besides, I am not sorry to have an opportunity of showing my husband that vigilance is a less certain safeguard than virtue, and that, jealous and mistrustful as he is, I am more difficult to surprise than himself.'

"She had hardly spoken when the captain appeared. He had indistinctly heard a portion of his wife's discourse, and requested to be informed of the subject of their conversation. 'We were speaking,' replied Aurora, 'of those youthful cavaliers who dare to hope for love from ladies of a tender age, because united to a husband for whom respect claims the place of passion. As you entered I was saying, that should such a gallant dare to address himself to me,--should he endeavour to introduce himself beneath your roof by some of those artifices to which such madmen have recourse, I should know well how to punish his audacity.'

"'And you, Madam,' said Zanubio, turning to Don Garcia, 'after what fashion should you treat a youthful cavalier in such a case?' Our assumption of a virgin was so much disconcerted at this question, that he was unable to reply; and his embarrassment would certainly have attracted Zanubio's attention, had not, at the moment, a servant entered the apartment, to inform the captain that a person who had just arrived from Madrid wished to speak with him.

"Zanubio had no sooner gone out than Don Garcia, throwing himself at Aurora's feet, exclaimed: 'Ah, madam, how can you delight thus to perplex me? Could you be cruel enough to expose me to the wrath of an enraged husband?' 'No, Pacheco,' replied the lady, smiling; 'youthful dames who are so unfortunate as to have aged spouses are not so resentful. Be not alarmed! I could not resist the temptation to amuse myself at the expense of your fears; but that is the sum of your punishment; and it is surely not exacting too great a price for my kindness in permitting your continuance here.' At these consoling words all Don Garcia's alarms were dispelled, and they yielded to hopes, of which Aurora was too kind long to delay the realization.

"One day, while their reciprocal affection was manifested in a form too clear to be misunderstood, the captain surprised them. Had he been the most confiding of men, it would have been impossible, unless his confidence were not extended to his own eyes, to doubt that the lovely unknown was a man in disguise. Furious at the scene which presented itself, he hastened to his dressing-room in search of his pistols; but, in the meanwhile, the fond couple escaped,--in their hurry to leave the apartment, double-locking the door, and taking with them the key. They lost no time in gaining a neighbouring village, in which Don Garcia had taken the precaution to leave his valet with two good horses. There, our hero, having abandoned his petticoats, and placed Aurora on a crupper on one of the steeds, mounted and rode with her to a convent, where she prayed him to leave her in the care of an aunt, its abbess; after which he returned to Madrid to await the termination of his adventure.

"Poor Zanubio, finding himself imprisoned, shouted with all his lungs, and a servant, hearing his voice, hastened to his assistance: but, if Love laughs at locksmiths, locks are sometimes extremely unaccommodating. In vain did the servant and captain try to force the door; and at last the latter, his wrath increasing with his efforts, rushed to the window, and threw himself from it, his pistols in his hands: he fell upon his back, wounded his head, and when his attendants arrived they found him senseless. He was carried bleeding to his chamber, and by deluging him with water, and by other gentle torments used on such occasions, they succeeded in bringing him to life; but his fury returned with his senses. 'Where is my wife?' he cried. To this interrogatory they replied, by informing him that they had seen her pass from the garden, in company with the unknown lady, by a little private door. He immediately demanded his pistols, which they dared not refuse him, ordered a horse to be saddled, and without reflecting on his wound, set out, but by another road, in pursuit of the lovers. The day passed in this fruitless search; and when he stopped for the night at a village inn, to repose himself, the fatigue and irritation of his wound brought on a fever and delirium, which nearly cost him his life.

"The rest is told in a few words. The captain, after being confined to his bed for a fortnight, in the village, returned still unwell to his country seat; and there, by continually dwelling on his misfortune, he shortly afterwards lost his reason. The relations of Aurora were no sooner informed of this event, than they caused him to be brought to Madrid, and confined where you now see him; and they have resolved that his wife shall remain in the convent for some years to come, as a punishment for her indiscretion, or, more properly, for a fault which their own cupidity placed her in a situation to be tempted to commit.

"The next to whom I shall direct your attention," continued the Devil, "is the Signor Don Blaz Desdichado, a worthy cavalier, whose deplorable malady is also owing to the loss of his wife, but by death." "That indeed surprises me," said Don Cleophas. "A husband whom the death of his wife renders insane! Well! that is more than I ever expected to spring from conjugal love." "Not so fast!" interrupted Asmodeus: "Don Blaz did not lose his reason with his wife; but because, having no children, he was obliged to return to the parents of the deceased fifty thousand ducats which he had received with her, and which the marriage contract compelled him to restore."

"Ah! that is another affair," replied Leandro; "the matter is by no means so wonderful as I imagined. But tell me, if you please, who is that young man that is skipping about like a kid in the next room, and from time to time stopping to laugh until he holds his sides? He is a lively fool enough." "Yes," replied the Cripple, "and it was excess of joy which made him mad. He was porter to a person of quality; when one day, hearing of the death of a rich contador, to whose wealth he was sole heir, he was so affected by the joyous news that his head was not proof against his good fortune.

"We have now come to that tall youth who is twanging the guitar, and accompanying the pathetic strain with his voice: his is a melancholy madness. He is a lover, whom the excessive severity of his mistress reduced to despair, until they were obliged to enclose him here." "Alas! how I pity him," exclaimed the Student; "permit me to express my sorrow for his misfortune;--it is one to which every susceptible heart is exposed. Were it my own fate to love a disdainful beauty, I know not but that I too should love to madness." "I can believe you," replied the Demon: "that sentiment would stamp you for a true Castilian. One must be born in the centre of that ancient kingdom to be capable of loving until reason sinks with a despised heart. Your Frenchman is not so tender; and would you appreciate the difference between a gay Parisian and a fiery Spaniard in this respect, I need only repeat to you the song which yon poor fool is singing, and which his passion inspires even at this moment:

SPANISH SONG.

    'Mine eyes gush o'er with floods of wild desire,
        And hopeless love burns fiercely in my breast;
    Yet not my tears can quench my bosom's fire,
        Nor passion's fire my scalding tears arrest.'[4]

"It is thus sings a true Castilian whom his lady slights; and now I will repeat to you the words in which a Frenchman told his griefs, in a similar case, only a few days ago:

FRENCH SONG.

    'She who within my bosom reigns,
        A tyrant's stern control maintains;
    Nor sighs, nor tears, nor prayers can move
    The least relenting look of love.

> A kind word, kindly spoken, might
> Have turn'd my darkness into light;
> But, since my suit is urged in vain,
> I fly to feed my griefs with Payen.'⁵

"This Payen is undoubtedly a tavern-keeper?" said Don Cleophas. "Exactly so," replied the Devil. "But let us continue our observations." "Let us then turn to the women," exclaimed Leandro; "I am impatient to hear their histories." "I will yield to your impatience," answered the Spirit; "but there are yet two or three unfortunates on this side of the house, whom I would first show to you: you may profit by their unhappiness.

"You observe, close by the melancholy songster, that pale and haggard face; those teeth, which gnash as though they would make nothing of the iron bars that ornament the window. Yon is an honest man, born under influence of malignant star, who, with all the merit in the world, has vainly striven, during twenty years, to secure a modest competence; he has scarcely, with all his efforts, succeeded in gaining his daily bread. His reason fled its seat, on his perceiving a worthless fellow of his acquaintance suddenly mount the top of fortune's wheel by a lucky speculation.

"His neighbour, again, is an old secretary, whose head was cracked by a stroke of ingratitude, which he received from a courtier, in whose service he lived during sixty years. No praises were too great for the zeal and fidelity of this ancient servant; who, however, never claimed their just reward, content to let his assiduity and services speak for themselves. His master, far from resembling Archelaus, king of Macedonia, who refused favours when demanded, and bestowed them when unasked, died forgetful of his merits, leaving him just enough to pass his days in misery, and the refuge of a madhouse.

"I will only detain you with one more, and it is with the man who, leaning with his elbows on the window, appears plunged in profound meditation. You see in him a Signor Hidalgo, of Tafalla, a small town of Navarre, which he left for Madrid that he might make the best use of his wealth. He was bitten with a rage for surrounding himself with the literati of the day; and as these animals are always seen to most advantage at feeding-time, he kept open house for their entertainment. Authors are an unpolished and ungrateful race; but, although they despised and snarled at their keeper, he was not contented until they had eaten him out of house and home." "Poor fellow," said Zambullo: "he no doubt went mad with rage at his awful stupidity." "On the contrary," replied Asmodeus, "it was with regret at finding himself unable to keep up his menagerie. Well! now let us pay our respects to the ladies," added the Devil.

"Why! how is this?" exclaimed the Student: "I only see seven or eight of them. I had expected to have found them here by scores." "Ah!" said the Devil, smiling, "but they are by no means all confined within these walls. I will take you instantly, if you wish it, to another quarter of the city, where there is a larger house than this, full of mad-women to the very roof." "Do not trouble yourself, I beg," replied Don Cleophas; "I am by no means anxious for their acquaintance: these will suffice." "You are right," replied the Devil; "and these too, are almost all youthful ladies of distinction. You may perceive by the attention which is paid to their persons, that they are not ordinary subjects. And now for the story of their madness.

"In the first room is the wife of a corregidor, who went mad with rage at being termed plebeian by a lady of the court; in the second, is the spouse of the treasurer-general of the council of the Indies: anger also made her mad, at being obliged, in a narrow street, to turn back her carriage to make way for that of the duchess of Medina-Coeli. The third room is the residence of a merchant's widow, whom regret for the loss of a noble signor's hand robbed of her senses; and the fourth is occupied by a girl of highest rank, named Donna Beatrice, whose misfortunes are worth your attention.

"This young lady was united by the most tender friendship with the Donna Mencia: they were indeed inseparable. It happened, however, that a handsome chevalier of the order of St. James became acquainted with them both, and they soon were rivals for his heart. As he could not marry the two, and as his affections inclined towards the Donna Mencia, he paid his court to that lady, and she shortly became his wife.

"Donna Beatrice, jealous of the power of her charms, and mortified to excess by the preference shown to another, conceived a passion for revenge, which, like a woman, or a good Spaniard, she nourished at the bottom of her heart. While this passion was yet in its infancy, she received from Don Jacintho de Romarate, a neglected lover of the Donna Mencia, a letter stating that, being as much insulted as herself by the marriage of his mistress, he had resolved to demand satisfaction of the chevalier for their united wrongs.

"This letter gave great delight to Beatrice, who desiring but the death of the sinner, wished for nothing more than that his rival should fall beneath Jacintho's hand. While anxiously awaiting for so christianly a gratification, it happened, however, that her own brother, having chanced to quarrel with this same Jacintho, came to blows with her champion, and fell pierced with wounds of which he died. Although duty prompted Donna Beatrice to avenge her brother's death by citing his murderer before the

Alain René Le Sage

tribunals of his country, she neglected to do so, as this would have interfered with her revenge; which demonstrates, if such proof were needed, that there is no interest so dear to a woman as that of her beauty. Need I remind you, that when Ajax violated Cassandra in the temple of Pallas, that goddess did not on the instant punish the sacrilegious Greek? No! she reserved her wrath until its victim should have first redressed the insult offered to her charms by the Judgment of the hated Paris. But, alas! Donna Beatrice, less fortunate than Minerva, never tasted the sweetness of her anticipated vengeance. Romarate perished by the sword of the chevalier, and chagrin for her wrongs, still unpunished, drove the lady into this asylum.

"The next who offer themselves to your notice are an attorney's grandmother and an aged marchioness. The ill-temper of the first so annoyed her descendant, that he very quietly got rid of her by placing her here: the other is a lady who has ever been an idol to herself, and instead of aging with becoming resignation, has never ceased to weep the decay of that beauty which formed her only happiness; and at last, one day, when her mirror told, too plainly to be doubted, that all her charms were flown, went mad."

"So much the better for the ancient dame," added Leandro. "In the derangement of her mind, she will no more perceive the ravages of time." "Most assuredly not," replied the Devil; "far from beholding in her face the marks of age, her complexion seems to her now a happy blending of the lily and the rose; she sees around her but the Graces and the Loves,--in a word, she thinks that she is Venus herself." "Ah! well!" exclaimed the Student, "were it not better that thousands should be mad, than that they should know themselves for what they are?" "Undoubtedly," replied Asmodeus; "but come, we have only one other female to observe; and that is she who dwells in the furthest room, and whom sleep has just visited with rest, after three days and nights of raving. Look at her well! What think you of the Donna Emerenciana?" "That she is beautiful, indeed," answered Zambullo. "What horror, that so lovely a creature should be mad! By what fatal accident is she reduced to this dreadful situation?" "Listen!" replied the Demon; "I will tell you the story of her woes.

"Donna Emerenciana, only daughter of Don Guillem Stephani, lived tranquilly at Siguença, in the mansion of her father, when Don Kimen de Lizana came to trouble her repose by those attentions with which he sought to win her heart. Flattered by his gallantries, she received their homage with delight; she even had the weakness to lend herself to the artifices to which he resorted that he might speak with her in private; and in a short time exchanged with him vows of eternal love and fidelity.

"The lovers were of equal birth; but the lady was one of the richest heiresses of Spain, while Don Kimen was a younger son. But there was still another obstacle to their union,--Don Guillem hated the family of the Lizana. This he never affected to conceal, whenever they were mentioned; and he seemed more averse to Don Kimen himself, than to any other of his race. Emerenciana, though deeply afflicted at her father's sentiments on this subject, which she felt boded unhappily for her passion, could not resolve to abandon its object; and she therefore continued her secret interviews with her lover, who from time to time, through the assistance of a waiting-maid, ventured even into her chamber by night.

"It happened, one of these nights, that Don Guillem chanced to be awake when the gallant was thus introduced, and thought he heard a noise in his daughter's apartment, which was not far from his own. This was quite enough to arouse a father, and especially one so mistrustful as Don Guillem. Suspicious as he was, he had never imagined the possibility of his daughter's intelligence with Don Kimen; but not being of a disposition to place too much confidence in any one, he rose quietly from his bed, opened a window which looked into the street, and there patiently waited until he saw that cavalier, whom the light of the moon enabled him to recognize, descending from the balcony by a silken ladder.

"What a sight for Stephani!--for the most vindictive, the most relentless mortal, that even Sicily, which gave him birth, had ever produced. He controlled the first emotions of his terrible wrath, and repressed every exclamation of surprise at what he beheld, that the chief victim which his wounded pride demanded might not be warned of his fate, and attempt to escape the avenger's hand. He so far constrained himself as to wait until the morning, when his daughter had risen, ere he entered her apartment. She was alone, as he approached her, with fury sparkling in his eyes; and, with a voice that made her tremble, he addressed her thus: 'Unworthy wretch! whom not the honour of thy race restrains from deeds of infamy, prepare to meet their due reward! This steel,' he added, as he drew a dagger from his bosom, 'shall find a sheath within your heart, unless with truth upon your lips you name the daring villain who brought, last night, dishonour on my house.'

"Emerenciana was so overcome by this unexpected discovery and her father's threats, that her tongue refused its office. 'Ah! miserable,' continued Don Guillem, 'thy silence and confusion tell me too plainly all thy guilt! Dost think, child, whom I blush to call mine own, that I know not what has passed? I know too well! I saw, myself, the villain, and recognized him for Don Kimen. 'Twas not enough, then, to receive a cavalier at night within thy room!--that cavalier must be the man whom most I loathe! But come! tell me how much I owe him. Speak without disguise,--thy sincerity alone can save thy shameful life.'

"These last words, terrible as they were, brought with them some slight hope to the unfortunate girl of escaping the fate which menaced her, and she recovered from her fright sufficiently to enable her to reply: 'Signor, I cannot deny that I am guilty of listening to Lizana; but I call Heaven to witness for the purity of his sentiments and conduct. Aware as he was of your hatred for his name, he dared not to ask your sanction for his addresses; but it was for no other end than to confer with me how that sanction might be obtained that he sought, and I permitted, his coming here.' 'And who, then,' asked Stephani, 'was the willing instrument through which you exchanged your communications?' 'It was,' replied his daughter, 'one of your pages to whom we were indebted for that kindness.' 'Enough,' interrupted the father; 'and now to execute the design for which I come!' Thereupon displaying his poniard, he made Emerenciana sit down, and placing paper and ink before her, compelled her to write to her lover the following letter which he dictated:--

"'Dearest Love,--only delight of my life,--I hasten to inform you that my father has just set out for his estate, whence he will not return until to-morrow. Lose not this happy opportunity. I doubt not you will watch for the coming night with as much impatience as your beloved

"'EMERENCIANA.'

"As soon as this treacherous letter was written and sealed, Don Guillem said to his daughter: 'And now summon the page who so well performs the duties you impose on him, and direct him to carry this note to Don Kimen: but hope not to deceive me; I shall conceal myself behind the drapery of your room, whence I can observe your slightest movement; and if while you charge him with this commission you speak one word, or make the smallest sign which may give him suspicion of your message, I will plunge this dagger in your heart.' Emerenciana knew her father too well to dare to disobey him: the page was called, and the letter placed as usual in his hands.

"Not until then did Stephani put up his weapon; but he did not leave his daughter for a moment during the day, nor would he let any one approach her, so that she could communicate to Lizana intelligence of the snare which was spread for him. Accordingly, when night came, the youthful gallant hastened to the wished-for meeting; but hardly had he entered the door of his mistress's house before he found himself seized by three powerful men, who disarmed him in a moment, tied a bandage over his mouth to prevent his cries, another over his eyes, and bound his hands behind his back. They then placed him in a carriage, which was waiting for the purpose, and having all mounted therein for complete security of the betrayed cavalier's person, they carried him to the seat of Stephani, situated near the village of Miedes, four leagues from Siguença, where they arrived before daybreak.

"The first care of the signor was to cause Don Kimen to be placed in a vault which received but a feeble light from a hole near the top, so small, that escape by that was impossible. He then ordered Julio, a confidential servant, to feed him with bread and water only, to give him but a truss of straw to sleep on, and to say to him every time he carried him food: 'Here, base seducer: it is thus that Don Guillem treats those who are mad enough to dare to insult him!' The cruel Sicilian was hardly less severe in his treatment of his daughter: he imprisoned her in a chamber which looked into a small courtyard, deprived her of her attendants, and placed her in the custody of a duenna whom he had chosen, because she was unequalled for her skill in tormenting those committed to her charge.

"Having thus disposed of the two lovers, he was by no means contented with the punishment already inflicted on them: he had resolved to get rid of Don Kimen, and had only not done so at once because he wished to avoid any unpleasant consequences which might follow his crime; to manage which, appeared to be somewhat difficult. As he had employed three of his servants in the abduction of the cavalier, he could hardly hope that a secret known to so many persons would always remain undiscovered:--what then was he to do, to shun any impertinent explanations which justice might think it necessary to demand? His resolve was worthy of a conqueror; he assembled his accomplices in a small pavilion, a short distance from the chateau, and after telling them how highly satisfied he was with their zeal, he stated that he had brought them there to receive a substantial reward for their services in money, and that he had prepared a little festival, which he invited them to share. They sat down to enjoy themselves, little dreaming that it was a feast of death; for when their brains were heated with wine, the worthy Julio by his master's order brought in a poisoned bowl, which soon ended their rejoicing. The pair then fired the pavilion, and before the flames had brought around them the inhabitants of the neighbouring village, they assassinated Emerenciana's two female attendants and the page of whom I have spoken, and threw their bodies into the burning heap. It was really amusing, while the remains of these poor wretches were consuming in this infernal pile, which the peasants strove in vain to extinguish, to witness the profound grief displayed by our Sicilian: he appeared inconsolable for the loss of his domestics.

"Nothing remaining to be feared from any want of discretion on the part of his coadjutors, which might have betrayed him, he thus addressed his confidant: 'My dear Julio, my mind is now at peace, and the life of Don Kimen is at my mercy; but, before I immolate him to my wounded honour, I would enjoy the sweet delight of making him feel how much he has offended me;--the misery and horror of a long and solitary confinement will be more dreadful to him than death itself.' In truth, Lizana was by no means comfortable; and, hopeless of ever leaving the dungeon where he wasted, he would have welcomed death as a cheap release from his sufferings.

"But, despite his boast of peace, the mind of Stephani knew no rest after the exploits he had recently achieved; and ere many days had passed, a new source of inquietude presented itself in the fear lest Julio, as he daily saw the prisoner for the purpose of taking him food, should suffer himself to be corrupted by promises. This fear made Don Guillem resolve to get rid of Lizana without loss of time, and then to blow out the brains of his friend Julio. But the latter was also not without his own misgivings; and, as he shrewdly suspected that were Don Kimen once out of the way, he would be found in it, he had made his resolution to take himself off some fine night, with all that was portable in the house, when the darkness would excuse his not distinguishing his master's property from his own.

"While these honest gentlemen were each meditating an agreeable surprise for the other, they were one day both unwelcomely accosted at a short distance from the chateau, by about twenty archers of St. Hermandad, who surrounded, and greeted them in the name of the king and the law! At this salutation Don Guillem was somewhat confounded; but, calling the colour to his cheeks, he asked the commandant of the archers whom he sought. 'Yourself!' replied the officer: 'you are accused of having unlawfully seized on Don Kimen de Lizana; and I am directed to make strict search for that cavalier within your mansion, and further to make you my prisoner.' Stephani, convinced by this answer that he was lost, drew from his person a brace of pistols, exclaiming that he would suffer no one to enter his house; and that he would shoot the commandant without ceremony if he did not instantly take himself off with his troop. The leader of the holy brotherhood, despising this threat, advanced at once towards the Sicilian; who, as good as his word, fired, and wounded him slightly in the face. This wound, however, cost the life of the madman who gave it; for the archers in a moment stretched him lifeless at the feet of their injured chief. Julio surrendered himself without resistance; and, making a virtue of necessity, cleared his conscience by a frank avowal of all that had occurred,--except that, perceiving his master was really dead, he did him the honour to invest his memory with all the glory attaching to the transaction.

"He then conducted the archers to the vault, where they found Lizana on his straw bed, securely bound. The unfortunate gentleman, who lived in continual expectation of death, thought it was come at last when he saw so many armed men enter his prison; and was, as you may expect, agreeably surprised to find liberators in those whom he had taken for his executioners. When they had released him from his dungeon, and received his thanks, he asked them how they had learned that he was confined in the place where they found him. 'That,' replied the commandant, 'I will tell you in a few words.'

"'The night you were entrapped,' said the officer, 'one of Don Guillem's assistants, whose mistress resided in the neighbourhood, stole a few moments while they were waiting for you, to bid adieu to his sweetheart before his departure, and was indiscreet enough to reveal to her the project of Stephani. For a wonder, the lady kept the secret for three whole days; but when the news of the fire at Miedes reached Siguença, as every body thought it strange that all the servants of the Sicilian should have perished in the flames, she naturally took it into her head also that the fire was the work of Guillem himself. To revenge her lover's death, therefore, she sought the Signor Don Felix, your father, and related to him all she knew. Don Felix, alarmed at finding you were in the hands of a man capable of everything, accompanied the lady to the corregidor, who on hearing her story had no doubt of Stephani's intentions towards you, and that he was the diabolical incendiary the woman suspected. To make inquiries into all the circumstances of the case, the corregidor instantly despatched orders to me at Retortillo, where I live, directing me to repair with my brigade to this chateau, to find you if possible, and to take Don Guillem, dead or alive. I have happily performed my commission as regards yourself; and I only regret that it is out of my power to conduct the criminal to Siguença alive. He compelled us by his furious resistance to dispatch him on the spot.'

"The officer, having ended his story, thus continued: 'I will now, Signor Don Kimen, draw up a report of all that has happened here; I will not, however, detain you long, and we will then set out together to release your friends from the anxiety they suffer upon your account.' 'Stay, signor commandant,' interrupted Julio, 'I will furnish you with matter to lengthen your report: you have got another prisoner to liberate. Donna Emerenciana is confined in a dismal chamber of this chateau, guarded by a merciless duenna, who upbraids her without ceasing for her love of this cavalier, and torments her by every device she can imagine.' 'Oh Heaven!' cried Lizana, 'is it possible that the barbarous Stephani should not have been contented to exercise his cruelty on me alone? Let us hasten to deliver the unfortunate lady from the tyranny of her gaoler.'

"Julio lost no time in conducting the commandant, four or five of the archers, and Lizana, to the prison of Don Guillem's daughter. They knocked at the door; it was opened by the surprised duenna, and you may conceive the delight of Don Kimen at again beholding his mistress, after having lost her as he supposed for ever. All his hopes revived; nor could he reasonably conceive the possibility of their non-fulfilment, since he who alone stood between him and his happiness, was dead. He threw himself in ecstacy at the feet of Emerenciana; when,--picture his horror if you can,--he found, instead of the gentle girl who had listened with tender transport to his vows, a maniac. Yes! so well had the duenna succeeded in her efforts, that she had effaced the image of the lover by destroying the canvas on which it was depicted.

"She remained for some time in apparent meditation, then imagining herself to be the fair Angelica, besieged by the Tartars in the towers of Albraca, and the persons who filled her apartment to be so many Paladins come to her rescue, she received them with much politeness. Addressing the chief of the holy brotherhood as Roland, Lizana as Brandimart, Julio as Hubert of the Lion, and the archers as Antifort, Clarion, Adrian, and the two sons of the Marquis Olivier, she said to them: 'Brave chevaliers, I no longer fear the Emperor Agrican, nor Queen Marphisa: your valour would suffice for my defence against the world itself in arms.'

"The officer and his followers could not resist an inclination to laugh at this heroic reception; but poor Don Kimen was so much afflicted by the unexpected condition in which he found her for whom alone he had wished to live, that reason seemed to be on the point of abandoning him also. Recovering himself, however, from his first surprise, and hoping that she might be brought to recognize the unhappy author of her misfortunes, he addressed her tenderly: 'Dearest Emerenciana,' said he, 'it is Lizana speaks to thee: recall thy scattered thoughts, he comes to tell thee that thy griefs are at an end. Heaven has heard the prayer of those fond hearts itself united; and its wrath has fallen on the wicked head of him who would have separated two beings made for each other.'

"The reply to these words was another speech from the daughter of king Galafron to the valiant defenders of Albraca, who this time however restrained their mirth. Even the commandant, whose profession was not favourable to the kindlier feelings of humanity, was touched with compassion, and observing the profound affliction of Don Kimen, said to him: 'Signor Cavalier, do not despair! We have, in Siguença, physicians celebrated for their skill in curing the disorders of the mind, and there is yet hope for your unfortunate lady. But let us away! You, Signor Hubert of the Lion,' added he, addressing himself to Julio, 'you who know the whereabouts of the stables of this castle, take with you Antifort and the two sons of the Marquis Olivier, bring out the fleetest coursers from their stalls and harness them to the car of our princess; in the meanwhile I will prepare my dispatches.' "So saying, he drew out his writing materials, and having finished his report, he presented his hand to Angelica and conducted her to the court-yard, where he found a carriage with four mules, which had been prepared for her reception by the paladins. The lady was placed therein by the side of Don Kimen; and the commandant having compelled the duenna to enter also, as he thought the corregidor would be glad to have some conversation with the dame, he mounted, and they set out for Siguença. This is not all: by order of their chief, the archers bound Julio, and placed him in another carriage with the body of Don Guillem; then mounting their horses they followed the same route.

"During the journey, the daughter of Stephani uttered a thousand extravagancies, every one of which was as a dagger in the heart of her lover. The presence of the duenna was an additional source of disquiet to him. 'It is you, infamous old woman,' said he to her, 'it is you who by your cruelty have tortured Emerenciana to madness.' The old hypocrite endeavoured to justify herself by pleading the instructions of her defunct master. 'It is to Don Guillem alone,' said she, 'that her misfortunes are attributable: daily did that too rigid father visit her in her room; and it is to his reproaches and threats that the loss of her reason is owing.'

"On reaching Siguença, the commandant immediately went to give an account of his mission to the corregidor, who after examining Julio and the duenna found them lodgings in the prisons of that town, where they reside to this time. Lizana, after deposing to all he had suffered from Don Guillem, repaired to his father's house, where his presence restored joy to his alarmed relations. Donna Emerenciana was sent by the judge to Madrid, where she has a kind uncle by her mother's side, who desired nothing better than the administration of his niece's property, and who was nominated her guardian. As he could not creditably do otherwise than appear desirous of her restoration to sanity, he had recourse to the most famed physicians of this city; but he had nothing to fear, for, after having taken a becoming number of fees, they declared her incurable. On this decision, the guardian, no doubt very reluctantly, placed her here; and here, most likely, she is destined to end her days."

"And a sad destiny it is," cried Don Cleophas; "I am really touched by her misfortunes: Donna Emerenciana deserved a better fate. And Don Kimen," added he, "what is become of him? I am curious to learn how he acted." "Very reasonably," replied Asmodeus: "when he heard that the evil was past a remedy, he went to Spanish America. He hopes that by change of scene he may insensibly efface the remembrance of those charms that wisdom and his own peace require he should forget.----But," continued the Devil, "after having exhibited to you madmen who are confined, it is time I shewed to you those who deserve to be so."

Alain René Le Sage

Footnote:
4.
'Ardo y lloro sin sosiego:
 Llorando y ardiendo tanto,
 Que ni el llanto apaga el fuego,
 Ni el fuego consume el llanto.'
5.
'L'objet qui règne dans mon coeur
 Est toujours insensible à mon amour fidèle,
    Mes soins, mes soupirs, ma langueur,
 Ne sauraient attendrir cette beauté cruelle.
 O ciel! est-il un sort plus affreux que le mien?
       Ah! puisque je ne puis lui plaire,
       Je renonce au jour qui m'éclaire;
 Venez, mes chers amis, m'enterrer chez Payen.'

CHAPTER X
THE SUBJECT OF WHICH IS INEXHAUSTIBLE.

"Run your eyes over the city, and as we discover subjects worthy of being placed in this museum, I will describe them to you. There is one, already; I must not let him escape: he is a newly-married man. It is just a week since, in consequence of reports which reached his ears relative to the coquetries of a damsel whom he affected, he went in a fury to her house, broke one portion of her furniture, threw the other out of windows, and on the next day mended the matter by espousing her." "A proper candidate, indeed," said Zambullo, "for a vacant place in this establishment!"

"He has a neighbour," resumed the Cripple, "who is not much wiser than himself, a bachelor of forty-five, who, with plenty to live on, would yet swell the train of some noble pauper. And yonder is the widow of an advocate, who, having counted three-score years and more, is about to seek the shelter of a convent, that her reputation may not, as she says, suffer scandal in this wicked world.

"I perceive also two virgins, or, to speak more properly, two girls of fifty years of age. They pray Heaven, in its mercy, to take to it their father, who keeps them mewed like minors; as they hope, when he is gone, to find handsome men who will marry them for love." "And why not?" inquired the Scholar; "there are stranger things than such men to be found." "I am perfectly of your opinion," replied Asmodeus: "they may find husbands, doubtless; but they ought not to expect to be so fortunate,--it is therein that their folly consists.

"There is no country in the world in which women speak the truth in regard to their age. At Paris, about a month ago, a maiden of forty-eight and a woman of sixty-nine had occasion to go before a magistrate as witnesses in a case which concerned the honour of a widow of their acquaintance. The magistrate, first addressing himself to the married lady, asked her age; and, although her years might have been counted by the wrinkles on her brow, she unhesitatingly replied, that she was exactly forty. 'And you, madam,' said the man of law, addressing the single lady in her turn, 'may I ask your age also?' 'We can dispense with that, your worship,' replied the damsel; 'it is a question that ought not to be asked.' 'Impossible!' replied he; 'are you not aware that the law requires....' 'Oh!' interrupted the lady sharply, 'the law requires nothing of the kind: what matters it to the law what my age may be? It is none of its business.' 'But, madam,' said the magistrate, 'I cannot receive your testimony unless your age be stated; it is a necessary preliminary, I assure you.' 'Well,' replied the maiden, 'if it be absolutely necessary, look at me with attention, and put down my age conscientiously.'

"The magistrate looked at her over his spectacles, and was polite enough to decree that she did not appear above twenty-eight. But when to his question, as to how long she had known the widow, the witness replied--before her marriage: 'I have made a mistake,' said he; 'for I have put you down for twenty-eight, whereas it is nine and twenty years since the lady became a wife.' 'You may state then,' cried the maiden, 'that I am thirty: I may have known the widow since I was one year old.' 'That will hardly do,' replied the magistrate; 'we may as well add a dozen years at once.' 'By no means,' said the lady; 'I will allow another year, if you please; but if my own honour were in question instead of the widow's, I would not add one month more to please the law, or any other body in the world.'

"When the two witnesses had left the magistrate, the woman said to the maiden: 'Do not you wonder at this noodle, who thinks us young enough to tell him our ages to a day? It is enough, surely, that they should be inscribed on the parish registers, without his poking them into his depositions, for the information of all the world. It would be delightful, truly, to hear recited in open court,--Madame Richard, aged sixty and so many years, and Mademoiselle Perinelle, aged forty-five, depose such and so forth. It is too absurd: I have taken care to suppress a good score of years; and you were wise enough to follow my example.'

'What do you mean by following your example?' cried the ancient damsel, with youthful indignation: 'I am extremely obliged to you; but I would have you to know that thirty-five years are the utmost I have seen.' 'Why! child,' replied the matron, with a malicious smile, 'you forget yourself: I was present at your birth--ah! what a time it is ago! And your poor father! I knew him well. But we must all die; and he was not young, either: it is nearly forty years since we buried him.' 'Oh! my father,' interrupted the virgin, hastily, irritated at the precision of the old dame's tender recollections,--'my father was so old when he married my mother, that she was not likely to have any children by him.'

"I perceive in that house opposite," continued the Spirit, "two men, who are not over-burdened with sense. One is a youth of family, who can neither keep money in his pocket, nor do entirely without it: he has discovered, therefore, an excellent means of always having a supply. When he is in cash, he lays it out in books, and when his purse is empty, he sells them for the half of their cost. The other is a foreign artist, who seeks for patronage among the ladies as a portrait painter: he is clever, draws correctly, colours to perfection, and is extraordinarily successful in the likeness; but--he never flatters his originals, yet expects the women will flock to him. Sheer stupidity! Inter stultos referatur."

"What?" cried the Scholar, "have you studied the classics?" "You ought hardly to be surprised at that," replied the Devil: "I speak fluently all your barbarous tongues--Hebrew, Greek, Persic, and Arabic. Nevertheless, I am not vain of my attainments; and that, at all events, is an advantage I have over your learned pedants.

"You may see in that large mansion, on the left, a sick lady surrounded by several others, who are in attendance upon her: she is the rich widow of a celebrated architect, whose love for her husband's profession has extended itself to the most foolish admiration of the Corinthian capital of society--the higher classes. She has just made her will, by which she bequeaths her immense wealth to grandees of the first class, who are ignorant of her very existence, but whose titles have gained for them their legacies. She was asked whether she would not leave something to a person who had rendered her most important services. 'Alas! no,' she replied, with an appearance of regret; 'and I am sorry that I cannot do so. I am not so ungrateful as to deny the obligation which I owe to him; but his humble name would disgrace my will.'"

"Signor Asmodeus," interrupted Leandro, "tell me, I pray you, whether the old gentleman whom I perceive so busy reading in his study, does not chance to be one of those who merit to be here confined." "He does, indeed, deserve it," answered the Demon: "he is an old licentiate, who is reading a proof of a book which he is passing through the press." "Doubtless, some work on morals or theology?" said Don Cleophas. "Not it," replied the Cripple; "it is a collection of amatory songs, which he wrote in his youth: instead of burning them, or at least suffering them to fall into the oblivion to which he is fast hastening, he has resolved to print them himself, for fear his heirs should be tempted to do so after his death, and that, out of respect for his memory, they should deprive them of their point by rendering them decent.

"There is a little lady living in the same house with our Anacreon, whom I must not forget: she is so entirely convinced of the power of her attractions, that no man ever spoke to her whom she did not at once place in the list of her admirers.

"But let us turn to a wealthy canon, whom I see a few paces beyond her. He has a very singular phantasy. If he lives frugally, it is not with a view to mortify the flesh, or from a dislike to the grape; if his humility does without a coach and six, it is not from avarice. Ah! for what object then does he husband his resources? What does he with his revenues? Does he bestow them in alms? No! he expends them in the purchase of paintings, expensive furniture, and jewellery. Now, you would naturally expect he bought these things to enjoy them while he lived?--No such thing; he only seeks to swell the inventory of his effects when he shall be no more."

"Oh! impossible!" cried Zambullo: "such a madman as you describe cannot exist on the earth!" "I repeat, nevertheless," replied the Devil, "that such is his mania. The only pleasure he derives from these things is in the imagination of how they will figure in his said inventory. Does he buy, for instance, a superbly inlaid cabinet; it is neatly packed upon the instant, and carefully stowed away; that it may appear quite new in the eyes of the brokers who may come when he is dead to bargain for his relics.

"I will show you one of his neighbours that you will think quite as mad as he,--an old bachelor, recently arrived from the Philippine Isles, with an enormous fortune which he derived from his father, who was auditor of the court at Manilla: his conduct is extraordinary enough. You may see him daily in the antechambers of the king, or of the prime minister. Do not fancy, however, that it is ambition which leads him there, to solicit some important charge: he seeks no employment; he asks for nothing. 'What then!' you will say to me, 'does he go there simply to pay his devoirs?' Colder still! He never speaks to the minister, to whom indeed he is not even known, nor does he desire to be so. 'What then is his object?'--I will tell you. He wishes to persuade the world of his credit at Court."

"An amusing original, indeed!" cried the Student, bursting with laughter; "he takes great pains to little purpose, truly: you may well place him in the list of madmen." "Oh! as to that," replied Asmodeus, "I shall shew you many others whom it would be unreasonable to think more wise. For instance, look in yonder house, so splendidly illuminated, and you will perceive three men and two ladies sitting round a table. They have just supped together, and they are now playing at cards to while away the night, with which only will they leave their occupation. Such is the life these gentle cavaliers and ladies lead. They meet regularly every evening, and break up like fogs only with the sun; when they retire to sleep until darkness again calls them to light and life: they have renounced the face of day and the beauties of nature. Would not one say, to behold them thus surrounded with waxen tapers, that they were corpses, waiting for the last sad offices that are rendered to the dead?" "There is no necessity to shut those people from the world," said Don Cleophas;--"they have ceased to belong to it."

"I perceive in the arms of sleep," resumed the Cripple, "a man whom I esteem, and who is also attached devotedly to me,--a being formed in my own mould. He is an old bachelor, who idolises the fair sex. You cannot speak to him of a pretty woman, without remarking the delight with which he hears you; if you say that her mouth is small, her lips rubies, her teeth pearls, her cheeks roses on an alabaster vase; in a word, if you paint her in detail, at every stroke he sighs and lifts his eyes, and is visibly excited by his voluptuous imagination. Only two days ago, passing the shop of a ladies' shoemaker, he stopped to look with admiration on a pair of diminutive slippers which were there exposed. After contemplating them for some time, with more attention than they deserved, he exclaimed with a languishing air, to a cavalier who accompanied him: 'Ah! my friend; there now are slippers which enchant my soul! what darling feet for which they were made! I look on them with too much interest: let us away! the very atmosphere around this place is dangerous.'"

"We may mark that gentleman with black, at all events," said Leandro Perez. "We may indeed," replied the Devil; "and you may tar his nearest neighbour with the same brush, while you are about it--an original of an auditor, who, because he keeps a carriage, blushes whenever he is obliged to put his foot into a public vehicle. He again may be worthily paired with one of his own relations, a wealthy dignitary of the church here, who almost always rides in a hired coach, in order to save two very neat ones, and four splendid mules, which he keeps in his stables.

"In the immediate neighbourhood of the auditor and our amatory bachelor, I discover a man to whom, without injustice, no one could deny his title to a strait waistcoat. There he is--a cavalier of sixty, making love to a damsel of sixteen. He visits her daily, and thinks to win her affections by a recital of the conquests of his youth; he hopes that she will love him now for the charms of which he formerly could boast.

"We may place in the same category with the aged swain, another who is sleeping about ten paces from us--a French count, who came to Madrid to see the court of Spain. This old gentleman, who is nearly seventy years of age, shone with great lustre in the court of his own sovereign, fifty years ago; he was indeed perfectly the rage; all the world envying his manly form, his gallant deportment, and above all the exquisite taste which he displayed in his apparel. He scrupulously preserved the dresses so much admired, and has continued to wear them on all occasions despite the changes of fashion, which in Paris occur every day. What, however, is most amusing in the matter is, that he fancies himself at this time as graceful and attractive as in the days of his youth."

"There is not the slightest doubt," said Don Cleophas, "that we may book a place in the Casa de los locos for this French signor." "I must reserve another though," replied the Demon, "for a lady who resides in a garret, next to the count's mansion. She is an elderly widow, who, from excess of affection for her children, has had the kindness to make over to them all her property; reserving only a small stipend for herself, which, with proper filial gratitude, they take good care never to pay.

"I have another subject for the same establishment, in a youth of family, who no sooner has a ducat than he spends it; and who, as he cannot do without the ready, is capable of anything to obtain it. A fortnight ago, his washer-woman, to whom he owed thirty pistoles, came to dun him for that sum, stating that she wanted it particularly, as she was going to be married to a valet-de-chambre, who sought her hand. 'You must have more money than this,' said he, 'for where the devil is the valet-de-chambre who would take you to wife for thirty pistoles?' 'Oh! yes,' replied the sudorific dame, 'I have two hundred ducats besides.' 'The deuce!' replied our hero, with emotion--'two hundred ducats! You have only to give them to me, I will marry you myself, and we may then cry quits.' He was taken at his word, and the laundress became his wife.

"We must retain three places also for the same number of persons, whom you see returning from supper at a celebrated countess's, and now stopping before that house on the left, where they at present reside. One is a nobleman of an inferior grade, who piques himself on his passion for the belles lettres; the second is his brother, your ambassador to Timbuctoo, or some such place; and the third is their foster-brother, a literary toady who follows in their train. They are almost always together, and especially when visiting in the clique to which they belong. The noble praises himself only; the ambassador praises his brother and himself also; but the toady has three things to look after,--the praises of the other two, and the mixing of his own praises with theirs.

"Two places more! One for a floricultural citizen, who, scarcely gaining his own bread, must need keep a gardener and his wife to look after a dozen plants that languish at his suburban villa; the other for an actor, who, complaining the other day to his brethren on the disagreeables inseparable from a strolling life, observed: 'Well, my friends, I am utterly disgusted with my profession; yes, so much so, that I would rather be a humble country gentleman with a thousand ducats a year.'

"On whichever side I turn my eyes," continued the Spirit, "I see nothing but addled brains. There, for instance, is a chevalier of Calatrava, who is so proud, or rather vain, of being privately encouraged by the daughter of a noble signor, that he thinks himself on a par with the first persons of the court. He reminds me of Villius, who thought himself son-in-law of Sylla, because he was on good terms with the daughter of that dictator; and the resemblance is the more striking, because this chevalier, like the

Roman, has a Longarenus; that is to say, a rival of low degree, who, nevertheless, is still more favoured by the lady than himself.

"One would be inclined to affirm that the same men are born anew from time to time, but under other circumstances. I recognize, in that secretary of department, Bollanus, who kept measures with nobody, and who affronted all whose appearance was, at first sight, unpleasing to him. I behold again, in that old president, Fufidius, who lent his money at five per cent. per month; and Marsoeus, who gave his paternal mansion to the actress Origo, lives once more in that noble stripling, who is spending with a dancer of the ballet the proceeds of a country seat which he has near the Escurial."

Asmodeus was about to continue, when, suddenly hearing the sound of instruments which were tuning in the neighbourhood, he stopped, and said to Don Cleophas: "There are musicians at the end of this street, who are just commencing a serenade in honour of the daughter of an alcade de corte; if you would like to witness this piece of gallantry, you have only to say so." "I am a great admirer of this sort of concert," replied Zambullo; "let us by all means get near them; there may chance to be some decent voices among the lot." He had hardly spoken, when he found himself on a house adjoining that of the alcade.

The serenade was commenced by the instruments alone, which played some new Italian airs; and then two of the voices sang alternately the following couplets:

"List, while the thousand charms I sing,
Which round thee such enchantment fling,
That even Love has plumed his wing

To seek thy bower.

"Thy neck, that shames the mountain snow,
Thy lip, that mocks the peach's glow,
Bid Cupid's self a captive bow

Beneath thy power.

"Thine arched brows as bows are bent
To speed the shafts thine eyes have sent;
E'en armed Love's own mail is rent,

Resisting them.

"Thou art, in sooth, a queenly maid;
Yet hast thou every heart betray'd,
That thee its trusting pole-star made;

Thou priceless gem!

"Oh! would that I some spell possess'd,
While painting thee, to touch thy breast;
Thou evening star, thou heaven of rest,

Thou morning sun!"[6]

"The couplets are gallant and delicate," cried the Student. "They seem so to you," replied the Demon, "because you are a Spaniard: if they were translated into French, for instance, they would not be greatly admired. The readers of that nation would think the expressions too figurative; and would discover an extravagance of imagination in the conceptions, which would be to them absolutely laughable. Every nation has its own standard of taste and genius, and will admit no other: but enough of these couplets," continued he, "you will hear music of another kind.

"Follow with your eyes those four men who have suddenly appeared in the street. See! they pounce upon the serenaders: the latter raise their instruments to defend their heads, but their frail bucklers yield to the blows which fall on them, and are shattered into a thousand pieces. And now see, coming to their assistance, two cavaliers; one of whom is the gallant donor of the serenade. With what fury they charge on the four aggressors! Again, with what skill and valour do these latter receive them. What fire sparkles from their swords! See! one of the defenders of the serenade has fallen,--it is he who gave it,--he is mortally wounded. His companion, perceiving his fall, flies to preserve his own life; the aggressors, having effected their object, fly also; the musicians have disappeared during the combat; and there remains upon the spot the unfortunate cavalier alone, who has paid for his gallantry with his life. In the meanwhile, observe the alcade's daughter: she is at her window, whence she has observed all that has passed. This lady is so vain of her beauty,--although that is nothing extraordinary either,--that instead of deploring its fatal effect, she rejoices in the force of her attractions, of which she now thinks more than ever.

"This will not be the end of it. You see another cavalier, who has this moment stopped in the street to assist, were it possible, the unfortunate being who is swimming in his blood. While occupied in this charitable office, see! he is surprised by the watch. They are taking him to prison, where he will remain many months: and he will almost pay as dearly for this transaction as though he were the murderer himself."

"This is, indeed, a night of misfortunes!" said Zambullo. "And this will not be the last of them," added the Devil. "Were you, this moment, at the Gate of the Sun, you would be horror-stricken at the spectacle which is now exhibiting. Through the negligence of a domestic, a mansion is on fire, which in its rage has already reduced to ashes the magnificent furniture it contains, and threatens to consume the whole building; but great as might be his loss, Don Pedro de Escolano, to whom the house belongs, would not regret it for a moment, could he but save his only daughter, Seraphina, who is likely to perish in the flames."

Don Cleophas expressing the greatest anxiety to see this fire, the Cripple transported him in an instant to the Gate of the Sun, and placed him in a house exactly opposite to that which was burning.

Footnote:
6.
"Si de tu hermosura quieres
Una copia con mil gracias;
Escucha, porque pretendo

El pintarla.

"Es tu frente toda nieve
Y el alabastro, batallas
Offreciò al Amor, haziendo

En ella vaya.

"Amor labrò de tus cejas
Dos arcos para su aljava:
Y debaxo ha descubierto

Quien le mata.

"Eres duena de el lugar
Vandolera de las almas,
Iman de los alvedrios,

Linda alhaja.

"Un rasgo de tu hermosura
Quisiera yo retratarla;
Que es estrella, es cielo, es sol;

No es sino el alva."

Alain René Le Sage

CHAPTER XI

OF THE FIRE, AND THE DOINGS OF ASMODEUS ON THE OCCASION, OUT OF FRIENDSHIP FOR DON CLEOPHAS.

In the street beneath them nothing was to be heard but a confused noise, arising from cries of fire from one half of the crowd, and the more appropriate one of water from the other. As soon as Leandro was able to comprehend the scene, he saw that the grand staircase, which led to the principal apartments of Don Pedro's mansion, was all in flames, which also were issuing with clouds of smoke, from every window in the house.

"The fire is at its height," said the Demon; "it has just reached the roof, and its thousand tongues are spitting in the air millions of brilliant sparks. It is a magnificent sight: so much so, that the persons who have flocked from all parts around it, to assist in extinguishing the flames, are awed into helpless amazement. You may discern in the crowd of spectators an old man in a dressing-gown: it is the Signor de Escolano. Do you not hear his cries and lamentations? He is addressing the men who surround him, and conjuring them to rescue his child. But in vain does he implore them,--in vain does he offer all his wealth,--none dares expose his life to save the ill-fated lady, who is only sixteen, and whose beauty is incomparable. The old man is in despair: he accuses them of cowardice; he tears his hair and beard; he beats his breast; the excess of his grief has made him almost mad. Seraphina, poor girl, abandoned by her attendants, has just swooned with terror in her own apartment, where, in a few minutes, a dense smoke will stifle her. She is lost to him for ever: no mortal can save her."

"Ah! Signor Asmodeus," exclaimed Leandro Perez, prompted by feelings of generous compassion, "if you love me, yield to the pity which desolates my heart: reject not my humble prayer when I entreat you to save this lovely girl from the horrid death which threatens her. I demand it, as the price of the service I rendered but now to you. Do not, this time, oppose yourself to my desires: I shall die with grief if you refuse me."

The Devil smiled on witnessing the profound emotion of the Student. "The fire warms you, Signor Zambullo," said he. "Verily! you would have made an exquisite knight-errant: you are courageous, compassionate for the sufferings of others, and particularly prompt in the service of sorrowing damsels. You would be just the man, now, to throw yourself in the midst of the furnace yonder, like an Amadis, to attempt the deliverance of the beauteous Seraphina, and to restore her safe and sound to her disconsolate father." "Would to heaven!" replied Don Cleophas, "that it were possible. I would undertake the task without hesitation." "Pity that your death," resumed the Cripple, "would be the sole reward of so noble an exploit! I have already told you that human courage can avail nothing on the occasion. Well! I suppose, to gratify you, I must meddle in the matter; so observe how I shall set about it: you can watch from hence all my operations."

He had no sooner spoken these words than, borrowing the form of Leandro Perez, to the great astonishment of the Student, he alighted unobserved amid the crowd, which he elbowed without ceremony, and quickly passing through it, rushed into the fire as into his natural element. The spectators who beheld him, alarmed at the apparent madness of the attempt, uttered a cry of horror. "What insanity!" said one; "is it possible that interest can blind a man to such an extent as this? None but a downright idiot could have been tempted by any proffered recompence to dare such certain death." "The rash youth," said another, "must be the lover of Don Pedro's daughter; and in the desperation of his grief has resolved to save his mistress or to perish with her."

In short, they predicted for him the fate of Empedocles,[7] when, a minute afterwards, they saw him emerge from the flames with Seraphina in his arms. The air resounded with acclamations, and the people were loud in their praises of the brave cavalier who had performed so noble a feat. When rashness ends in success, critics are silent; and so this prodigy now appeared to the assembled multitude as a very natural result of a Spaniard's daring.

As the lady was still insensible, her father did not dare to give himself up to joy: he feared that, although thus miraculously delivered from the fire, she would die before his eyes, from the terrible impression made upon her mind by the peril she had encountered. He was, however, soon reassured, when, recovering from her swoon, her eyes opened, and looking on the old man, she said to him with an affectionate voice: "Signor, I should have had more occasion for affliction than rejoicing at the preservation of my life, were not yours also in safety." "Ah! my child," replied her father, embracing

65

her, "nothing is lost since you are saved. But let us thank," exclaimed he, presenting to her the double of Cleophas,--"let us testify our gratitude to this young cavalier. He is your preserver; it is to him you owe your life. How can we repay that debt? Not all that I possess would suffice to cancel the obligation he has conferred upon us."

To these observations the Devil replied, with an air which would have done Don Cleophas credit: "Signor, I am noble, and a Castilian. I seek no other reward for the service I have had the happiness to render you than the pleasure of having dried your tears, and of having saved from the flames the lovely object which they threatened to devour;--surely such a service is its own reward."

The disinterestedness and generosity of their benefactor raised for him the highest feelings of admiration and esteem in the breast of the Signor de Escolano, who entreated him to call upon them, and offered him his warmest friendship. The Devil replied in fitting terms to the frank advances of the old man; and, after many other compliments had passed, the father and daughter retired to a small building which remained uninjured, at the bottom of the garden. The Demon then rejoined the Student, who, seeing him return under his former guise, said to him: "Signor Asmodeus, have my eyes deceived me? Were you not but now in my shape and figure?" "Excuse the liberty," replied the Cripple; "and I will tell you the motive for this metamorphosis. I have formed a grand design: I intend that you should marry Seraphina, and, under your form, I have already inspired her with a violent passion for your lordship. Don Pedro, also, is highly satisfied with you, because I told him that in rescuing his daughter I had no other object than to render them both happy, and that the honour of having happily terminated so perilous an adventure was a sufficient reward for a Spanish gentleman. The good man has a noble soul, and will not easily be outdone in generosity; and he is at this moment deliberating within himself whether he shall not give you his daughter, as the most worthy return he can make to you for having saved her life.

"Well! while he is hesitating," added the Cripple, "let us get out of this smother into a place more favourable for continuing our observations." And so saying, away he flew with the Student to the top of a high church filled with splendid tombs.

Footnote:
    7. A Sicilian poet and philosopher, who threw himself into the crater of Mount Ætna.

Alain René Le Sage

CHAPTER XII
OF THE TOMBS, OF THEIR SHADES, AND OF DEATH.

Asmodeus now said to the Student: "Before we continue our observations on the living, we will for a few moments disturb the peaceful rest of those who lie within this church. I will glance over all the tombs; reveal the secrets they contain, and the feelings which have prompted their elevation.

"The first of those which are on our right contains the sad remains of a general officer, who, like another Agamemnon, on his return from the wars found an Ægisthus in his house; in the second, reposes a young cavalier of noble birth, who, desirous of displaying in the sight of his mistress his strength and skill at a bull-fight, was gored to death by his furious opponent; and in the third lies an old prelate who left this world rather unceremoniously. He had made his will in the vigour of health, and was imprudent enough to read it to his domestics, whom, like a good master, he had not forgotten: his cook was in a hurry to receive his legacy.

"In the fourth mausoleum rests a courtier who never rested in his lifetime. Even at sixty years of age, he was daily seen in attendance on the king, from the levée until his majesty retired for the night: in recompense for all these attentions the king loaded him with favours." "And was he, now," said Don Cleophas, "the man to use his influence for others?" "For no one," replied the Devil: "he was liberal of his promises of service to his friends, but he was religiously scrupulous of never keeping them." "The scoundrel!" exclaimed Leandro. "Were we to think of lopping off the superfluous members of society,-- men that like tumours on the body politic draw all its nourishment to themselves, it is with courtiers like this one would begin."

"The fifth tomb," resumed Asmodeus, "encloses the mortal remains of a signor, ever zealous for the interests of his country, and jealous of the glory of the king his master, in whose service he spent the best years of his life as ambassador to Rome or France, to England or Portugal. He ruined himself so effectually by his embassies that he did not leave behind him enough to defray the expenses of his funeral, which the king has therefore paid out of gratitude for his services.

"Let us turn to the monuments on the other side. The first is that of a great merchant who left enormous wealth to his children; but, lest they should forget, in its flood, the humble source from which it, like themselves, was derived, he directed that his name and occupation should be graven on his tomb, to the no small annoyance of his descendants.

"The next stone which surpasses every other in the church for its magnificence, is regarded with much admiration by all travellers." "In truth," said Zambullo, "it appears to me deserving of its reputation. I am absolutely enchanted by those two kneeling figures--how exquisitely are they chiselled? Not Phidias himself could have surpassed the sculpture of this splendid work! But tell me, dear Asmodeus, what in their lives were those whom these all-breathing marbles represent?"

The Cripple replied: "You behold a duke and his noble spouse: the former was grand chamberlain to his majesty, and the duchess was celebrated for her extreme piety. I must, however, relate to you an anecdote of her grace, which you will think rather lively for a devotee;--it is as follows.

"She had been for a long time in the habit of confessing her sins to a monk of the order of Mercy, one Don Jerome d'Aguilar, a good man, and a famous preacher, with whom she was highly satisfied, when there suddenly appeared at Madrid a Dominican, who captivated the town by the novelty of his style, and the comfortable doctrines on which he insisted. This new orator was named the brother Placidus: the people flocked to his sermons as to those of Cardinal Ximenes; and as his reputation grew, the court, led to hear him by curiosity, became more loud in his praises than the town.

"Our duchess at first made it a point of honour to hold out against the renown of the new-comer, nor could even curiosity induce her to go to hear him, that she might judge for herself of his eloquence. She acted thus from a desire to prove to her spiritual director, that, like a good and grateful penitent, she sympathised with him in the chagrin which the presence of brother Placidus must have caused him. But the Dominican made so much noise, that at last she yielded to the temptation of seeing him, still however assured of her own fidelity: she saw him, heard him preach, liked him, followed him; and the little inconstant absolutely formed the project of putting herself under his direction.

"It was, however, necessary to get rid of her old confessor, and this was not an easy matter; a spiritual guide cannot be thrown off like a lover; a devotee would not like to be thought a coquette, or to lose the esteem of the director whom she abandons; so what did the duchess? She sought Don Jerome,

Asmodeus; or, The Devil on Two Sticks

and with an air of sorrow which spoke a real affliction, said to him: 'Father, I am in despair: you see me in amazement;--in a grief,--in a perplexity of mind which I cannot depict.' 'What ails you then, Madam?' replied d'Aguilar. 'Would you believe it?' she replied; 'my husband, who has ever had the most perfect confidence in my virtue, after having seen me for so long a time under your guidance, has, without appearing in the least suspicious of myself, become suddenly jealous of you, and desires that you may no longer be my confessor. Did you ever hear of a similar caprice? In vain have I objected that by his suspicions he insulted not only myself, but a man of the strictest piety, freed from the tyranny of the passions; I only increased his jealous fears by my vindication of your sacred honour.'

"Don Jerome, despite his shrewdness, was taken in by this story: it is true that it was told with such demonstrations of candour as would have deceived all the world. Although sorry to lose a penitent of such importance, he did not fail to exhort her to obey her husband's will; but the eyes of his Reverence were opened at last, and the trick discovered, when he learned that the lady had chosen brother Placidus as his successor.

"After the grand chamberlain and his cunning spouse," continued the Devil, "comes a more modest tomb, which has only recently received the ill-assorted remains of a president of the council of the Indies and his young wife. This president, in his sixty-third year, married a girl of twenty: he had by a former wife two children, whom he was about to leave penniless, when a fit of apoplexy carried him off; and his wife died twenty-four hours after him from vexation at his not having lived three days longer.

"And now we have arrived at the most respectable monument this church contains. For it every Spaniard has as much veneration, as the Romans had for the tomb of Romulus." "Of what great personage, then, does it contain the ashes?" asked Leandro Perez. "Of a prime minister of Spain," replied Asmodeus; "and never did that monarchy possess his equal. The king left, with confidence, the cares of government to this great man; who so worthily acquitted himself of the charge, that monarch and subjects were equally contented. Under his ministry the state was ever flourishing, and its people happy; for his maxims of government were founded on the sure principles of humanity and religion. Still, although his life was blameless, he was not free from apprehension at his death,--the responsibility of his office might indeed make the best of mortals tremble.

"In a corner, a little beyond the tomb of this worthy minister, you may discern a marble tablet placed against one of the columns. Say! shall I open the sepulchre beneath it, and display before your eyes all that remains of a lowly maiden who perished in the flower of her youth, when her modest beauty won for her the love and admiration of all who beheld her? It has returned to its primeval dust, that fragile form, which in its life possessed so dangerous a beauty as to keep her fond parent in continual alarm, lest its bright temptation should expose her to the wiles of the seducer;--a misfortune which might have befallen had she lived much longer, for already was she the idol of three young cavaliers, who, inconsolable for her loss, died shortly afterwards by their own hands. Their tragical history is engraven in letters of gold on the stone I shewed you, with three little figures which represent the despairing lovers in the act of self-destruction: one is draining a glass of poison; another is falling on his sword; and the third is tying a cord about his neck, having chosen to die by hanging."

The Demon finding that the Student laughed with all his might at this sorrowful story, and that the idea of the three figures thus depicted on the maiden's monument amused him, said: "Since you find food for mirth in the artist's imagination, I am almost in the mind to carry you this moment to the banks of the Tagus, and there shew you a monument erected by the will of a dramatic author, in the church of a village near Almaraz, whither he had retired, after having led a long and joyous life at Madrid. This scribe had produced a vast number of comedies full of ribald wit and low obscenity; but repenting of his outrages upon decency ere he died, and desirous of expiating the scandal they had caused, he directed that they should carve upon his tomb a sort of pile, composed of books, bearing the names of the various pieces he had written, and that beside it they should place the image of Modesty, who, with lighted torch, should be about to consign them to the flames.

"Besides the dead whose monuments I have described to you, there are within this church an infinity of others without a stone to mark the spot where their ashes repose. I see their shades wandering solemnly around: they glide along, passing and repassing one after another before us, without disturbing the profound quiet which reigns in this holy place. They speak not; but I read in their silence all their thoughts." "I am annoyed without measure," exclaimed Don Cleophas, "that I cannot, like you, have the pleasure of beholding them!" "That pleasure I can give you then," replied Asmodeus; "nothing is more easy." The Demon just touched the Student's eyes, and by a delusion caused him to perceive a great number of pallid spectres.

As he looked on these apparitions, Zambullo trembled. "What!" said the Devil to him, "you are agitated! Is it with fear of these ghostly visitants? Let not their ghastly apparel alarm you! Look at it well! It will adorn your own majestic person some of these days. It is the uniform of the shades: collect yourself, and fear nothing. Is it possible your assurance can fail you now,--you, who have had the daring to look on me? These gentry are harmless compared with myself."

Alain René Le Sage

The Student, at these words, recalling his wonted courage, looked on the phantoms with tranquillity; which the Demon perceiving: "Bravo!" said he. "Well! now," he continued, "regard these shadows with attention! You will perceive that the occupant of the stately mausoleum is confounded with the inhabitant of the unstoned grave. The ranks by which they were distinguished in their lives died with them; and the grand chamberlain and the prime minister are no more now than the lowliest citizen that moulders in this church. The greatness of these noble shades ended with their days, as that of the strutting hero of a tragedy falls with the curtain."

"I have a remark to make," interrupted Leandro. "I see a lonely spirit hovering about, and seeming to shun all contact with his fellows." "Rather say," replied the Demon, "and you will speak the truth, that his fellows shun all company with him: and what now think you is that poor ghost? He was an old notary, who had the vanity to be buried in a leaden coffin; which has so offended the self-love of the more humble tenants of the surrounding tombs, that they resolved to black-ball him, and will not therefore permit his shade to mix with theirs."

"I have another observation yet to make," resumed Don Cleophas. "Two shadows, just now, on meeting, stopped for a moment to look upon each other, and then passed each on his way." "They are, or rather were, two intimate friends," replied the Devil; "one was a painter, and the other a musician: they both drew their inspiration from the bottle; but were, otherwise, honest fellows enough. It is worthy of note that they both brushed off in the same year; and when their spirits meet, struck by the remembrance of their former delights, they say to each other by their sorrowful but expressive silence: 'Ah! my friend, we shall drink no more.'"

"Grammercy!" cried the Student, "what do I see. At the other end of the church are two spirits, who are passing along together, but badly matched. Their forms and manners are immensely different: one is of enormous height, and moves with corresponding gravity, while the other is of dwarf-like stature, and passes o'er the ground like a breath." "The giant," replied the Cripple, "was a German, who lost his life in a debauch, by drinking three healths with tobacco mixed inadvertently in his wine; and the little ghost is that of a Parisian, who, with the gallantry belonging to his countrymen, was imprudent enough, on entering this very church, to present the holy water to a young lady who was leaving it: as a reward for his politeness, he was saluted on the same day with the contents of a carbine, which left him here a moral for all too attentive Frenchmen.

"For myself," continued Asmodeus, "I have been looking at three spirits which I discerned among the crowd; and I must tell you by what means they were separated from their earthly companions. They animated the charming forms of as many female performers, who made as much noise at Madrid, in their time, as did Origo, Cytheris and Arbuscula, in theirs, at Rome; and, like their said prototypes, they possessed the exquisite art of amusing mankind in public, and of privately ruining the same amiable animal. But, alas! all things must have an end, and these were the finales of those celebrated ladies: one died suddenly of envy, at an apoplectic fit of applause, from the pit, which fell upon a lovely first-night; another found in excessive good cheer, at home, the infallible drop which follows it; and, the third, undertaking the dangerous character, for an actress, of a vestal, became so excited with her part that she died of a miscarriage behind the scenes.

"But we will leave to their reposes(!) all these shades," again continued the Demon; "we have passed them sufficiently in review. I will now present to your sight a spectacle which, as a man, must impress you with a deeper feeling than the sight of the dead. I am about, by the same power which has rendered the shades of the departed visible to your sight, to present to you the vision of Death himself. Yes! you shall behold that insatiable enemy of the human race, who prowls unceasingly in the haunts of man, unperceived by his victims; who surrounds the earth, in his speed, in the twinkling of an eye; and who strikes by his power, its most distant inhabitants at the same moment.

"Look towards the east! He rises on your sight. A million birds of baneful omen fly before his advent in terror, and announce his presence with funereal cries. His tireless hand is armed with the fatal scythe which mows successive generations as they spring from earth. But if, as mocking at humanity, on one wing is depicted war, pestilence, famine, shipwreck, conflagration, with other direful modes by which he sweeps upon his prey, the other shows the priests who offer to him daily hecatombs in sport; as youthful doctors, who receive from himself their diplomas, after swearing, in his presence, never to practise surgery or medicine contrary to the rules of the courts."

Although Don Cleophas suspected that all he saw was an illusion, and that it was merely to gratify his taste for the marvellous that the Devil raised this form of Death before his eyes, he could not look on it without trembling. He assumed, however, all the courage he was possessed of, and said to the Demon: "This fearful spectre will not, I suppose, pass vainly over Madrid: he will doubtless leave some awful traces of his flight?" "Yes! certainly," replied the Cripple; "he comes not here for nothing; and it depends but on yourself to be the witness of his visitation." "I take you at your word," exclaimed the Student; "let us follow in his train; let me visit with him the unhappy families on whom he will expend his present wrath. What tears are about to flow!" "Beyond a doubt," replied Asmodeus; "but many which come at convenience. Death, despite his horrors, causes at least as much joy as grief."

Asmodeus; or, The Devil on Two Sticks

Our two spectators took their flight, and followed the grim monarch in his progress. He entered first a modest house, whose owner lay in helpless sickness on his bed; the autocrat but touched the poor man with his scythe, and he expired in the midst of his weeping relations, who instantly commenced an affecting concert of cries and lamentions. "There is no mockery here," said the Demon: "the wife and children of this worthy citizen loved him with real affection: besides, they depended on him for their bread; and the belly is rarely a hypocrite.

"Not so, however, is it in the next house, in which you perceive his grisly majesty now occupied in releasing a bed-ridden old gentleman from his pains. He is an aged counsellor who, having always lived a bachelor of law, has passed his life as badly as he could, that he might leave behind him a good round sum for the benefit of his three nephews, who have flocked round his bed on hearing that he is about to quit it, at last. They of course displayed an extreme affliction, and very well they did it; but are now, you see, letting fall the mask, and are preparing to do their duties as heirs, after having performed their parts as relations. How they will rummage the old gentleman's effects! What heaps of gold and silver will they discover! 'How delightful!' said one of these heart-broken descendants to another, this moment,--'how delightful is it for nephews to be blessed with avaricious old uncles, who renounce the pleasures of life for their sakes!'" "A superb funeral oration," said Leandro Perez. "Oh! as to that," replied the Devil, "the majority of wealthy parents, who live to a good old age, ought not to expect a better from their own children.

"While these heritors are joyfully seeking the treasures of the deceased, Death is directing his flight to a large house, in which resides a young nobleman who has the small-pox. This noble, one of the brightest ornaments of the court, is about to perish, just as his star is rising, despite the famed physician who attends him,--or rather because he is attended by this learned doctor.

"But see! with what rapidity does the fatal scythe perform its operations. Already has it completed the destiny of the youthful lord, and its unblunted edge is turned elsewhere. It hovers over yonder convent; it darts into its deepest cell, sweeps over a pious monk, and cuts the thread of the penitent and mortifying life that he has led during forty years. Death, all-fearful as he is, had no terrors for this holy man; so, in revenge, he seeks a mansion where his presence will be unwelcome indeed. He flies towards a licentiate of importance, who has only recently been appointed to the bishopric of Albarazin. This prelate is busily occupied with preparations for repairing to his diocese with all the pomp which in our day accompanies the princes of the church. Nevertheless, he is about to take his departure for the other world, where he will arrive with as few followers as the poor monk; and I am not sure that he will be quite as favourably received."

"Oh heavens!" cried Zambullo; "Death stoops upon the palace of the king. Alas! one stroke of his fatal scythe, and all Spain will be plunged in dreadful consternation." "Well may you tremble," said the Cripple; "for the barbarian has no more respect for kings than for their meanest slaves. But be not alarmed," he added, a moment afterwards, "he aims not at the monarch yet; his business now is with a courtier only, one of those noble lords whose only occupation is to swell his master's train: such ministers as these are not exactly those the state can least afford to lose."

"But it would seem," replied the Student, "that the spectre king is not contented with so mean a prize as the parasite you speak of. See! he hovers still about the royal house; and, this time, near the chamber of the Queen." "Just so," replied the Devil, "and he might be worse employed: he is about to cut the windpipe of an amiable dame who delights to sow divisions in her sovereign's court; and who is now mortally chagrined, because two ladies whom she had cleverly set by the ears, have been unreasonable enough to become sincerely reconciled with each other.

"And now, my master, you will hear cries of real affliction," continued the Demon. "Death enters that splendid mansion to the left; and a scene as touching as the world's stage offers is about to be acted there. Look, if you can, on the heart-rending tragedy." "In truth," said Don Cleophas, "I perceive a lady struggling in the arms of her attendants, and tearing her hair with signs of deepest grief. Tell me its cause!" "Look in the room adjoining, and you will see cause enough," replied the Devil. "You observe the man stretched on that stately couch: it is her dying husband,--to her a loss indeed! Their story is affecting, and deserves to be written:--I have a great mind to relate it to you."

"You will give me great pleasure in so doing," interrupted Leandro: "the sorrows of this world do not move less than its vices and follies amuse me." "It is rather long," resumed Asmodeus, "but it is too interesting to annoy you on that account. Besides, I will confess to you, that, all Demon as I am, I am sick of following the track of Death: let us leave him in his search of newer victims." "With all my heart," replied Zambullo: "I am more curious to hear your promised narrative Of suffering humanity, than to see my fellow-mortals, one after another, hurried into eternity." The Cripple then commenced as follows, after having transported the Student on to the roof of one of the highest houses in the Strada d'Alcala.

Alain René Le Sage

CHAPTER XIII
THE FORCE OF FRIENDSHIP.

A young cavalier of Toledo, accompanied by his valet-de-chambre, was journeying with all possible speed from the place of his birth, in order to avoid the consequences of a tragical adventure in which he had unfortunately been engaged. He was about two leagues from the town of Valencia, when, at the entrance of a wood, he fell in with a lady who was alighting hastily from a carriage. No veil obscured her charms, which were more than enough to dazzle a youthful beholder; and, as the lovely damsel appeared in trouble, it is not to be wondered that the cavalier, imagining that she sought assistance, offered her his protection and his services.

"Generous unknown," said the lady, "I will not refuse your proffered aid: Heaven, it would seem, has sent you here to avert a dreadful misfortune. Two cavaliers have met to fight within this wood;--I this moment saw them enter. Hasten with me, I entreat you, and assist me to prevent their fatal design." As she spoke, she plunged into the forest, and the Toledan, throwing his horse's rein to his attendant, followed her as quickly as he was able.

They had not gone a hundred yards before they heard the clashing of arms, and almost immediately discovered the two gentlemen, who were thrusting at each other with becoming fury. The Toledan drew his sword but to separate theirs; and by its assistance, and by entreaties uttered in exclamations, he managed to suspend their pastime, while he inquired the subject of their difference.

"Brave cavalier," said one of the combatants, "you see in me, Don Fabricio de Mendoza, and in my opponent, Don Alvaro Ponza. We both love Donna Theodora, the lady by whom you are accompanied; but we love to little purpose, for, despite our endeavours to win her affections, she treats our attentions with disdain. For myself, I should have been contented to worship an unwilling deity; but my rival, instead of acting with as much wisdom, has resolved to have the shrine to himself, and so has brought me here."

"It is true," interrupted Don Alvaro, "that I have so determined; and it is because I believe that, my rival away, Donna Theodora might deign to listen to my vows. I seek then the life of Don Fabricio, to rid myself of a man who stands in the way of my happiness."

"Signor Cavalier," said the Toledan, "I cannot approve of your reasons for duelling; besides that, you are injuring the lady who is the object of your strife. You must be aware that it will soon be known that you have been fighting for her; and the honour of your mistress should surely be dearer to you than happiness or life itself. And what, too, can he who may be successful expect to gain by his victory? Can he hope that, after having staked a lady's reputation on the quarrel, she will thank him for his folly? What madness! Believe me, it were far better, that, acting as becomes the names you bear, you should control your jealous wrath. Be men and pledge me your sacred words to bind yourselves by the terms I shall propose to you, and your quarrel may be adjusted without a deed of blood."

"Ah! but how?" cried Don Alvaro. "Why," replied the Toledan, "let the lady determine the question; let her choose between yourself and Don Fabricio; and let the slighted lover, instead of seeking to injure his more fortunate rival, leave the field at once." "Agreed!" said Don Alvaro; "and I swear it by all that is sacred. Let Donna Theodora decide between us. She may prefer, if she will, my rival to myself: this even would be less unbearable than the dread suspense in which I now exist." "And I," said Don Fabricio in his turn,--"I call Heaven to witness, that if the divine object of my love declares not in my favour, I will fly from the sight of her perfections; and if I cannot forget them, I will at least behold them no more."

On this the Toledan, turning to Donna Theodora, said: "Madam, it is for you now, by a single word, to disarm these two rivals for your love: you have only to name him whose constancy your favours would reward." "Signor Cavalier," replied the lady, "try some other means of reconciling them. Why should I become the victim of their disagreement? I esteem, in all sincerity, both Don Fabricio and Don Alvaro; but I love neither: and it were surely unjust, that, to prevent the stain with which their disputes may sully my name, I should be compelled to excite hopes that my heart disavows."

"It is too late to dissemble, Madam," resumed the Toledan; "you must now declare yourself. Although these cavaliers are equally good-looking, I doubt not that you can discern more merit in one than in the other; and I am confirmed in that opinion by the alarm with which but now I saw you agitated."

"You misinterpret that alarm," replied Donna Theodora. "The loss of either of these gentlemen would affect me beyond a doubt, and I should never cease to reproach myself with his death, although its innocent cause; but if I appeared to you greatly agitated, I can assure you that it was the peril to which my own honour was exposed that excited all my fear."

The impetuous Don Alvaro Ponza now lost all patience. "Enough!" he exclaimed, with an air of fury; "since the lady refuses to end the matter peaceably, let the fate of arms decide;" and as he spoke, he raised his weapon against Don Fabricio, who on his part prepared to receive him.

On this, the lady, more alarmed by the fury of Don Alvaro than decided by her own inclination, exclaimed wildly: "Hold! noble cavaliers; I will do as you desire. Since there is no other means of preventing a strife in which my reputation is involved, I declare in favour of Don Fabricio de Mendoza."

These words had no sooner escaped her lips, than the discarded Ponza, without uttering a syllable, hastened to his horse, which he had fastened to a tree, released it, threw himself into the saddle, and disappeared, after casting one look of intense fury on his rival and implacable mistress. The fortunate Mendoza, on the contrary, was in ecstasies; now humbling himself in his joy at the feet of Donna Theodora, and now embracing the Toledan, unable to contain the satisfaction with which his heart was filled, or to find words to express his gratitude.

In the meanwhile the lady, freed from the presence of the burning Don Alvaro, had become more tranquil; and it was with grief she reflected that she had engaged to permit the addresses of a lover, whom, while she truly esteemed his merit, her heart told her she could never love.

"Signor Don Fabricio," she said to him, timidly, "I trust you will not abuse the preference I have just avowed for you; you owe it only to the necessity in which I found myself placed of declaring between yourself and Don Alvaro. I can say with truth that I have ever thought more highly of you than of him;--there are noble qualities that you possess of which Alvaro cannot boast; I have always looked on you with justice as the most perfect cavalier Valencia contains; I have even no hesitation in saying that the attentions of such a man would be flattering to the vanity of any woman; but, how honourable soever they might be to me, I feel bound to tell you that my heart is still untouched, and that it is with sorrow I behold in you an affection for myself so great as your every action displays. I will not, however, take from you all hope of winning my affections; my present indifference may arise from the effects of that grief which still fills my bosom for the loss of my late husband, Don Andrea de Cifuentes, who died about a year ago. Although we were not long united, and although he was advanced in years when my parents, dazzled by his riches, compelled me to espouse him, I was yet much afflicted by his loss, and the wound is still green which his death inflicted.

"Ah! was he not worthy of my regret?" she added. "He was indeed unlike those aged and jealous tyrants, who, unable to persuade themselves that a youthful wife can be virtuous enough to excuse their weakness, watch all her motions with suspicion, or place over her some hideous duenna as a spy. Alas! he had in my honour a confidence of which a young and much-loved husband would be hardly capable. His kindness was unbounded, and his only study, to anticipate my every wish. You may suppose, then, Mendoza, that such a man as Don Andrea de Cifuentes is not easily forgotten. No! he is ever present in my thoughts; and the fond recollection of his amiability and love for me may excuse my indifference for objects which might otherwise attract me."

"Ah! Madam," exclaimed Don Fabricio, interrupting Donna Theodora, "how great is my delight to learn from those lovely lips that it is from no dislike for myself that you have slighted all my cares! I can still then hope that the day will come when my constancy may be rewarded." "It will not be my fault if that do not happen," replied the lady, "since I consent that you should visit me, and will not forbid you to speak to me of love. You shall strive, then, to win me to the world and to yourself by your attentions; and I promise to conceal not from you any favourable impression you may make: but if, Mendoza, despite your efforts, my heart refuses to be happy, remember that I give you no right to reproach me."

Don Fabricio was about to reply; but the lady, placing her hand in that of the Toledan, turned away, and hastened towards her carriage. He therefore unbound his horse, and leading it through the thicket by the bridle, followed his mistress, and arrived just in time to see her enter the vehicle, which she did with as much agitation as she had left it, although arising from a very different cause. The Toledan and himself accompanied Donna Theodora to the gate of Valencia, where they separated,--she taking the road to her own house, and Don Fabricio taking the Toledan with him to his.

After a slight repose, Mendoza entertained the stranger with a sumptuous repast, and in the course of conversation asked him what had brought him to Valencia, and whether he proposed to stay there for any time. "For as short a time as possible," replied the Toledan; "I am here only on my way to the sea, that I may embark in the first vessel that leaves the shores of Spain. It matters little to me in what part of the world I go to end a life of unhappiness, except that the more distant from this fatal clime the better."

"What do I hear?" exclaimed Don Fabricio with surprise. "What can have disgusted you with your native land, and caused you to look with hate on that which all men love so fondly?" "After what has occurred to me," replied the Toledan, "my country is to me unbearable, and to leave it, for ever, my only desire." "Ah! Signor Cavalier," cried Mendoza, affected with compassion, "I am impatient to learn your misfortunes! If I cannot relieve them, I am at least disposed to share them. Your appearance from the first prepossessed me in your favour, your bearing and manners charmed me, and already I feel deeply interested in your destiny."

"You afford me, Signor Don Fabricio," replied the Toledan, "the greatest consolation I could receive; and in return for the kindness you are pleased to express for me, it delights me to be able to say, with truth, that on seeing you with Don Alvaro Ponza my heart inclined towards yourself. A feeling, with which I never was inspired at the first sight of any one before, made me fear lest Donna Theodora should decide in favour of your rival; and it was with joy I heard her state her preference for you. Since then, you have so gained upon that first impression, that, far from desiring to conceal my griefs, I seek with a sort of pleasure to unbosom them to you: Learn then my misfortunes.

"I was born in Toledo, and my name is Don Juan de Zarata. I lost my parents while almost in my infancy; so that at an early age I found myself in the enjoyment of a yearly income of four thousand ducats, which I inherited from them. As my hand was at my own disposal, and as I was rich enough to be able to bestow it where my heart should dictate, I married, early, a maiden of exquisite beauty; careless that she added nothing to my fortune, and that her rank was inferior to my own. I loved her, and I was happy; and that I might enjoy to the full the pleasure of possessing one so dear to me, I had not been long married before I sought with her a small estate which I possessed a few leagues from Toledo.

"We lived there, for some time, in unity and bliss; when it chanced that the Duke de Naxera, whose seat was in the neighbourhood, came one day, when he was hunting, to refresh himself at my house. He saw my wife, and unfortunately became enamoured of her. I suspected his passion from the first; and was not long before I was too certainly convinced of its existence by the eagerness with which he sought my friendship, that up to this time he had wholly neglected. His hunting parties were now never complete without me; he loaded me with presents, and still more with his offers of service.

"I became alarmed by his evident design, and prepared for our return to Toledo. Heaven doubtless inspired me with this resolution; for, had I acted upon it, and thus taken from the Duke his opportunities of seeing my wife, I should have avoided all the misfortunes which followed a contrary course. My confidence in her virtue, however, soon reassured me. It appeared to me impossible that a being whom I had raised from obscurity to her present position, from motives of affection alone, could be ungrateful enough to consent to my disgrace. Alas! I little thought that ambition and vanity, two feelings common to every woman, were the greatest vices in the character of my wife.

"No sooner, therefore, had the Duke managed to inform her of his sentiments towards her, than she took credit to herself for so important a conquest. The attachment of a man approached by all the world with the titles of Your Grace and Your Highness tickled her pride, and filled her mind with the most absurd notions; so that she was indefinitely exalted in her own opinion, and thought the less of me. All that I had done for love of her, instead of exciting feelings of gratitude, now appeared but a contemptible offering to her charms, of which she no longer thought me worthy; and she seems not to have doubted that if the noble duke, who flattered her by his homage, had seen her before she had thrown herself away on me, he would have eagerly sought her hand. Infatuated by these absurd notions, and seduced by some well-timed presents which flattered her vanity, she yielded to the secret assiduities of his grace.

"Although they corresponded frequently, I had not for some time the slightest suspicion of their communications; but, at last, my eyes were unfortunately opened to my disgrace. One day I returned from hunting somewhat earlier than usual, and went directly to the apartment of my wife, who expected nothing less than to see me. She had just received a letter from her paramour, and was at the moment preparing a reply. She could not disguise her emotion at my unexpected coming; and as I perceived on the table paper and ink, I trembled,--for the truth rushed on my mind with the speed of all unwelcome conclusions. I commanded her to show me what she was writing, which she refused; so that I was compelled to use violence in order to satisfy my jealous curiosity, and drew from her bosom, in spite of her resistance, a letter which was to the following effect:--

"'Must I for ever languish in the despair of seeing thee again? Hast thou then cruelty enough to call sweet hopes into my heart, and let the short-lived blisses perish from delay? Don Juan leaves thee daily for the chase, or to repair to Toledo: would not Love then snatch these happy opportunities with eager joy? Think of the passion which consumes my life! Pity me, lady! and remember that if the happiness is great we hope to share, the greater is the torment which bars us its possession.'

"As I read this epistle, my blood boiled with fury. My hand sought the hilt of my stiletto, and my first inclination was to plunge it in the unfaithful breast of her who had betrayed me; but a moment's reflection told me that I should thus revenge but half my shame, and that another victim was demanded to appease my wrath. I therefore controlled myself, and, dissimulating as well as I was able, said to my wife: 'Madam, you have done wrong in listening to the duke; the splendour of his rank should not have been sufficient to dazzle you. However, youth finds delight in the trappings of nobility; and I am willing to believe that your guilt extends no further, and that my honour is still in safe keeping with you. I forgive, then, your want of discretion; but it is on condition that you return to the paths of duty, and that henceforth, sensible to the affection which animates my bosom, you will think it enough to deserve it.'

"I did not wait for a reply, but left the apartment; as much to give her an opportunity of collecting herself, as to seek that solitude in which alone my mind could free itself from the anger which inflamed me. If I did not regain my tranquillity, I at least affected an air of composure during that and the following day; and on the third, pretending to have business of importance which called me to Toledo, I told my wife that I was obliged to leave her for some time, and that I did so in full confidence of her virtue and good conduct.

"I set out; but, instead of going to Toledo, as soon as night came to assist my project, I returned home secretly, and concealed myself in the room of a trusty servant, whence I could observe any one who entered the house. I had no doubt that the duke was informed of my absence, and that he would not fail to make the most of so desirable a circumstance. How I longed to surprise them together! I promised myself an ample vengeance.

"Nevertheless, I was deceived in my expectations. Instead of remarking any preparations for the reception of an expected lover, I on the contrary perceived that the doors were scrupulously closed against everybody; and three days having passed without the appearance of the duke, or any of his people, I began to think that my wife had repented of her fault, and that she had broken off all connection with her seducer.

"As this opinion took possession of my mind, my desire of revenge dissipated; until, at last, yielding to those emotions of affection for my wife which anger had only suspended, I hastened to her apartment, and, embracing her with transport, exclaimed: 'Madam, I restore you my esteem and my love. I come to tell you that I have not been to Toledo, but that I pretended to have gone there only to test your discretion. You can forgive this deception in a husband whose jealousy was not entirely without foundation. I feared lest your mind, seduced by too brilliant illusions, should be incapable of a return to virtue; but, thank Heaven! you have seen your error, and I trust that our felicity may henceforth be unbroken.'

"My wife appeared affected at these words, and, while tears fell from her eyes, exclaimed: 'Unhappy have I been, to give you reason to suspect my fidelity! In vain do I detest myself for having so justly excited your anger against me! In vain is it that, since I saw you, my eyes have unceasingly o'erflowed with tears; my grief and my remorse are alike unavailing; I can never regain the confidence I have lost.' 'I restore it to you,' I replied, interrupting her, afflicted by the sorrow which she displayed--'I restore it to you; you have repented of the past; and I will, too gladly, forget it.'

"I kept my word; and, from that moment, my love for her was as great and as confiding as ever. I began again to taste those joys which had been so cruelly interrupted; they came to me, indeed, with redoubled zest; for my wife, as though she had been anxious to efface from my recollection all traces of the injury she had done me, took greater pains to please me. I thought I found more warmth in her caresses; in short, I almost rejoiced at the event which had told me how much was still left for me to love.

"Shortly after our reconciliation I was seized with illness. Although my ailment was not alarming, it is inconceivable how deeply it appeared to afflict my wife. All day she was by my side; and at night, as I was in a separate room, she never failed to visit me frequently, that she might convince herself of the progress of my recovery: her whole care appeared devoted to me, and all her anxiety to anticipate my every want; it seemed as though her whole life depended solely on mine. You may suppose that I was not insensible to all this show of tenderness, and I was never weary of expressing to her my gratitude for her attentions. However, Signor Mendoza, they were not so sincere as I imagined.

"My health was beginning to improve, when, one night, my valet-de-chambre came to awaken me. 'Signor,' said he, with emotion, 'I am sorry to disturb your repose; but I am too much interested in your honour to conceal from you what is at this moment passing beneath your roof. The Duke of Naxera is with my mistress.'

"I was so astounded by this information, that I looked for some time at my servant without being able to speak; and the more I thought of what he told me, the more difficulty I found in believing it. 'No! Fabio,' at last I said to him; 'no, it is impossible that my wife can be capable of such infamy! You must be mistaken.' 'Signor,' replied Fabio; 'would to Heaven that I could think so! But my eyes are not easily deceived. Ever since you have been ill, I have suspected that the duke was introduced almost nightly into my lady's apartment. This evening, I concealed myself, to confirm or dispel my suspicions; and I have but too good reason to know that they were not unfounded.'

"I hesitated no longer; but arose, and putting on my dressing gown, armed myself with my sword, and went in a perfect phrenzy towards my wife's chamber, Fabio following with a light. As we entered the room, the alarmed duke, who was sitting on the bed, rose, and taking a pistol from his girdle, aimed at me and fired; but thanks to his confusion, he missed me. I rushed on him, and in a moment thrust my sword into his heart. Then turning to my wife, who was already more dead than alive: 'and you!' said I, 'infamous wretch, receive the reward of your perfidy.' And so saying, I plunged my sword, still reeking with the blood of her paramour, into her bosom.

Alain René Le Sage

"I am sensible of the crime my fury induced me to commit; and I acknowledge, Signor Don Fabricio, that a faithless spouse may be sufficiently punished without taking her life; but where is the man who, under such excitement, could have preserved the cool temperament of the judge? Picture to yourself this perfidious woman attending me in sickness; imagine if you can, all that display of affection which she lavished upon me; think of all the circumstances,--of the enormity of her deception, and then say if her death weighs heavily against a husband animated with rage, to whom all this comes suddenly as lightning from the cloud.

"My tragical history is finished in a few words. My vengeance thus fully satiated, I dressed hastily, certain that I had no time to lose; for I knew well that the duke's relations would search for me in every corner of Spain, and that, as the power of my own family would be but as a feather in the scale to turn their wrath, there was no safety for me but in a foreign country. I therefore chose two of my best horses, and taking with me all the jewels and money I possessed, I left my house before daybreak, followed by the servant of whose fidelity I had recently been so well assured, and took the road to Valencia with the intention of sailing in the first vessel which should steer for Italy. It thus happened that, passing yesterday near the wood in which you were, I met Donna Theodora, and, at her entreaty, followed to assist in separating yourself and Don Alvaro."

When the Toledan had ended this narrative, Don Fabricio said to him: "Signor Don Juan, you have justly avenged yourself on the Duke de Naxera. Be not alarmed as to anything his relations can do; you shall stay, if you please, with me, until an opportunity offers for your passage into Italy. My uncle is governor of Valencia; you will therefore be more secure from danger here than elsewhere, and you will remain with one who would be united with you henceforth in bonds of strictest friendship."

Zarata replied to Mendoza in terms which expressed his grateful sense of the former's kindness, and at once accepted the proffered asylum. "And now it is, Signor Don Cleophas," continued Asmodeus, "that I shall exhibit to you the power of sympathy: such was the inclination which drew these two young cavaliers towards each other, that, in a few days, there existed between them a friendship not surpassed by that of Orestes and Pylades. With dispositions alike formed for virtue, they possessed a similarity of tastes which was certain to render that which pleased Don Fabricio equally agreeable to Don Juan--their characters were identical; in short, they were formed for each other. Don Fabricio, especially, was charmed with the deportment of his new friend; and lost no opportunity of endeavouring to exalt him in the estimation of the Donna Theodora.

"This lady now received them frequently at her house; but, though her doors were open at the bidding of Mendoza, her heart was still inaccessible to his attentions. Mortified to find his love thus slighted, he could not forbear complaining of her indifference to his friend, who endeavoured to console him with the assurance that the most insensible of women might be won to feeling at the last, and that nothing was wanting to lovers but patience to await for the favourable moment: he bade him then to keep up his courage, and to hope that, sooner or later, his mistress would yield to his assiduity and affection. This advice, though philosophical enough, was insufficient to assure the timid Mendoza, who began to despair of success with the widow of Cifuentes; and the anxiety of suspense so preyed upon his spirits, that Don Juan could not behold him without feelings of compassion. Alas! poor Don Juan was himself ere long more to be pitied than his friend.

"Whatever reason the Toledan had to be disgusted with the sex, after the abominable treachery he had met with, he could not long look upon the Donna Theodora without loving her. Far, however, from yielding to a passion which he felt to be an injury to Mendoza, he struggled with all his might to vanquish it; and convinced that this was only to be accomplished by flying from the bright eyes which had kindled the flame, he wisely resolved to shun the lady who possessed them. Consequently whenever Don Fabricio asked his company to his mistress's house, he managed to find some pretext to excuse himself from going with him.

"On the other hand, Mendoza never went to see the Donna Theodora, but she asked him why he no longer was accompanied by Don Juan. One day, when, for the hundredth time she put this question to her lover, the latter answered, smiling, that his friend had his reasons for absenting himself. 'And what reasons, then, can he have for flying me?' said Donna Theodora. 'Why, madam,' replied Mendoza; 'yesterday, when I pressed him, as usual, to come with me, and expressed some surprise at his refusal to do so, he confided to me a secret, which I must reveal in order to justify him in your eyes. He told me that he had formed a liaison in Valencia; and, that as he had not long to stay in this town, every moment was precious to him.'

"'I cannot exactly admit the validity of his excuse,' replied the widow of Cifuentes, blushing; 'it is not permitted to lovers that they should abandon their friends.' Don Fabricio, who observed the colour which tinged the cheeks of the Donna Theodora, thought that self-love alone had caused the blush, and that, like all pretty women, she could not bear to be neglected, even by a person who was indifferent to her. He was, however, deceived. A deeper feeling than wounded vanity inspired the emotion she displayed. She loved: but for fear that Mendoza should discover her sentiments, she changed the subject, and, during the conversation that followed, affected a gaiety which would have deceived him,

Asmodeus; or, The Devil on Two Sticks

had he not already deceived himself.

"As soon as Donna Theodora was alone, she abandoned herself to reflection. Then, for the first time, she felt all the strength of the attachment she had conceived for Don Juan; and, little thinking how deeply that feeling was shared by its object,--'Oh Love!' she cried: 'cruel and unjust art thou, who delightest to kindle passion in the hearts of those who care not for each other! I love not Don Fabricio, and he adores me; I languish for Don Juan, and his heart is possessed by another. Ah! Mendoza, reproach me not with my indifference for thee; thy friend has indeed avenged thee.'

"As she spoke, grief filled her eyes with tears, and jealousy possessed her breast; but Hope, who loves to soothe the sorrows of despairing lovers, took refuge in her mind, and filled it with bright images of joys to come. It suggested to her that her rival could not be very formidable, and that Don Juan was less the captive of her charms than the object of her favours, and that the ties which bound them could not therefore be difficult to break. She resolved, however, to judge for herself, and at once to see the Toledan. With this view she sent word that she wished to speak with him: he came; and, when they were alone, she thus addressed him:

"'I could never have believed that love could make a gallant man forgetful of his duties to a lady; nevertheless, Don Juan, since it has possessed you, you have become a stranger to my house. I think I have a right to upbraid you for this neglect; I am unwilling, however, to believe that you have yourself resolved to shun me, and will suppose that your mistress has forbidden your coming here. Tell me, Don Juan, that it is so, and I will excuse you. I know a lover is not master of his will, and that he dares not disobey the woman to whom he has resigned it.'

"'Madam,' replied the Toledan, 'I confess that my conduct may reasonably surprise you; but, in pity, ask me not to justify myself: content yourself with hearing from my lips that I shun you not without good cause.' 'Whatever may be that cause,' interrupted Donna Theodora, visibly affected, 'I request you will not conceal it.' 'Well, madam,' replied Don Juan, 'you shall be obeyed; but be not angry if you learn from me more than you would wish to know.

"'Don Fabricio,' he continued, 'has doubtless related to you the adventure which compelled me to quit Castile. In flying from Toledo, my heart filled with hatred against womankind, I bade defiance to the sex ever to touch that heart again. With this disposition, I approached Valencia; I met you, and, what perhaps none have ever sustained before, I met your eyes without yielding to their influence. I saw you again and again with impunity; but, alas! dearly I have paid for my pride of heart. You have conquered! Your beauty, your mind,--all your charms were turned against a rebel to your sway; in a word, I feel for you now all the love that you were formed by nature to inspire.

"'This, madam, is what has driven me from your sight. The mistress, to whom they told you I was devoted, exists but in the imagination of Mendoza; and it was to prevent in him a suspicion of the truth, which my constant refusals to accompany him here might have engendered, that I conjured her into life.'

"This confession, unexpected as it was by Donna Theodora, could not fail to fill her bosom with delight, nor could she conceal it from the Toledan. It is true she took no great pains to do so, and that, instead of regarding him with indignation for his presumption, her eyes beamed with tenderness as she said: 'You have revealed to me your secret, Don Juan; it is fair that I should discover mine to you: Listen!

"'Regardless of the overtures of Alvaro Ponza, and little affected by the addresses of Mendoza, I lived in tranquil joy, when chance brought you to the wood where we met. Agitated as I was by the scene which then was passing, I was nevertheless struck by the gentle and respectful manner in which you offered me your services; and the frankness and courage which you displayed in separating the two furious rivals for my love inspired me with the most favourable opinion of your character. The means by which you proposed to terminate their disputes, indeed, displeased me, and it was with repugnance that I resolved to choose between the combatants; but, I believe I must not disguise from you, that yourself in great part contributed to increase the difficulty of my decision. At the moment when, compelled by necessity, my tongue proclaimed the name of Don Fabricio, I felt that my heart had already declared in favour of the unknown. From that day, which, after what you have just avowed, I may call a happy one, your virtues have constantly augmented the esteem you then inspired.

"'Why should I affect to hide these feelings from you? I confess them with no greater candour than I told Mendoza that I loved him not. A woman whose misfortune is to love a being whom she may not hope to wed, may bury in her heart the passion which consumes it; but when her bosom's lord is one who nourishes an equal tenderness for her, silence were weakness, and dissimulation shame. Yes, I am indeed happy that your love is mine, and I render thanks to Heaven which I trust has destined us for each other.'

"Having thus spoken, the lady waited for Don Juan's answer, and to give him an opportunity of expressing all the gratitude which she naturally thought the declaration she had made must inspire; but her lover, instead of appearing enchanted by the confession he had just listened to, remained sad and thoughtful.

"'What means this silence?' she at length exclaimed. 'What! when for you, Zarata, I forget my sex's pride; and, what another would have deemed a fate to envy, show you a heart all filled with love for you,--can you repel the bliss which such a heart bestows;--be coldly silent to its fond disclosure, and look with grief when all things promise joy? Alas! Don Juan, my kindness for you has a strange effect, indeed.'

"'And what other, madam, can it have upon a heart like mine?' replied the Toledan, mournfully. 'The greater kindness you avow for me, the greater is the misery I suffer. You are not ignorant of all I owe to Don Fabricio; you know the tender friendship which unites us: can I then build my happiness upon the ruins of his dearest hopes?' 'You are too scrupulous,' resumed the Donna Theodora: 'I have promised to Mendoza nothing. I can bestow my love, nor merit his reproaches; and you may well accept it, nor yet do him a wrong. I acknowledge that the sorrows of your friend may cause you some unhappiness; but, Don Juan, can that o'erbalance in your mind the destiny which waits you?'

"'Yes, madam,' replied the Toledan, with respectful firmness; 'a friend like Don Fabricio has greater weight with me than you can well imagine. Could you possibly conceive the tenderness, the strength of that feeling which binds us to each other, you would pity me indeed. Mendoza has no secrets now with me; my interests have become his own; the slightest matter which concerns myself commands his strict regard: in a word, madam, I share his soul with you.

"'Ah! if you wished me to profit by your kindness, you should have disclosed it ere those ties were formed which bind me now to him. Delighted to have won your affections, I should then have seen in Don Fabricio but a rival; and my heart, steeled against the friendship which he offered to me, would have escaped its bonds; I should then have been free from all obligation towards him: but, madam, it is now too late. I have received all the services it was in his power to render me; I have indulged all the feelings which those services induced; gratitude and esteem now unite to reduce me to the cruel necessity of renouncing the inestimable prize you present for my acceptance.'

"While the Toledan was speaking thus, tears fell fast from the eyes of Donna Theodora; and, as he concluded, she hid her face in her handkerchief to conceal her distress. Don Juan was of course affected; his constancy began to evaporate, and he felt that his stay was dangerous. 'Adieu, madam,' he continued, while sighs impeded his utterance,--'adieu! I must fly to preserve my honour; your tears overcome me--all else I could withstand. I leave you for ever; and go, far hence, to deplore the loss of that happiness which my friendship for Don Fabricio inexorably demands as a sacrifice.' And as he finished, he hastily retired, with as much resolution as just enabled him to do so.

"After his departure, the widow of Cifuentes was distracted by a thousand conflicting emotions. She felt ashamed at having declared her love to a man whom its bright temptation had not won; but, unable to doubt his affection for her person, and assured that his refusal of her hand originated in no other feeling than an unexampled constancy for his friend, she was sufficiently reasonable to admire so rare an instance of virtue. Nevertheless, as it is in the nature of men, and more particularly in the nature of women, to feel annoyed when all things do not happen as they wish, she resolved to go into the country on the morrow, in order to dissipate her grief, or rather to augment it; for Solitude is nurse to Love, and strengthens the young passion while he strives to hush its cries.

"Meanwhile, Don Juan, not finding Mendoza on his return, shut himself in his own apartment, and gave way to the affliction he had restrained during his interview with Donna Theodora; for, after what he had sacrificed to friendship, he felt himself at liberty to indulge in grief for its loss. It was not long, however, before Mendoza came to break on his retirement, and judging by his friend's appearance that he was ill, he displayed so much uneasiness that Don Juan was obliged to plead a want of rest, in order to account for his altered looks. Mendoza left him to repose; but he went out with so much grief depicted on his countenance, that the Toledan was still more afflicted by his sympathy. 'Oh Heaven!' he exclaimed, 'why is it that the most tender friendship should bring to me nothing but misfortune?'

"On the following day, Don Fabricio was yet in bed, when they came to inform him that Donna Theodora had set out, with all her establishment, for her seat at Villareal, and that it was unlikely she would shortly return to Valencia. This information caused him less inquietude on account of his severance from the object of his devotion, than because a mystery had been made to him of her departure. Without being able to determine on its cause, a gloomy presentiment pervaded his mind as to its effect on his happiness.

"He instantly arose, that he might seek his friend, as much to converse with him on the subject which occupied his mind, as to inquire the state of Zarata's health; but, before he had completed his toilet, Don Juan entered his room, saying: 'I come to dissipate whatever apprehension you may entertain for me; I feel myself again restored to health.' 'The good news you tell me,' replied Mendoza, 'consoles me somewhat for the unwelcome intelligence I have just received.' 'Ah! what is that?' asked the Toledan anxiously. 'Why,' replied Don Fabricio, after having dismissed his attendants, 'Donna Theodora has gone this morning into the country, where they expect she will remain for some time. This sudden resolution astonishes me. Why has it been concealed? What think you, Don Juan? Have I not cause to be alarmed?'

"Zarata took good care not to communicate his real thoughts upon the subject, but endeavoured to persuade Mendoza that Donna Theodora might change her residence without giving him any reason for alarm. Don Fabricio, however, unconvinced by the arguments of his friend, interrupted him, saying: 'That is all very well, Zarata; but you cannot remove my fears of having imprudently done or said something which has displeased the Donna Theodora; and it is to punish my indiscretion that she leaves me without deigning even to inform me of my fault.

"'I will not, however, remain in uncertainty. Let us hasten, Don Juan, to follow her; I will at once order our horses.' 'I would advise you,' said the Toledan, 'to seek her alone; if it be as you think, witnesses are worse than needless.' 'Don Juan cannot be unwelcome,' replied Mendoza; 'Donna Theodora is aware that you know all that passes in my heart: she esteems you; and far from being in my way, you will assist me to appease her anger against me.'

"'No, no, Fabricio,' replied the Toledan, 'my presence will avail you nothing. Take my advice, and go alone, I conjure you!' 'Again no, my dear Don Juan,' interrupted Mendoza, 'we will go together; I expect this kindness of your friendship.' 'What tyranny! exclaimed the Toledan, with evident vexation; 'why ask you of my friendship what that very feeling should deny you most?'

"These words, which Don Fabricio could not comprehend, and the tone in which they were uttered, surprised him greatly. He looked at his friend for some time without speaking. At last, he said to him gravely: 'Don Juan, what mean you? What horrible suspicion breaks upon my mind? Ah! it is too much, to wound me by your terrible constraint! Speak! Whence arises this unwillingness to accompany me to Donna Theodora?'

"'I would have concealed it from you,' replied the Toledan, 'but, since you compel me to disclose the truth, I will dissimulate no longer. Let us, my dear Mendoza, no more rejoice in the similarity of our dispositions; it is but too perfect: the shafts which wounded you, have neither spared your friend. Donna Theodora----' 'What! you my rival?' interrupted Don Fabricio, turning pale as death. 'From the instant that my love for the widow of Cifuentes became apparent to myself,' replied Don Juan, 'I strove to stifle the passion. I have, as you know, sedulously avoided her sight: I at least triumphed over my feelings, if I could not destroy them.

"'Yesterday, however, Donna Theodora sent word that she desired to see me. I went to her; when she asked me why I seemed to shun her. I endeavoured to excuse myself as well as I was able; but, as my excuses did not satisfy her, I was compelled at last to avow the real cause of my absence. I imagined that, after this declaration, she would have approved the motives of my apparent neglect; but my unlucky star had decreed--shall I tell you? yes, Mendoza, it is useless attempting to deceive you,--I found Theodora disposed to favour my love.'

"Although Don Fabricio was one of the mildest and most reasonable of men, yet, at this confession, he was seized with a fury beyond his control; and, again interrupting his friend, he exclaimed: 'Hold! Don Juan, plunge at once your dagger in my breast; but continue not this fatal recital. What! not contented with avowing your passion for her whom I adore, must you tell me too that your love is returned? By Heaven! this is a strange confidence you dare to venture on with me. You put our friendship to a test indeed. But what say I! our friendship? You have broken it, in nourishing the traitorous feelings you have just imparted.

"'Oh! how have I been deceived! I thought you generous even to excess, and find you basely false; stooping to win the heart of her whose love were insult to your friend. This is indeed an unexpected blow; and falls with double weight since coming from the hand ...' 'Do me more justice,' in his turn interrupted the Toledan; 'reflect with patience ere you speak: I am not the traitor which you deem me. Hear me. You will repent the injuries you heap upon your friend.'

"Don Juan then related all that had passed between the widow of Cifuentes and himself, the tender confession she had made to him of love, and all the arguments she used to win him to indulge his own. He repeated to him then his firm reply; and, as he spoke of the determination he displayed, the wrath of Don Fabricio yielded by degrees. 'In short,' added Don Juan, 'friendship conquered love; and I rejected that of Donna Theodora, despite her tears. But, Gods, those tears! what trouble filled my soul at sight of them! I cannot recollect them now without trembling at the danger I encountered. I began to feel myself relent; and, for a few moments, Mendoza, my heart indeed betrayed you. I did not, however, yield to my weakness, but escaped those dangerous tears by hasty flight. Still it is not enough to have gone safely through the past,--the future must be feared. I shall therefore hasten my departure from Valencia; I will no more behold the lovely Theodora. And now, will Don Fabricio accuse his friend of ingratitude and perfidy?'

"'No!' replied Mendoza, embracing the Toledan; 'my eyes are opened, and I find him faithful as my heart could wish. Pardon those unjust reproaches to a jealous lover, who in a moment finds himself deprived of all his hopes. Alas! should I have expected that the Donna Theodora could have long beheld you, and have failed to love?--that she could resist the influence of those attractions which at once so drew you to myself? No! and I embrace my friend again. I attribute my misfortunes but to destiny; and, far from feeling hatred to yourself, my affection is increased by your noble conduct. What! can you renounce for me possession of the lovely Theodora,--can you yield for friendship's sake so great a prize, and shall I be insensible of the sacrifice? Can you conquer the passion which consumes you, and shall I make no endeavour so to vanquish mine? No! I will not be outdone in generosity of soul. Obey, Don Juan, the dictate of your heart; espouse the object of our mutual affections; my heart may groan in secret if it will; be it so! Mendoza intreats you to consult your own.'

"'In vain do you intreat me,' replied Zarata: 'I love her but too dearly, as I have told you; but, Mendoza, your happiness shall never be the price of mine.' 'And the happiness of Donna Theodora,' said Don Fabricio, 'shall that then count for nothing? Let not false delicacy weigh with us now: her passion for yourself has ended all my hopes. What though, for me, you shunned those fatal eyes, to lead in distant lands a life of woe,--what would it serve me now? She loves me not, and never will; Heaven reserved that bliss for you alone. From the moment that she saw you, her heart declared for you; nature prompted the emotion: in a word, you alone can render her happy. Receive then the heart she offers with her hand; crown her desires and your own; leave me to my fate; and make not three persons miserable, when the wretchedness of one alone is all that destiny requires.'"

Asmodeus was here obliged to suspend his narration, and listen to the Student, who said to him: "Well, all that you tell me is sufficiently surprising; but are there really such amiable people upon earth? I never met within this nether world but friends who strive, not for such mistresses as you depict the Donna Theodora, but for the arrantest coquettes. What! a lover to renounce the being he adores, by whom his love is shared, and all lest he should render some poor friend unhappy? That may do well for some romancer's pen, which fain would picture men the creatures they should be, for fear of telling them the things they are." "I own, with you," Asmodeus replied, "the virtue that I tell you of is rare; but still, my dear Cleophas, it exists; not in romances only, but in the principles of man's own nature. It is true that, since the deluge, I have seen but two examples of the like, and this is one; but, let us return to our history.

"The two friends continued still their amicable strife, and, as each was still unwilling to yield the palm of generosity to the other, their amorous sentiments remained suspended, during several days. They ceased to talk of Donna Theodora, each seemed afraid to breathe her very name; but, while Friendship triumphed over Love in the city of Valencia, Love, as though he would revenge the insult offered to his power, reigned with tyranny without its walls, and was there obeyed without scruple.

"Donna Theodora was all this time in the solitude of Villareal, which was not far distant from the sea. There, abandoning herself to her passion for Don Juan, she dreamt of its reward; and nuptial visions floated in her mind, despite the friendship the Toledan had recently displayed for Don Fabricio, his too much loved rival.

"One day, while the glorious splendour of the setting sun chained her to the margin of its bed, she perceived a boat which made towards the shore. As it approached, she saw that it contained seven or eight men, whose aspect was far from prepossessing; and as they came still nearer, she observed that their faces were covered with masks, and that they were armed.

"Trembling with fear, for it was not easy to divine any good object for this unlooked-for descent, she turned hastily towards her home. Looking from time to time behind her as she fled, she saw them land; and, as they instantly appeared to be endeavouring to overtake her, she began to run with all her might. But as she was not as swift of foot as Atalanta, and as the masks were light and fleet, they came up with her, just as she had reached the entrance of her grounds, and seized her.

"The shrieks of the Donna Theodora, and a girl who accompanied her, were loud enough however to attract the attention of some servants without the house; and these giving the alarm to those within, the whole establishment, to a man, turned out armed with clubs and pitchforks. But in the meantime, two of the most robust among the masqueraders had taken the lady and her damsel in their arms, and bore them towards the boat, while the remainder remained to give battle to the domestics, who, albeit not paid for fighting, did their utmost. The combat was long, but swords carried the day against pitchforks, and the gentlemen in dominoes were fast regaining the vessel to join their prize. It was time indeed they did so; for ere their embarkation was completed, four or five cavaliers were to be distinguished on the road from Valencia, riding at their topmost speed, and apparently anxious to be in time for the rescue of the Donna Theodora. The ravishers saw them; and made such good haste to get out to sea, that the cavaliers arrived too late to attain the accomplishment of their object.

"These cavaliers were Don Fabricio and Don Juan. Mendoza had received a letter, only a few hours before, informing him, on good authority, that Don Alvaro was in the island of Majorca; that he had equipped a sort of sloop, and that with some twenty scoundrels who had nothing to lose, he intended to carry off the widow of Cifuentes on the first occasion of her visiting her seat at Villareal. On this, the Toledan and himself, with their personal attendants, had set out immediately from Valencia, in order to inform Donna Theodora of the projected attempt. They had, unfortunately, arrived just in time to discern on the sea-shore a number of persons who appeared to be engaged in mortal strife; and, suspecting that it might be as they feared, had hastened with all expedition to oppose the infamous design of Don Alvaro. But, with all their haste, they arrived but to witness the abduction they had especially come to prevent.

Asmodeus; or, The Devil on Two Sticks

"In the meanwhile, Alvaro Ponza, joyful at his success, was hurrying from the coast with his prey, and was observed to join a small armed vessel which was awaiting him in the distance. Words cannot convey an idea of the grief of the two friends; the air rang with imprecations against Don Alvaro: their grief and rage, however, were alike unavailing. The domestics of the Donna Theodora, excited by so laudable an example, were not sparing of their lamentations; the shore resounded with cries: fury, desolation, and despair reigned where all before had been tranquil joy, or the sweet grief of love. The rape of the beauteous Helen herself did not excite at the court of Sparta an equal consternation."

CHAPTER XIV

THE SQUABBLE BETWEEN THE TRAGIC POET AND THE COMIC AUTHOR.

Leandro Perez, at this point of the narrative, could not help again interrupting the Devil: "Signor Asmodeus," said he, "I really cannot control my curiosity to know the meaning of something which attracts my attention, in spite of the pleasure I receive in listening to you. I see, in a room near us, two men fighting in their shirts, and several others in their dressing-gowns who are hastening to part them: tell me, I pray you, what it is all about." The Demon, ever ready to please the Student, without further pressing replied as follows:

"The persons whom you behold in their shirts, or so much of them as is left in the struggle, are two French authors; and the mediators in the strife are two Germans, a Fleming, and an Italian. They all lodge in that same house, which is a sort of lodging-house devoted exclusively to foreigners. One of these authors writes tragedies, and the other comedies. The former, disgusted for some reason or other with his own country, has come to Spain; and the latter also, discontented with his prospects in Paris, has performed the same journey, in the hope of finding in Madrid a better fortune.

"The tragic poet is vain and presumptuous, having obtained, despite the opinions of those whose breath should be fame, a tolerable reputation in his own country. To keep his Pegasus in wind, he rides it daily; and not being able to sleep this night, he commenced a piece, the subject of which is taken from the Iliad. He has finished one scene; and as his smallest fault is that, so common to his brethren, of cramming into other people's throats the trash which he has ejected, he rose from his table, where he was writing in his shirt, took a candle, and, as he was, went to rouse the comic author, who, making a better use of his time, was sleeping profoundly.

"The latter, awakened by the noise made at his door, went to open it to the other, who, with the air of one possessed, entered the room exclaiming: 'Down on your knees, my friend; down, and worship a genius whom Melpomene inspires. I have given birth to poetry--: but, what do I say?--I have done it! Apollo himself dictated the verses to me. Were I at Paris, I should go from house to house to read the precious lines; I only wait for day that I may charm with them our talented ambassador, and every other Frenchman who has the luck to be within Madrid; but, before I shew them to a soul, I come to recite them to you.'

"'I am much obliged by the preference,' replied the comic author, yawning with all his might; 'it is rather unlucky though, that you did not choose a better time. I went to bed extremely late,--can hardly keep my eyes unclosed,--and I will not answer for hearing all the verses you have to read to me, without tumbling to sleep again.' 'Oh! I will answer for that myself,' interrupted the tragic poet. 'Were you dead, the scene that I have just composed would recall you to life again. In my writings, there are none of your namby-pamby sentiments,--none of your common-place expressions, sustained alone by rhyme: masculine thoughts, and easy versification, move the heart and strike upon the mind. I am none of those wretched poetasters, whose pitiable creations glide upon the stage like shadows, and like them depart;--which go to Utica to amuse the Africans. My compositions, worthy to be consecrated with my statue in the library of Apollo Palatinus, draw crowds after thirty representations. But come,' added this modest poet, 'you shall hear the verses of which I wish to offer you the first incense.

"'This is my tragedy, THE DEATH OF PATROCLUS. Scene the first, Brisëis and the other captives of Achilles appear. They tear their hair and beat their breasts, to express the grief with which they are filled by the death of Patroclus. Unable even to support themselves, utterly prostrated by despair, they fall upon the stage. This, you will say, is a little daring; but that is exactly what I aim at. Let the small fry who swim in the waters of Helicon keep within the narrow bounds of imitation, without daring to o'erleap them; it is well, there is prudence in their timidity: but for me, I love invention; and I hold that, to move and overcome your spectators, you must present to their minds images which they could never have expected.

"'The captives, then, are lying on the earth. Phoenix, governor of Achilles, is with them. He assists them to rise, one after another; and, having placed them on their feet, he commences the argument of the drama in these lines:--

> Hector shall fall; and Troy itself be spread
> In ruins, to avenge Patroclus dead.
> Proud Agamemnon, Camelus the grave,
> Nestor the wise, and Eumelus the brave,
> Leontes, skilled to hurl the spear along,
> Smooth-tongued Ulysses, Diomed the strong,
> Arm with Achilles. Lo! that hero drives
> Tow'rds Ilium's gates--appalling Ilium's wives--
> His steeds immortal, urged across the plain
> So swift, the eye toils after them with pain.
> But still he cries: Dear Xanthus, Balius, fly!
> And when around ten thousand corses lie,
> When pallid Trojans scamper off like fillies,
> Regain your camp, but not without Achilles.
> Xanthus replies, bowing his head: You may
> Be sure, Achilles, we'll your will obey;
> But, while our pace with your impatience strives,
> Know that to you the fatal hour arrives--
> The ox-eyed Juno thus the steed enlightening,--
> And now the car moves with a speed quite frightening.
> The Greeks, beholding, utter cries of joy,
> So loud, they shake the very walls of Troy.
> Achilles, armed by Vulcan for the war,
> Appears more brilliant than the morning star;
> Or like the sun, when, in its bright career,
> It bursts on earth, dispelling night and fear;
> Or brilliant as the fires on mountains lighted,
> To guide poor swains, bewilder'd or benighted.[8]

"'I stop,' continued the tragic poet, 'to let you breathe a moment; for if I were to recite to you the whole of my scene at once, the beauty of my versification, and the great number of brilliant passages and sublime ideas that it contains, would smother you to a certainty. But remark the aptness of this comparison,--

> Or brilliant as the fires on mountains lighted,
> To guide poor swains bewilder'd or benighted.

"'It is not all the world who could appreciate that; but you, who have mind, and a clearness of perception,--you must be enchanted with it.' 'I am so, doubtless,' replied the comic author, smiling contemptuously; 'nothing can be more beautiful; and I am persuaded you will not fail to describe, in your tragedy, the care taken by Thetis to drive away the Trojan flies which approach the body of Patroclus.' 'You may spare your jests as to that,' replied the tragic poet;--'an author who has talent may venture everything. The very incident you mention is perhaps the one most capable of being rendered into heroic verse; and I shall not lose the opportunity, you may depend upon it.

"'All my works,' he continued complacently, 'bear the impress of genius; so that when I read them it would delight you to witness the applause they elicit: I am compelled to stop after every verse, to receive its laudatory tribute. I remember that one day, at Paris, I was reading a tragedy in the house of a wealthy patron of literature, in which all the wits of the capital generally assemble about dinner-time, and in which I may say, without vanity, that I do not pass for a Pradon. The dowager countess of Vieille-Brune was there, a lady of exquisite taste--I am her favourite poet. Well, at the first scene, the hot tears ran down her cheeks; during the reading of my second act, she was obliged to change her handkerchief; her sobs were beyond her control in the third; at the end of the fourth she was nearly in hysterics; and I expected, at the catastrophe, that she would have absolutely died with the hero of my piece.'

"At these words, although the comic author endeavoured strenuously to preserve his gravity, a burst of laughter escaped him. 'Ah!' he exclaimed, 'how well do I recognize her ladyship by your description! The good countess is one who cannot endure comedy: so strong is her aversion for the merry muse, that she hurries from her box after the dagger or the bowl has done its work, that she may not lose an atom of her mimic grief. Tragedy is her pet passion; and be it good or bad, so long as it presents unhappy love, so surely may you bid her tears to flow. Honestly, did I pretend to the heroics, I should wish for other admirers than the countess.'

"'Oh! as to that, I have others too,' replied the tragic poet. 'I am the approved of thousands, male and female, of the highest rank----' 'I should also mistrust the suffrages of the quality,' interrupted the comic author; 'I should have no great confidence in their judgment: I will tell you why. Auditors of this description are, for the most part, too much occupied with themselves to pay great attention to the reading of a poem; or are caught for the moment by high-sounding verse, or the feeble delicacy of some sickly sentiment. Either is sufficient to induce their praise of an author's labours, whatever else of better they may lack. On the contrary, let but a line rustle their gentle ears too harshly, and it is enough that they exclaim against the piece, however good.'

"'Well!' resumed the lachrymose inditer, 'since you would have me suspicious of this tribunal, I rely on the applauses of the pit.' 'Bah! talk not to me of your pit,' replied the other; 'its judgment is guided by caprice. Stupidly won by the novelty of a first representation, it will be for months enraptured by a wretched piece. It is true that in the end it discovers its folly; and, then, it never forgives an author for having received from it an undeserved renown, or cheated it into mercy.'

"'That is a misfortune for which I have nothing to fear,' said the tragic poet; 'my pieces are reprinted as often as they are played. This, now, never occurs with comedies; printing exhibits their feebleness. Comedies being but trifles,--the lighter productions of mind....' 'Softly! my tragic friend; softly!' interrupted the other: 'you are getting somewhat warm. Speak, I beg of you, of comedy with less irreverence to me. Do you think, now, a comic piece less difficult to write than tragedy? Undeceive yourself! It is far less easy to make good men laugh, than it is to make them weep. Learn that a subject drawn from ordinary life requires talent of as high an order as do the stilted heroes of antiquity.'

"'I'faith,' cried the tragic poet with an air of raillery, 'I am delighted to hear you so express yourself.' 'Well! monsieur Calidas, to avoid disputation, I agree henceforth to as greatly admire your productions as I have heretofore despised them.' 'I care little for your contempt, monsieur Giblet,' hastily replied the comic author; 'and in return for your insolence, I will plainly tell you my opinion of the rubbish you have just been inflicting on me: your verse is a mixture of bombast and absurdity, and the ideas, although borrowed from Homer, have, in passing through your brain, become tinctured with its vulgarity. Achilles talks to his horses, and his horses reply to him; what nonsense! It is a pity they were not asses, for then you could have put into their mouths with propriety your splendid comparison of the village bonfire on the top of a mountain. It is doing no honour to the ancients to pillage them after this fashion: their works are undoubtedly filled with beauties; but it requires greater taste than you possess to make of them a fitting use, or to enable you to borrow from them to advantage.'

"'Since you have not sufficient elevation of soul,' retorted Giblet, 'to appreciate the merits of my poetry, and to punish you for having dared to criticise my scene, I will not read to you the remainder.' 'What, I wonder, have I done, that I should have been punished by being compelled to listen to the beginning?' replied Calidas. 'It well becomes you indeed to despise my comedies! Learn that the very worst that I could write will be compared with anything that you can compose, and that it is much easier to inflate the cheeks with hollow sentiments and sounding words, than it is to enlighten the mind by pointed wit or a delicate irony.'

"'Thank Heaven!' exclaimed the tragic poet, with an awful expression of disdain, 'if in its rigour it denies me your esteem, I may easily console myself for my misfortune. The court, however, thinks more favourably of my tragedies; and the pension with which in its grace it has been pleased----' 'Pshaw! think not to dazzle me with your pensions,' interrupted Calidas; 'I know too well how they may be obtained to esteem your works the more for that. And to prove to you your folly, in thinking more highly of yourself than of comic authors, and that it is easier to compose serious dramas than comic pieces, I am resolved if I return to France, and do not succeed in my own line, that I will descend to making tragedies.'

"'For a scribbler of farces,' said the tragic poet, 'you are not over modest.' 'For a versifier who only owes his reputation to borrowed plumes,' replied the comic author, 'you would fain have one think rather too highly of you.' 'You are an insolent scoundrel,' exclaimed the sombre genius. 'If I were not in your room, little monsieur Calidas, the catastrophe of this adventure should teach you to respect the buskin.' 'Let not that consideration restrain you, I entreat, lanky monsieur Giblet,' replied Calidas; 'if you wish to receive a thrashing, I would as soon give it you in my own room as elsewhere.'

"Immediately, they seized each other by the throat and hair; and kicks and cuffs were exchanged with generous ardour. An Italian, who lay in a neighbouring chamber, having listened to the overture of this drama, and hearing the noise of the incidental combat, judged that it was quite time for the spectators to assemble when the play had begun. He rose, therefore, and out of compassion for the French authors, although Italian, he filled the house with his cries. On this the Fleming and the two Germans hastened with himself in their dressing-gowns to the theatre of strife, and the piece is, as you see, just terminating by the separation of the combatants."

"This squabble is amusing enough," said Don Cleophas. "But, it would appear from what you tell me that tragic writers in France imagine themselves to be much more important personages than those who devote themselves to comedy." "Certainly!" replied Asmodeus. "The former think themselves as much exalted over the latter, as are the stately heroes of tragedies above the intriguing servants of comic pieces." "Indeed! and on what do they found this opinion of themselves?" inquired the Student. "Is it then really so much more difficult to write the one than the other?" "The question you put to me," replied the Devil, "is one which has been a hundred times debated, and is so to this day. For myself, this is my decision, with all deference to those who differ from me in opinion. I say that it is not more easy to compose a comic than a tragic piece; for if it were so, we must conclude that a tragic poet would be more capable of writing a comedy, than the best comic author; the which is not borne out by experience. According to me, then, each of these two descriptions of poem requires a genius of a different character, but of an equal capability.

"It is time, however, to end this digression. I will therefore resume the thread of the history, which you so unceremoniously interrupted."

Footnote:
8.
    Priam va perdre Hector et sa superbe ville;
    Les Grecs veulent venger le compagnon d'Achille,
    Le fier Agamemnon, le divin Camélus,
    Nestor, pareil aux dieux, le vaillant Eumélus,
    Léonte, de la pique adroit à l'exercice,
    Le nerveux Diomède, et l'éloquent Ulysse.
    Achille s'y prépare, et déjà ce héros
    Pousse vers Ilium ses immortels chevaux;
    Pour arriver plus tôt où sa fureur l'entraîne,
    Quoique l'oeil qui les voit ne les suive qu'à peine,
    Il leur dit: Chers Xanthus, Balius, avancez;
    Et lorsque vous serez du carnage lassés,
    Quand les Troyens fuyant rentreront dans leur ville,
    Regagnez notre camp, mais non pas sans Achille.
    Xanthus baisse la tête, et répond par ces mots:
    Achille, vous serez content de vos chevaux,
    Ils vont aller au gré de votre impatience;
    Mais de votre trépas l'instant fatal s'avance.
    Junon aux yeux de boeuf ainsi le fait parler,
    Et d'Achille aussitôt le char semble voler.
    Les Grecs, en le voyant, de mille cris de joie
    Soudain font retentir le rivage de Troie.
    Ce prince, revêtu des armes de Vulcain,
    Paraît plus éclatant que l'astre du matin,
    Ou tel que le soleil, commençant sa carrière,
    S'élève pour donner au monde la lumière;
    Ou brillant comme un feu que les villageois font
    Pendant l'obscure nuit sur le sommet du mont.

CHAPTER XV

CONTINUATION, AND CONCLUSION, OF THE FORCE OF FRIENDSHIP.

Success had not attended the endeavours of the servants of Donna Theodora to prevent her being carried away; but they had at least opposed it with courage, and their resistance had been fatal to some of the companions of Alvaro Ponza. Among others, whose wounds had not permitted them to follow their comrades, there was a man, stretched almost lifeless on the sand, whom they recognized as one of Alvaro's own attendants. Perceiving that he still breathed, they carried him to the house, and spared no pains to restore him to his senses. In this they at last succeeded, although the quantity of blood which had escaped from his numerous wounds had reduced his stream of life to its lowest ebb, and left him extremely weak. To induce him to speak, they promised to take every care to prolong his days, and not to deliver him into the hands of justice, provided that he would inform them of the place to which his master had designed to take the Donna Theodora.

Gratified by these assurances, although the state to which he was reduced left him but small hope to profit by their realization, he rallied all his remaining strength, and, with a faltering voice, confirmed by his confession the information that Don Fabricio had received. He added, however, that Don Alvaro designed to conduct the widow of Cifuentes to Sassari, in the island of Sardinia, where he had a relation whose protection and power promised him a safe asylum.

The deposition of the dying man, for he expired a few hours afterwards, raised Mendoza and the Toledan from complete despair; and as their stay at Donna Theodora's seat was now useless, they at once returned to Valencia. After debating for some time on the steps most expedient to be taken, they resolved to seek their common enemy in his chosen retreat, and in a few days embarked, without attendants, at Denia, for Port Mahon, not doubting that they would there find some means of transport to the island of Sardinia. It so happened that scarcely had they reached their destined port, when they learned that a vessel freighted for Cagliari was about to sail, and in it they immediately secured a passage.

The vessel left the island of Minorca with breezes friendly to their hopes; but five or six hours after their departure there came on a calm, and night brought with it winds directly in their teeth; so that they were obliged to tack about and wait for a favourable change. Three days were thus passed in sailing without progress; when, on the fourth, about two hours after noon, they discovered a strange sail, all its canvas spread, and bearing down directly upon them. At first they took it for a merchantman, bound for the shores they steered from; but observing that it came within the range of cannon-shot without showing its colours, they began to fear it was a corsair.

They were not deceived: it was a Tunisian pirate, which approached them in full expectation that the Christians would yield without a blow. As it came near enough, however, for the corsairs to discern what was passing on board of their expected prey, and to observe that the sails were reefed and the guns run out, they guessed that the affair was likely to turn out more seriously than they had expected. They therefore shortened sail, wore round, hurriedly cleared the deck, and prepared for action.

A brisk exchange of shots soon commenced, and the Christians, taking advantage of the surprise which their unexpected resistance had occasioned, began to prevail over their opponent; but an Algerine pirate, larger and of heavier metal than either of the others, arriving in the middle of the action, took part with its brother of Tunis, and the Christians were thus placed between two fires.

Discouraged by this unlooked-for circumstance, and feeling that it was useless to continue the unequal strife, they gradually slackened their fire, and at last it ceased altogether. On this a slave appeared on the bow of the Algerine vessel, who hailed them in their own language, bidding them, if they hoped for mercy, to strike to Algiers. A Turk then advanced, holding in his hand a green silk flag studded with silver crescents interlacing each other, which he waved in the air. The Christians, looking upon further resistance as hopeless, gave themselves up to all the grief that the idea of slavery inspires in the breasts of freemen, until the master of the vessel, fearing that a further delay of submission would only serve to irritate their barbarian conqueror, hauled down his colours, threw himself into a boat with some of his sailors, and went to surrender to the Algerine corsair.

The latter immediately sent a portion of his crew on board the Spanish vessel to examine, or rather to pillage it of all that it contained. The Tunisian pirate gave similar orders to some of his men, so that all the passengers it contained were in an instant disarmed and plundered, and were shortly afterwards

Asmodeus; or, The Devil on Two Sticks

exchanged into the Algerine vessel, when the two pirates divided their prisoners by lot.

It would have been at least some consolation for Mendoza and his friend to have both fallen into the hands of the same corsair; they would have found their chains somewhat the less heavy to have borne them together; but Fortune, apparently disposed to make them feel the terrors of her caprice, allotted Don Fabricio to the pirate of Tunis, and Don Juan to his competitor of Algiers. Picture to yourself the grief of the two friends, when told that they must part. They threw themselves at the feet of the corsairs, and entreated them that they might not be separated. But their entreaties were vain; the barbarians before whom they knelt were too much accustomed to the sight of human misery not to be proof against the prayers of their present victims. On the contrary, judging by their demeanour that the two captives were men of wealth and station, and that they would consequently pay a weighty ransom, they were the more resolved to divide them.

Mendoza and Zarata, perceiving that they were in the power of men with hearts insensible to all but gain, turned towards each other, their looks expressing the depth of their affliction. But when the booty had been shared, and the Tunisian pirate prepared to return to his own vessel with his proportion, and the slaves which it included, they seemed as though they would expire with despair. Mendoza rushed into the arms of the Toledan, and embracing him, exclaimed: "Must we then separate? Cruel necessity! Is it not enough that we should be borne to slavery, and unavenged? Must we even be denied to bear in union the sorrows to which we are destined? Ah! Don Juan, what have we done that Heaven should thus visit us with its terrible wrath?" "Seek not elsewhere the cause of our disgrace," replied Don Juan: "I only am to blame. The death of two unfortunates, immolated to my revenge, although excused to mortal eyes, is deep offence to Heaven; and you, my friend, are punished for the fault of loving one who took upon himself the vengeance that belongs to God alone."

While they spoke thus, tears, strangers to the eyes of men, streamed down their cheeks, and sighs but choked their utterance. So touching was their grief, that those who shared their fate were yet as much affected by the sight as with their own misfortune. Not so the wretches who formed the crew of the Tunisian corsair. Perceiving that Mendoza was the last to quit the Algerine vessel, they tore him without ceremony from the arms of the Toledan; and, as they dragged him away, added blows to insult. "Adieu, dear friend," he cried: "adieu for ever! Donna Theodora is yet unavenged! and, parted from you, the miseries that these wretches prepare will be the least that slavery can bring to me."

Don Juan was unable to reply to the exclamations of his friend; the treatment that he saw him endure filled his breast with a horror which deprived him of speech. And so, Signor Don Cleophas, as the course of my narrative requires that we should follow the Toledan, we will leave Don Fabricio, in solemn silence, to be conducted on board of the Tunisian pirate.

The Algerine returned toward his port, where, having arrived, he conducted his slaves to the house of the superintending basha, and thence to the public market. An officer of the Dey, Mezzomorto, purchased Don Juan for his master; and the new slave was at once employed as an assistant in the gardens of the harem. This occupation, although laborious for a gentleman, was however, the less disagreeable to Don Juan, on account of the solitude to which it left him; for, situated as he was, it was a pleasure to have at least the liberty of indulging his own melancholy thoughts. Incessantly occupied with his misfortunes, his mind, far from endeavouring to lighten them with hope, seemed to delight in dwelling on the past, and to inspire his bosom with gloomiest presages for the future.

One day he was occupied with his work, murmuring the while one of his now usual songs of sorrow, when the Dey, who was walking in the garden, came upon him without being perceived, and stopped to listen. Pleased with his voice, and moved by curiosity, he approached the captive and asked his name. The Toledan replied, that he was called Alvaro; for, following the usual custom with slaves, of concealing their station, he thought fit to change his name, and, as the outrage upon Donna Theodora was ever uppermost in his thoughts, the name of the detested Alvaro had come soonest to his lips when suddenly asked his own. Mezzomorto, who spoke the Spanish language tolerably well, then questioned him as to the customs of Spain, and particularly as to the conduct observed by those of its cavaliers who would render themselves agreeable to their ladies;--to all of which Don Juan replied in such a manner as to greatly please the Dey.

"Alvaro," said he to him at last, "you appear to be intelligent; and I judge you to have been a man of rank in your own country: but, however that may be, you are fortunate enough to please me, and I will honour you with my confidence." At these words, Don Juan prostrated himself before the Dey, and with well-affected humility, kissed the hem of his master's robe, and after touching with it his eyes and forehead, arose, and stood before him in silence.

"To begin by giving you proof of my regard," resumed the Dey, "you know, that in my seraglio, I have some of the fairest women which Europe can offer for my pleasures. Among these, however, there is one whose beauty is beyond compare; nor do I believe that the Grand Signor himself possesses so exquisite a creature, although for him the winds of heaven daily waft ships with their lovely burden from all quarters of the globe. In her visage the dazzling sun seems reflected, and her form is graceful as the rose's stem which grows in the gardens of Eram. My soul is enchanted with her perfections.

Alain René Le Sage

"Alas! this miracle of nature, all beauteous as she is, maintains and nourishes the deepest grief; which neither time nor all the efforts of my love can dissipate. Although fortune has yielded her to my will, I have ever respected her grief, and controlled my desires; and unlike those who, placed as I am, seek but the momentary gratifications of sense, I fain would win her heart, and have striven to gain it by respectful attentions, such as the vilest Mussulman that lives would feel degraded to offer to the fairest Christian slave.

"Still, all my cares seem but to add to her affliction; and I will not disguise that its obstinacy begins to weary me. The sense of slavery is not imprinted in the minds of others of my slaves in characters so deep, but that a look of favour from myself can soon efface or gild them; so that I may well tire of this incessant grief. Nevertheless, before I abandon myself to the passion which transports me, I would make one last endeavour to touch her insensible heart; and I will leave this task to you. As my fair slave is Christian, and even of your own country, she may confide in you, and you may persuade her to my wishes better than another. Go, then! tell her of my riches and my power; tell her that among my many slaves, I care for only her; and, if it must be so, bid her even hope that she may one day be the honoured wife of Mezzomorto. Tell her that I would rather win her love, than receive the hand of a Sultana from the grace of his Highness the Sultan himself."

Don Juan threw himself a second time before the Dey; and although not over-delighted with this commission, assured him that he would do his utmost to execute it to his satisfaction. "Enough!" replied Mezzomorto, "leave your work and follow me. I am about, contrary to our usages, to permit you privately to see this slave. But, tremble, if you dare abuse the confidence I place in you! Tortures, such as even were never yet inflicted by the Turks, shall punish your temerity. Strive to overcome your own sorrows, and dream of liberty as the reward of ending the sufferings that I endure." Don Juan threw down his hoe, and silently followed the Dey, who, when they entered the palace, left him, that he might prepare the afflicted captive to receive his messenger of love.

She was with two aged slaves, who retired as soon as Mezzomorto appeared. The beauteous slave herself saluted the Dey with great respect, but she could not behold him without greater fear, as indeed had ever been the case when he presented himself before her. He perceived it, and to reassure her mind: "Amiable captive," he said, "I come but to inform you that among my slaves there is a Spaniard with whom you would perhaps be glad to converse. If you wish to see him, I will give him permission to speak with you, and even alone."

As the lovely slave expressed no objection to receive her countryman: "I go," resumed the Dey, "to send him to you: may he, by the information he conveys, serve to relieve you of your troubles!" He left her as he spoke; and as he went out, meeting the Toledan, said to him in a low voice: "Enter! and when you have communicated what I desire, come to my cabinet and inform me of the result."

Zarata entered as he was directed, closed the door, and bowed before the favoured slave, who returned his salute, without either particularly observing the other. When, however, their eyes at last met, a cry of surprise and joy escaped them both: "Oh Heaven!" exclaimed the Toledan, approaching the captive, "is it not a vision that deceives mine eyes? Can it be the Donna Theodora whom I see?" "Ah! Don Juan," ere he had uttered these words, cried the lady he addressed, "is it indeed yourself who speaks to me?" "Yes, madam," replied the Toledan, while he fell upon his knee and tenderly kissed her hand, "it is Don Juan. Let these tears, that my eyes, rejoiced to behold you again, cannot restrain; let this transport, that you alone can excite in the heart of him who kneels before you, witness for my presence! I murmur no longer against my destiny, since it conducts me to you--Alas! what does my ecstacy inspire? I forget that you are in chains. By what unhappy chance do I find you here? How have you escaped from the frantic passion of Alvaro? Ah, what horror fills my soul to mention his very name! How do I tremble to learn the fate for which Heaven reserved you, when it abandoned you to his perfidy!"

"Heaven," replied the Donna Theodora, "has avenged me on Alvaro Ponza. Had I but time to relate to you----" "Time!" interrupted Don Juan,--"you have plenty, and to spare. The Dey himself permitted me to see you, and, what may well surprise you, alone. Profit by the happy moments which his confidence affords, and inform me of all that has happened to you since you were carried off by Alvaro." "And who, then, told you that it was by him I was taken away?" inquired Donna Theodora. "Alas! madam, I know it but too well," replied the Toledan. He then shortly narrated the manner in which he had become acquainted with Alvaro's design, and had witnessed its execution; how Mendoza and himself had followed him in the hope of preserving her from his violence, or to revenge it; and of their unfortunate, but for this meeting, encounter with the pirates, and its consequence.

As soon as he had finished this recital, Donna Theodora began the story of heir own sufferings, as follows: "I need not dwell upon my astonishment at finding myself seized by a masked band of ruffians--indeed, I had hardly time to wonder at the outrage, for I swooned in the arms of the first who laid hold of me; and when I recovered my senses, which must have been after the lapse of some hours, I found myself alone with Agnes, one of my own attendants, in a cabin on the poop of a vessel, in the open sea, sailing with all its canvass spread before the wind.

Asmodeus; or, The Devil on Two Sticks

"The perfidious Agnes, on perceiving my tears, exhorted me to bear my misfortune with patience; but from a few words which dropped from her as she spoke, I was not long in divining that she was in the confidence of Alvaro, who shortly afterwards appeared. Throwing himself at my feet: 'Madam,' he exclaimed, 'pardon to a too fond lover the means by which he has dared to possess himself of your person! You know how deeply I have loved you, and how ardently I disputed with Mendoza for your heart, up to the fatal day when you declared your preference for him. Had my passion been the cold and empty feeling that mortals dignify with the name of love, I might have vanquished it as easily as such a feeling is inspired; but my misfortune was beyond consolation. I live but to adore those charms; and, despised though I be, I cannot free myself from their spell. But, madam, let not the fury of my passion alarm you! I have not deprived you of liberty, that I may rob you of honour; I seek only that, in the retreat unto which we are hastening, a sacred tie may unite our hearts for ever.'

"He continued in this strain for some time, but in terms which I cannot remember. To hear him, it would have seemed that, in forcing me to wed him, he did me no wrong; and that where I saw but an insolent ravisher, I should have beheld alone an impassioned lover. As, however, while he spoke thus, I answered him but with tears, and exhibited an evident despair, he left me; but not without making signs to Agnes, which I plainly understood as directions for her to second, as well as she was able, the splendid arguments by which he had sought to dazzle my weak understanding.

"She did her best; representing to me that, after the éclat of an abduction, I could not do otherwise than graciously accept the offered hand of Alvaro Ponza; that, whatever aversion I might feel for his excessive tenderness, my reputation demanded of my heart this sacrifice. As, however, the necessity which she painted, of a hated marriage, was not exactly the way to dry my tears, I still remained inconsolable; and Agnes had exhausted all her eloquence, when we suddenly heard upon the deck a noise which attracted the attention of us both.

"This noise, which proceeded from Alvaro's people, was caused by the apparition of a large ship, which was sweeping with its wings all spread upon us; and from which, as our vessel was by no means so good a sailer, there was no escaping. Down it came, and we soon heard cries of 'Lie to, and send a boat aboard!' But Alvaro Ponza and his men, who knew what they had to expect from yielding, chose rather to die, or at least to run the chance of a combat. The action was sharp, but of short duration: I cannot pretend to give you its details, and will therefore only say, that Alvaro and every one of his crew perished, after fighting like men who preferred death to slavery. For myself and Agnes, we were removed into the other vessel, which belonged to Mezzomorto, and was commanded by Aby Aly Osman, one of his officers.

"Aby Aly looked at me for some time, with much surprise; and recognizing me, by my dress, for a Spaniard, he said to me in almost pure Castilian: 'Moderate your grief, lady, for having fallen into slavery: it is a consolation in our woes to know that they are inevitable. But what do I speak of?--Woe! Happiness alone awaits you. You are far too lovely for the homage of Christian dogs. Heaven never made you for the pleasure of the miserable wretches whom we trample under foot. You were formed to receive the admiration of the men of the world; a Mussulman alone is worthy to possess such beauty. I shall return at once,' he added, 'to Algiers. Albeit I have made no other prize, I know our Dey too well not to be persuaded that with you I shall not be all unwelcome. I have no great fear that he will condemn my impatience to place within his hands a beauty whom our Prophet must have sent on earth expressly for his enjoyment, and to be the light of his harem.'

"These compliments, Don Juan, told me too plainly all I had to fear, and my tears flowed the faster as he spoke. Aby Aly was pleased, however, to interpret my fears after his own fashion; and, laughing at my timidity, gave orders to sail towards Algiers. Never was port so dreaded by the ship-bound habitant of ocean! Sometimes I threw myself on my knees, and implored Heaven for its protection; at others, my doubting spirit wished for the assistance of man in Christian guise who might come to my rescue, or sink the pirate vessel, which contained me, in the waves,--or that these in their mercy would engulph us. Then, again, I hoped that my tears, and the sorrow which caused them, would render me so unsightly that the tyrant to whom they bore me might fly my sight with horror. Vain wishes, that my modesty had formed! We arrived at the dreaded port; they conducted me to the palace; I appeared before Mezzomorto.

"I know not what Aby Aly said on presenting me to his master, nor what the latter replied, for they spoke in their own tongue; but I thought I could perceive by the looks and gestures of the Dey that I had the misfortune to please him. But what, after they had conversed thus for some time, was addressed to me in my own language, completed my despair by confirming me in the opinion I had formed.

"Vainly I cast myself before him, offering him whatever sum he chose to name as my ransom; in vain did I tempt his avarice by the promise of all that I possessed, or could command: he answered me by saying, that I offered him in my own person more than all the riches in the world could bestow. He then conducted me to this apartment, the most splendid his palace contains, and from that hour to the present moment, he has spared no pains to dispel the grief with which he sees me overcome. All his slaves who either dance, sing, or play, have tried by his command their skill before me. He removed from me Agnes, because he thought that she served to remind me of my home, and I am now attended by two aged female slaves, whose sole discourse is of love and the Dey, and of the happiness which through his favour I may secure.

"Need I say, Don Juan, that all their efforts to divert my grief add but to its intensity, and that nothing can console me? Captive in this detestable palace, which resounds from day to day with the cries of innocence oppressed, I suffer less from the mere loss of liberty than from the terror which the hated tenderness of the Dey inspires. It is true I have hitherto found in him but a lover gentle and respectful; but I am not the less alarmed. I fear lest, wearied by a semblance of devotion, which cannot but constrain him to put on, he should resume the rights of power; and this fear agitates me without ceasing, making of my life but one long torment."

As Donna Theodora finished these words, she wept; and her tears fell like iron on the heart of poor Don Juan. "It is not without cause," he at last exclaimed, "that you look on the future with dread; I am, myself, as much alarmed for it as you. The respect of the Dey is melting faster than even you imagine; your submissive lover will soon abandon all the mildness he assumes. Alas! I know too well the dangers which surround you.

"But," he continued, his voice changing as he spoke, "shall I calmly witness your dishonour? Slave though I be, he may feel the weight of my despair. Before Mezzomorto injures you, I will plunge in his heart----" "Ah! Don Juan," interrupted the widow of Cifuentes, "what dreadful project do you dream of? For Heaven's sake, think of it no more! With what dreadful cruelties would they avenge his death! Torments the most refined--I cannot think of them without trembling! Besides, to what end would you encounter such a peril? In taking the life of the Dey, would you restore me to liberty? Alas! I should be sold to some other tyrant who would treat me with less respect than Mezzomorto. No!" she exclaimed, throwing herself on her knees, "it is thou, Almighty Father, who canst alone protect me. Thou knowest my weakness, and the infamous designs of him in whose power I am placed. Thou, who forbiddest me to save myself by poison or the steel, Thou wilt save me in Thy justice from a crime that is abhorrent in Thy sight."

"Yes, madam," replied Zarata, "Heaven will avert the misfortune with which you are threatened! I feel already that it inspires me;--the ideas which flash across my mind are doubtless prompted by its mercy. Hear me! The Dey has permitted me to see you, only that I might induce you to return his love. It is time that I rendered him an account of our interview; and, in so doing, I shall deceive him. I will tell him that your grief may be overcome; that his conduct towards you has already won for him your esteem, and that, from a continuance in that conduct, he has everything to hope. Do you assist me in my design? When he comes next to visit you, let him find you less sorrowful than usual; and appear, at least, to be interested in his conversation."

"What a task would you impose on me!" interrupted Donna Theodora. "How is my soul, always frank and open, to assume such a disguise, and what will be the fruit of so painful a deception?" "The Dey," replied Zarata, "will be flattered by this change in your deportment, and will be anxious to complete his conquest of you by gentle means. In the meanwhile, I will endeavour to effect your freedom: it will be difficult, I acknowledge; but I am acquainted with a slave on whose address and enterprise some reliance may be placed.

"I leave you," he continued, "as no time is to be lost: we shall meet again. I now go to the Dey; whose impetuous ardour I hope to restrain by some well-invented fables. And you, madam, prepare to receive him; constrain yourself to deceit. Let your eyes, which his presence offends, display neither hatred nor pride; let your lips, which now unclose but to express your affliction, form for him honeyed words of respect; you must indirectly promise all, in order that you may concede nothing." "Enough!" replied the lady, "I will do as you desire, since the danger that impends over me compels me to this cruel necessity. Go! Don Juan, employ all your thoughts to end my slavery: my freedom will be doubly sweet, if owing to you."

As soon as the Toledan repaired to Mezzomorto, the latter cried with great emotion: "Well! Alvaro, what news do you bring to me of my lovely captive? Have you inclined her to listen to my vows? Tell me not that her ceaseless grief refuses to yield to my tenderness; or I swear, by the head of the Commander of the Faithful himself, that force shall wring from her what affection cannot win." "Signor," replied Don Juan, "that oath were useless now: you will have no need of violence to gratify your passion. Your slave is young,--has never loved;--and she whose pride disdained the offers of the noblest of her native land, in which she lived as queen, and here exists in chains, may well ask time to reconcile her haughty spirit to her new condition. This, proud as she is, habit will soon effect; and even now, I dare affirm, the yoke is felt less heavy: the kindness you have shown, the respectful cares which she could never have expected from yourself, have already lessened her misfortune, and must triumph over her disdain. Continue, Signor, this gentle observance; continue--and complete the charm which dissipates her grief, by new attentions to each fond caprice; and you will shortly find her yield to your desires, and lose her love of liberty, encircled in your arms."

"Your words enrapture me," exclaimed the Dey: "the hopes which you inspire engage me to what you will. Yes! I will restrain my impatient love, that I may satisfy it the more worthily. But, do you not deceive me, or are you not deceived yourself? I will this moment see my lovely mistress; I will endeavour to discern in her eyes some expression of the flattering appearances you speak of." And so saying, he hastened to seek Theodora; while the Toledan returned to the garden, where he found the slave whose skill he proposed to employ in the liberation of the widow of Cifuentes.

This slave, named Francisco, was a Navarrese, and was perfectly acquainted with Algiers and its customs, having there served two or three masters before he was purchased by the Dey as a gardener. "Francisco, my friend," said Don Juan, accosting him, "you see me in deep affliction. There is, in the harem of the Dey, a young lady of the highest distinction of Valencia: she has entreated Mezzomorto to name a ransom of any amount; but he refuses to do so, having fallen in love with her." "And why should that annoy you so much?" asked Francisco. "Because I come from the same town," replied the Toledan; "her relations and my own are intimately connected; and there is nothing which I would not do to restore her to liberty."

"Well! though that is no easy matter to accomplish," said Francisco, "I dare undertake to bring it about, provided her relations are disposed to come down pretty handsomely." "Be assured of that," replied Don Juan; "I answer for their gratitude, and especially for her own. Her name is Donna Theodora: she is the widow of a man who has left her immense possessions, and she is generous as rich. For myself, I am a Spaniard, and a noble; my word may suffice to convince you of what I state."

"Well, again!" resumed the gardener: "on the faith of your word then, I will seek a Catalonian renegade whom I know, and propose to him----" "What say you?" interrupted the Toledan, in alarm;-- "would you confide in a wretch who has not been ashamed to abandon his religion for----" "Although a renegade," interrupted Francisco, in his turn, "he is nevertheless an honest man. He is rather deserving of your pity than contempt; and, if the crime he has committed can be excused at all, I think he may be pardoned. I will tell you his history in a few words.

"He was born in Barcelona, where he practised as a surgeon. Finding, however, that he was worse off there than his patients, he resolved to establish himself at Carthagena, thinking of course to better his condition. He accordingly embarked with his mother, for that town; but they were taken on the way by a pirate, who brought them hither. They were sold; his mother to a Moor, and he to a Turk, who used him so badly that he assumed the turban to release himself from slavery, as also to enable him to free his parent, who was no better off in the house of the Moor, her master. With this view, he entered into service with the Dey, and made several voyages, in which he gained four hundred patacoons: he employed a portion of this in the ransom of his mother; and, to make the best use of the remainder, took it in his head to scour the seas on his own account.

"Appointed captain, he purchased a small open vessel, and with some Turkish seamen who had sailed with him before, he set out to cruize between Alicant and Carthagena, and returned to Algiers, laden with booty. He repeated this several times; and succeeded always so well that at last he was able to arm a large vessel, with which he made several prizes, but was in the end unfortunate. One day, he was imprudent enough to attack a French frigate, which so mauled his ship that it was with difficulty he escaped, and regained Algiers. As pirates are judged here, like their betters elsewhere, according to their success, the renegade gained the contempt of the Turks as the reward of his misfortune. Disgusted by this injustice, he sold his vessel, and retired to a house without the town; where, since then, he has lived on the produce of his ship, and what remained of the fruits of his former enterprises, in company with his mother, and attended by several slaves.

"I often go to see him, for he served with me under my first master, and we are intimate friends. He conceals nothing from me; and, only three days ago, he told me, with tears in his eyes, that, despite his wealth, he had known no peace since he had renounced his faith; that to appease the remorse which preyed on him without ceasing, he was sometimes tempted to trample his turban under foot, and, at the risk of being burned alive, to repair, by a public avowal of his repentance, the insult he had offered to the Mediator whom in secret he still adored.

"Such is the renegade whom I am about to consult," continued Francisco: "surely, a man like him may be trusted by you. I will seek him, under pretext of going to the bagnio; I will represent to him, that instead of consuming his life in vain regret at his exclusion from the bosom of the church, he should act so as to assure his forgiveness and reception; that to do this he has only to equip a vessel, as if, disgusted with a life of inaction, he intended to resume his piracies; and that, with this vessel, we may gain the coast of Valencia, where, once arrived, Donna Theodora will give him wherewith to pass the remainder of his life in tranquillity at Barcelona."

"Yes! my dear Francisco," cried Don Juan, transported with joy at the hope thus raised by the Navarrese slave,--"yes! you may promise all this, and more, to your renegade friend; both he and yourself may be sure of a rich reward. But, do you conceive it possible to execute the project you conceive?" "There may be difficulties," replied Francisco, "which I do not contemplate; but, rely on it, that I and my friend will overcome them all." "Alvaro," he added, as they parted, "I hope well for our enterprise; and I trust that, when we meet again, I shall have good news to tell you."

Alain René Le Sage

With what anxiety did the Toledan await the return of Francisco! At last he came. "I have seen the renegade," he said, "and have opened to him our design. After much deliberation, we have arranged that, to save time, he shall purchase a vessel already fitted for sea; that, as it is permitted to employ slaves as sailors, he shall take with him those who now serve him; that, however, to guard against suspicion, he shall also engage some dozen others, as if he really designed what he pretended; but that, two days before the time fixed for his departure, he shall embark, by night, with his own people, and weigh anchor, after coming for us with his boat to a little door which leads from the garden, close by the sea. This is our plan; of which you can inform the captive lady, assuring her that in a fortnight from this time she shall be free."

How great was the joy of Zarata, to be able to convey such welcome intelligence to the Donna Theodora! To obtain permission to see her, on the following day, he sought, without appearing to do so, Mezzomorto; and, having met with him: "Signor," said he, "dare I enquire how you have found your lovely slave? Are my hopes fulfilled?--" "I am delighted," interrupted the Dey; "her eyes no longer shun the tender glance of mine; her words, which heretofore presented but the picture of her griefs, no longer breathe complaint; and for the first time, she seemed to listen to my own without aversion.

"It is to you, Alvaro," he continued, "that I owe this happy change: I see," he added, good-humouredly, "that you are in favour with the ladies of your country. I will trust you, however, to speak with her again, that you may finish well what you have so well begun. Exhaust thy fertile genius to attain the bliss I seek, and thy chains are turned to gold. Yes! I swear, by the spirit of our Holy Prophet, that I will restore you to your home, so loaded with my favours, that your Christian friends shall not believe you, when you tell them you return from slavery."

The Toledan, although somewhat conscience-stricken, did not fail to continue Mezzomorto in the flattering error he indulged. Affecting gratitude for his kindness, and under pretext of hastening its accomplishment, he left the Dey at once to see the charming slave; and, finding her alone in her apartment, he lost no time in informing her of what the Navarrese and the renegade intended on her behalf.

The lady was of course greatly delighted to hear that already such strides were making towards her deliverance. "Is it possible," she cried, "that I may hope again to see Valencia, my own dear native land? Joy, joy!" she continued,--"after so many dangers and alarms, to live in peace once more with you! Ah! Don Juan, this is happiness indeed! Can I doubt that your heart partakes of it? Remember, Zarata, that, in snatching me from the Dey, you bear away your wife!"

"Alas!" replied the Toledan, sighing deeply, "how delicious were those words to my expecting soul, did not the remembrance of an unhappy aspirant for thy love dash their sweet fragrance with alloy! Pardon me, madam, that at such a moment I should think of aught but you! But you must acknowledge that a friend like Mendoza merits thy pity as my own. It was for thee he left Valencia; it was in search of thee that he became a slave; and I feel sure that, at Tunis, he is not bowed down so much by the weight of his chains, as with despair at failing to avenge thee."

"He merited indeed a happier lot," said Donna Theodora; "and I call Heaven to witness that I am deeply affected at what he suffers on my account. Yes! I accuse myself of the pains which he endures; but, such is my destiny, my heart can never be their recompense."

This conversation was interrupted by the coming of the two old dames who attended on the widow of Cifuentes. Don Juan immediately assumed the confidant of the Dey: "Yes, fair lady," said he to Theodora, "you have deprived him of liberty who keeps you in chains. Mezzomorto, your master and my own, the most loving and the most amiable of Turks, is your slave. Treat him with the favour you now deign to show him, and soon will a joyous end arrive to his sufferings and your own." Zarata bowed respectfully as he pronounced these words, the purport of which was well understood by the lady to whom they were addressed, and left the apartment.

During the following week, affairs remained in this position in the palace of the Dey. In the meantime, however, the renegade had purchased a small sloop, and was making preparations for its putting to sea; but, six days before it was ready, a new subject for alarm occurred to Don Juan.

Mezzomorto sent for him, and, taking him into his cabinet: "Alvaro," he said, "thou art free!--free to return when thou wilt to Spain; the reward that I have promised now awaits thee. I have seen my lovely slave this day;--ah! how unlike the creature whose sorrow filled my breast with anguish! Daily does the feeling of captivity grow weaker; and so bright are now her charms, that I have resolved at once to make her mine: in two days she shall be my wife."

Don Juan changed colour at these words, and, with all the effort that he made to constrain them, could not conceal his trouble and surprise from the Dey, who asked him the cause of this emotion.

"Signor," replied the Toledan, with embarrassment, "I cannot control my astonishment at hearing one of the greatest princes of the Ottoman empire avow his intention of so far humbling himself as to wed with a slave. I know that this is not without precedent; but, for the illustrious Mezzomorto, who might aspire to the daughter of the highest in the service of the Sultan, to"--"I agree to what you say," interrupted the Dey; "I might marry with the daughter of the Grand Vizier, and even hope to succeed

91

him in his office: but I have great wealth, and small ambition. I prefer repose, and the delights I enjoy here in my vice-royalty, to the dangerous honours to which we are no sooner elevated, than the fear of our sovereign, or the jealousy of the envious who surround him, prepares for us a fall. Besides, I love this slave; and her beauty and virtue render her worthy of the rank to which my affection calls her.

"It is however necessary," he added, "that she should at once renounce her religion, to attain the honour for which I destine her. Think you that absurd prejudices will induce her to despise that honour?" "No, Signor," replied Don Juan; "I am persuaded that on reflection, she will hold her faith as too small a sacrifice to your love. But, permit me to say that this should not be proposed too hastily. There is no doubt that the idea of abandoning the creed she lisped almost on her mother's bosom will at first revolt her: give her therefore time to reflect on the inducements to a change. When she remembers that, instead of using your power over her person, and then abandoning her to grow old among the neglected slaves of your caprice, you seek to unite her to yourself for ever, by a marriage which crowns her with honour, her gratitude--her woman's vanity--will by degrees vanquish her scruples. Defer therefore for a week, at least, the execution of your design."

The Dey remained for some time in deep thought: the delay that his confidant proposed suited but ill to his desires; nevertheless, the counsel appeared judicious. "I yield to your advice, Alvaro," at last he said, "impatient as I am to press the lovely captive to my heart. I will wait a week, as you request. Go!" he continued, "see her at once, and dispose her to fulfil my wishes, when that time shall have passed. I am anxious that Alvaro, who so well has tutored the fair one to my will, should have the honour of tendering to her my hand."

Don Juan hastened to the apartment of Theodora, and informed her of what had passed between the Dey and himself, that she might conduct herself accordingly. He also informed her that in six days the vessel would be ready; and, as she was anxious to know how, when the time arrived, she was to escape, seeing that all the doors of the rooms she had to traverse, in the usual way of reaching the staircase, were well secured: "Let not that embarrass you," he answered; "a window of your ante-room looks upon the garden; and you may thence descend, by a ladder which I will take care to provide."

The six days added their units to eternity, and Francisco informed the Toledan that the renegade was prepared to sail on the coming night: you may guess with what impatience it was expected. It came, and, graciously for the fugitives, shrouded in its thickest mantle to cover their flight. At the appointed moment, Don Juan placed the ladder against the window of the ante-room, and the watchful captive hastened to descend, trembling with agitation and suspense. She reached the ground in safety, and leaning on the arm of the Toledan, the latter lost no time in conducting her to the little door which opened on the sea.

They walked with hasty steps, enjoying, by anticipation, the happiness of recovered freedom; but fortune, not even now disposed to favour these unhappy lovers, plunged them into grief more dire than they had yet experienced, and of a nature that they least expected.

They had already left the garden, and were advancing to the shore, where the sloop awaited them, when a man whom they took for an accomplice in their escape, and of whom, therefore, they had no suspicion, came upon Don Juan, sword in hand, and thrust it in his breast. "Perfidious Alvaro Ponza!" he exclaimed, "it is thus that Don Fabricio de Mendoza punishes a base seducer: you deserve not that I should attack you openly as an honest man."

The Toledan could not resist the force of the blow, which stretched him on the earth; and, at the same moment, Donna Theodora, whom he supported, struck with surprise, with grief and fear, fell in a swoon beside him. "Ah! Mendoza," cried Don Juan, "what have you done? It is your friend whose bosom you have pierced!" "Gracious Heaven!" exclaimed Don Fabricio, "is it possible that I have assassinated----" "I pardon you my death," interrupted Zarata; "destiny is alone to blame, or rather it has so willed it, to end our misfortunes. Yes! my dear Mendoza, I die contented, since I restore to your hands the Donna Theodora, who will convince you that my friendship for you has never belied itself for an instant."

"Too generous friend," said Don Fabricio, prompted by a feeling of despair, "you shall not die alone; the same point which wounded you shall punish your assassin: if my error may excuse my crime, it cannot console me for its committal." As he spoke, he turned his sword against his breast, plunged it therein nearly to the hilt, and fell upon the body of Don Juan, who fainted less from loss of blood, than from horror at the frenzy of his friend.

Francisco and the renegade, who were not ten paces from the spot, and who had their reasons for not having defended the slave Alvaro, were amazed to hear the last words of Don Fabricio, and still more so to witness his last act. They had heard enough, however, to know that he had been mistaken, and that the wounded pair were friends, instead of deadly enemies, as they had believed. They now therefore hastened to their assistance; but, finding them both senseless, as also the Donna Theodora, they were at a loss how to proceed. Francisco advised that they should content themselves with bearing off the lady, leaving the two cavaliers on the shore; where, according to him, if they were not already dead, they would soon be so. The renegade, however, was not of this opinion: he said that it would be cruel to abandon the two unfortunates; that their wounds were probably not mortal, and that he would look to them when on board his vessel, where he had been provident enough to stow away all the implements of his ancient trade.

To this, Francisco made no objection; so, as they both agreed that there was no inducement to stay where they were, by the assistance of some slaves, they carried the unhappy widow of Cifuentes, and her still more unfortunate lovers, to the boat, and soon joined their ship. There, no time was lost in spreading the sails; while some upon their knees poured forth to Heaven the most fervent prayers which fear could suggest, that they might escape the cruisers of the Dey.

The renegade, having left the management of the vessel to a French slave whom he could trust, gave his attention to his passengers. The lady, of course, claimed his first care; and, having restored her to life, he took his measures so skilfully, that Don Fabricio and the Toledan also speedily recovered their senses. Donna Theodora, who had swooned the instant Don Juan was struck, was greatly astonished on her recovery to behold Mendoza; and, although she soon comprehended that the latter had wounded himself for having incautiously assailed his friend, she could not look upon him but as the murderer of the man she loved.

"You would have been affected, Don Cleophas, could you have seen these three persons at the moment I speak of: the deathlike stillness from which they had emerged would not have commanded half your pity. There was Donna Theodora, gazing on Don Juan with eyes which spoke all the feelings of a soul filled with grief and despair; while the two friends, each fondly turning upon her their dying looks, were striving to control the sighs which rent their hearts."

The scene lasted for some time in silence, which Mendoza was the first to break. "Madam," said he, addressing Donna Theodora, "I die; but I have the satisfaction of knowing you are free. Would to Heaven that thy liberty were owing to myself! But it has decreed that you should owe that obligation to him whose image you cherish in your heart. I love too much my rival to complain; and trust that the blow which my blindness dealt may be too light to prevent his sweet reward." The lady answered not this touching speech. Insensible, for the time, to the fate of Mendoza, she could not restrain the feelings of aversion which the condition of the Toledan, over whom she hung, inspired in her bosom towards him who had caused it.

The regenade surgeon now examined and probed the wounds of the two friends. Beginning with Zarata, he pronounced it favourable, inasmuch as the sword had only glanced through the muscles of the left breast, without touching any of the vital parts. This report, while it lessened the grief of Donna Theodora, gave great delight to Don Fabricio, who, turning his head towards the lady, exclaimed, "Madam, I die without regret, since the life of my friend is out of danger: you will forgive me now."

He pronounced these words with so much pathos, that the widow of Cifuentes was moved beyond expression. As she no longer feared for Don Juan, she ceased to hate Mendoza, and beheld in him now but an object of the deepest pity. "Ah! Don Fabricio," she exclaimed, her generous nature resuming its influence, "let them attend to your wound; it is, I trust, not more dangerous than that of your friend. Let not your feelings interfere to render the cares of those who love you useless. Live!--if I cannot yield felicity to you, at least I will never bestow it on another. Friendship and compassion shall restrain the hand that I would give to Don Juan: I will sacrifice for you, as he has done, the dearest wishes of my heart."

Don Fabricio would have replied; but the surgeon, fearing that in his case, as in trouble generally, talking would only increase the ill, imposed silence, while he examined his wound. On so doing, he saw that it was likely to prove mortal, as the sword had penetrated the lungs, and the consequent loss of blood had been excessive. Having however dressed it with care, he left the cavaliers to repose; and that a matter so essential to them, in their present state, might be secured, he took with him, as he left the cabin, Donna Theodora, whose presence seemed likely to disturb it.

But despite all these precautions, Mendoza was seized with fever, and towards midnight the wound began to bleed afresh. The renegade then thought it right to inform him that all hope of recovery was over, and that, if he had anything which he wished to communicate to his friend, or to Donna Theodora, he had no time to lose. The Toledan was greatly affected on hearing the declaration of the surgeon: for Don Fabricio, he listened to it with indifference. He calmly requested that the regenade would summon the widow of Cifuentes to his side.

Donna Theodora hastened to the dying man, in a state more easy to conceive than to describe: tears streamed down her cheeks, and sobs choked her utterance;--so violent was her affliction, that Mendoza could not repress his agitation at the sight. "Madam," he exclaimed, "I am unworthy of the precious drops which dim those lovely eyes: restrain them, I entreat you, and listen to me for a few moments. And you also, my dear Zarata," he continued, observing the excess of grief in which his friend indulged, "control your feelings for a while, and hear me. I well know that to you this separation is a painful shock; your friendship is too well assured for me to doubt it; but wait, both of you, until the earth shall have hidden me from your sight; and honour, with those marks of tenderness and pity, my silent grave.

Asmodeus; or, The Devil on Two Sticks

"Suspend until then your affliction; I feel it now more than the loss of life. Let me relate to you the way by which the fate that pursues me conducted me this night to the fatal shore which I have stained with the blood of my friend, and my own. You must be anxious to learn how it happened that I mistook Don Juan for Alvaro; I will tell you, if the short time which it is permitted me to live will enable me to do so.

"Some hours after the vessel in which I was had quitted that wherein I had left Don Juan, we met a French privateer, which attacked and took the Tunisian pirate, and landed us near Alicant. I was no sooner free, than I thought on the ransom of my friend; and, to effect this I went to Valencia to obtain the necessary funds. There, learning that at Barcelona some brothers of the Holy Order of Redemption were just about to sail for Algiers, I set out for the former town. Before leaving Valencia, however, I begged my uncle the governor, Don Francisco de Mendoza, to use all his influence with the court of Madrid to obtain the pardon of Zarata, that, on his return with me, he might be reinstated in his former possessions, which had been confiscated in consequence of the death of the Duke of Naxera.

"As soon as we had arrived at Algiers, I went to all the places frequented by the slaves; but in vain did I run them through, I found not the object of my search. This morning, I met the regenade Catalonian, to whom this vessel belongs, and whom I recognized as a man who had formerly attended my uncle. I told him the motive of my voyage, and requested him to make strict inquiry for my friend. 'I am sorry,' he replied, 'that it is out of my power to serve you. I leave Algiers to-night, with a lady of Valencia, one of the Dey's slaves.' 'And who is this lady,' I demanded. 'She is called the Donna Theodora,' was his startling answer.

"The surprise which I exhibited at this information told the regenade at once that I was interested in this lady's fate. He therefore informed me of the design which he had formed for her liberation; and as, during his recital, he mentioned the slave Alvaro, I had no doubt that it was Alvaro Ponza himself of whom he spoke. When he had finished: 'Assist me in my resentment!' I exclaimed, with transport; 'furnish me with the means of avenging myself upon my enemy!' 'You shall soon be satisfied,' replied the regenade; 'but, tell me first what subject of complaint you have against this same Alvaro.' I related to him all our history; which, when he had heard: 'Enough!' he cried, 'you shall accompany me to-night. They will point out to you your rival; and, when you have punished him for his villany, you shall take his place, and join with us in conducting Donna Theodora to Valencia.'

"Nevertheless, my impatience did not cause me to forget Don Juan. I left the money for his ransom in the hands of Francisco Capati, an Italian merchant, who resides at Algiers, and who promised me to effect it, if by any means he could discover him. At last, the night arrived; I went to the house of the regenade, who led me, as he had promised to the sea shore. We concealed ourselves near a little door, whence shortly issued a man who came directly towards us, and, pointing to two persons who followed him, said 'There are Alvaro and Donna Theodora.'

"Furious at this sight, I drew my sword, ran to meet the unfortunate Alvaro, and, imagining that it was my hated rival whom I struck, I thrust my weapon into the bosom of the faithful friend whom I had come to seek. But, Heaven be praised!" he continued with emotion, "my error will not cost him his life, nor cause eternal grief to Donna Theodora."

"Ah! Mendoza," interrupted the lady, "you do injustice to my tears; never shall I console myself for your own loss. Even should I espouse your friend, it will be only to unite our griefs: your love, your friendship, your misfortunes will ever be present to our recollection,--the sole topic for our tongues." "It is too much, madam," replied Don Fabrido; "I am not worthy thus to trouble thy repose. Permit, I entreat thee, Zarata to call thee his, on the day when he shall have revenged thy wrongs on Alvaro Ponza." "Don Alvaro," said the widow of Cifuentes, "is no more; on the same day that he forced me from my home, he was killed by the pirate who enslaved me."

"Madam," replied Mendoza, "my wavering soul rejoices at the welcome news; my friend will be the sooner happy. Follow without control your mutual inclinations. I see, with joy, the hour approach which removes from you, for ever, the obstacle which your generous compassion has raised against your happiness. May your days glide in peace, and in an union which the envy of fortune may never dare to trouble! Adieu, Madam;--adieu, Don Juan!--think sometimes, in your joy, of one who has never loved but you."

Donna Theodora and the Toledan were unable to reply to this affectionate address, except by tears, which redoubled as he spoke. Mendoza, therefore, perceiving their grief, thus continued: "But I have done with earth! Death already points me out my way; and I have not yet supplicated the Divine mercy to pardon me for having, by my own folly, shortened a life of which it should have alone disposed." He spoke no more; but, raising his eyes to Heaven, appeared to be engaged in mental prayer for its forgiveness; when a gurgling in his throat told that a last outbreaking of his wound had taken place, and he expired.

Don Juan, as he heard the fatal rattling which indicated what was passing, was maddened with despair. His hands sought his own wound; and tearing it open, he would have soon joined his friend, but that the renegade and Francisco threw themselves upon him, and withheld his fury: Donna Theodora, woman-like, forgetful of her own woes at sight of the transport of the Toledan, hastened to soothe him by her tenderness; and--what will not love do?--soon brought him to himself: in short, the lover triumphed over the friend. But, if reason regained its sway, it was only to resist the insensate frenzy of his grief, and not to weaken its sentiment.

The renegade, who, among the many things which he was bearing from Algiers, happened to have balsam of Arabia, and other precious requisites, undertook to embalm the body of Mendoza, at the request of Donna Theodora and her now unrivalled lover; who were anxious to render to their friend's remains all proper honours of sepulture at Valencia. Love, with them, did nothing but sigh and moan, during the voyage; not so, however, with their companions: they were rejoiced by favourable winds, which soon brought them in sight of the coast of Spain, to the inexpressible delight of those, which included the whole crew, who had never expected to behold it again.

When the vessel had happily arrived at the port of Denia, every one took his own course. For the widow of Cifuentes and the Toledan, they sent a courier to Valencia, with letters for the governor and the friends of Donna Theodora. Alas! while the intelligence of the return of this lady brought joy to her relations, that of the death of his nephew caused the deepest affliction to Don Francisco de Mendoza.

The poor old man, accompanied by the relatives of the released lady, lost no time in repairing to Denia; and there, insisting on beholding the body of the unhappy Don Fabricio, he bathed it with his tears, uttering such deep complaints as melted the hearts of the beholders. Then, turning to the Toledan, he requested to be informed of the unfortunate events which had brought his nephew to so sad an end.

"I will tell you," replied Zarata: "far from seeking to efface them from my memory, I feel a mournful pleasure in recalling them to my mind, and in indulging my grief." He then related to Don Francisco all that had occurred; and this recital, while it brought fresh tears to his own eyes, added to those which flowed from those of his aged listener. Meanwhile the friends of Theodora were occupied in testifying the delight which was elidted by her unexpected return, and in felicitating her on the miraculous manner in which she had been delivered from the tyranny of Mezzomorto.

After all things had been satisfactorily explained, they placed the body of Don Fabricio in a hearse, and bore it to Valencia. It was not, however, buried there, because, as the period of the vice-royalty of Don Francisco was nearly expired, that nobleman was preparing to return to Madrid, where he had resolved that his nephew should be interred. While the preparations for the funeral were making, the widow of Cifuentes was employed in loading Francisco and the renegade with the fruits of her gratitude. The Navarrese retired to his own province, and the surgeon returned with his mother to Barcelona, where he sought once more the bosom of the church, in which he lives to this day snugly enough. And now, when all was completed, Don Francisco received an express from the court, conveying the pardon of Don Juan, which the king, notwithstanding his consideration for the house of Naxera, had been unable to refuse to all the Mendozas who had united to ask the grace. This pardon was the more welcome to the Toledan, inasmuch as it gave him liberty to accompany the body of his friend to its last home, which he would not otherwise have dared to do.

At last the sorrowful procession, attended by a numerous concourse of noble mourners, set out for Madrid; where it was no sooner arrived, than all that remained of Don Fabricio was deposited in yonder church, where Zarata and the Donna Theodora, with the permission of the Mendozas, erected a splendid monument to his memory. Nor did they bury their grief with their friend: they bore at least its outward sign for the unusual space of an entire year, that the world might know how deeply they deplored his loss.

After having exhibited such signal proofs of their affection for Mendoza, they married; but by an inconceivable effort of the force of friendship, Don Juan for a length of time still preserved a melancholy that not even love could banish. Don Fabricio, his dear Don Fabricio, was ever present in his thoughts by day; and, by night, he saw him in his dreams, and mostly as he had beheld him when the last sigh escaped him. His mind, however, began to be relieved from these saddening visions,--the charms of his beloved Theodora, which had ever possessed his soul, commenced their triumph over his baneful remembrances; in short, Don Juan once more touched upon happiness. But, a few days since, while hunting, he was thrown from his horse, fell upon his head, and fractured his skull. Physicians could not save him; he is just dead: and it is Theodora whom you see, in the arms of the two women, and who will probably soon follow him to the grave.

CHAPTER XVI

THE DREAMERS.

Leandro Perez, as soon as Asmodeus had finished this narrative, said to him: "A very pretty picture of friendship have you presented! But, rare though it be to see two men so bound by love as the Toledan and Don Fabricio, I imagine it were quite impossible to find two rivals of the softer sex, who could so generously sacrifice to each other, for friendship's sake, the man they love."

"Doubtless!" replied the Devil: "that is a sight the world ne'er saw, and one that, as it grows older, it probably never will see. Women have no affection for each other. I will suppose two who think themselves friends; I will even go the length to suppose that they never speak ill of one another when apart,--so extraordinary are the ties which bind them. Well! see them together; and incline the least towards the one, and rage shall fill the bosom of the other; not that she cares an atom for yourself, but because she would be preferred by all. Such is the character of woman: jealousy occupies too large a portion of her heart to leave room for friendship."

"The history of these peerless friends," replied Don Cleophas, "possesses a slight touch of the romantic, and has led us somewhat from our object. The night is far advanced, and we shall soon behold the brilliant heralds of the coming day: I expect of you, therefore, a new pleasure. I perceive a great number of persons still sleeping, and wish you to satisfy my curiosity by informing me of their dreams." "Willingly!" replied the Demon. "You are, I see, an admirer of les tableaux changeants; I will gratify your taste."

"Thanks!" said Zambullo: "I expect that I am about to hear of rare absurdities in these same dreams." "And why?" asked the Cripple: "you, so well versed in Ovid, do you not know that it is towards break of day that dreams visit the mind with presages of truth, because at that time the soul is disengaged from the vapours of digestion?" "Oh! as to that," replied the Student, "despite of master Ovid, I have no faith in dreams." "You are wrong, then," exclaimed Asmodeus: "you should neither treat them as fantastic visions, nor yet believe them all; they are liars, who sometimes speak the truth. The emperor Augustus, whose head had well adorned a student's shoulders, despised not dreams which turned upon his fate; and nearly took it in his head, at the battle of Philippi, to strike his tent, on hearing of a dream which regarded himself. I could cite a thousand examples to you, which would convince you of your folly in this respect; but I forbear to do so, that I may at once satisfy the new desire which prompts you.

"We will begin by this handsome mansion on our right. Its proprietor, whom you see ensconced in that superb apartment, is a liberal and gallant noble. He is dreaming that he is at the opera, listening to a new prima donna; and that the voice of the syren is just enslaving his heart.

"In the next apartment lies the countess, his wife, who loves play to madness. She dreams that she has no money, and that she is pawning her diamonds with a jeweller, who is lending her thereon three hundred pistoles, deducting only a very moderate discount.

"In the next house, on the same side, lives a marquis of the same stamp as the count, and who, for the moment, is in love with a celebrated, but capricious, beauty. He dreams that he is borrowing largely of an usurer for the purpose of securing her to himself; while his steward, who is sleeping at the top of the house, is dreaming that he is growing rich as fast as his master is hastening to ruin. Well! what think you of these dreams? Is there anything in them so extravagant?" "No! on my life," replied Don Cleophas, "I begin to think Ovid is right: but who is that man whom I see, lying with his mustachios in paper, and preserving in his sleep an air of gravity which would indicate that he is no ordinary cavalier." "He is a country gentleman," replied the Demon,--"a viscount of Aragon, imbued with all the pride of that province. His soul at this moment swims in delight; he dreams that he is with a grandee who is yielding to him precedence in a public ceremony.

"But," continued Asmodeus, "I observe in the same house two brothers, apothecaries, whose dreams are particularly unpleasant. One of them is reading, in his sleep, an ordinance which decrees that doctors shall not be paid, except when they have cured their patients; and his brother is occupied with a similar law, which ordains that medical attendants shall head the procession at the funeral of all who die in their hands." "I could wish," interrupted Zambullo, "that these decrees were as true as they would be just; and that your doctor were thus compelled to be present at the burial of his innocent patient, as a lieutenant criminel, in France, is bound to witness the execution of the guilty wretch whom he has

Alain René Le Sage

condemned." "I like your comparison," exclaimed the Devil: "it might be said in such a case, however, that the one merely superintends the execution of his own sentence; but that the other, having already performed his especial function, pursues his victim after death."

"Hollo!" cried the Student, "who is that personage rubbing his eyes, and rising in such tremendous haste?" "He," replied Asmodeus, "is a noble signor who is soliciting an appointment, as governor, in the Indies. A frightful dream has startled him from sleep: he fancied himself at court, and that the premier had passed him with averted eyes. And there, too, is a youthful damsel, waking to the world, not over contented with her dream. She is a lady of rank, and not more handsome than discreet. She has two lovers; for one of whom she nourishes a passion the most tender, and for the other an aversion, almost amounting to horror. Well! in her sleep just now, she saw, upon his knees before her, the gallant she detests; and he was so impassioned, so assiduous, that had she not awakened, she would have treated him with even greater kindness than she ever bestowed on the lover whom she favours: nature, during sleep, signor Student, throws off the yoke of reason, and of virtue.

"Cast your eyes upon that house at the corner of this street: it belongs to an attorney. Behold him and his wife sleeping in twin bedsteads, in that room hung with ancient tapestry, embroidered with grotesque figures. The man of law dreams that he is about to visit one of your hospitals for the charitable purpose of relieving a sick client with his own money; while the lady imagines that her husband is driving out of his house a sturdy clerk, of whom he has become suddenly jealous."

"I hear ungentle snorings break on the stillness round us," said Leandro Perez; "and I fancy they proceed from yonder plump old man, whom I discern in the house adjoining that of the attorney." "Precisely so," answered Asmodeus. "It is a canon chanting in his sleep his Benedicite.

"His neighbour, there, is a silk-mercer, who vends his costly wares, at his own price, to titled customers, for their time. His lordly ledger is inscribed with debts amounting to above a hundred thousand ducats; and he is dreaming that his debtors are bringing him their gold; while his creditors are horrified with visions of his own bankruptcy." "These dreams," said the Student, "certainly have not emerged from Sleep's dark temple by the same gate." "I fancy not, indeed," replied the Demon: "the first has passed by the ivory portal of the leaden god, and the other from that of horn.

"The house adjoining that of the mercer is occupied by a celebrated bookseller. He has recently published a work which has been extremely successful. On bringing it out, he promised to give the author fifty pistoles, in addition to the price agreed for, should the book run to a second edition; and he is at this moment dreaming that he is reprinting it without informing the unfortunate scribe of the fact."

"Ah!" exclaimed Zambullo, "there is no need to ask from which door that dream proceeded; and I have not the slightest doubt of its proving one of the least deceitful visions he ever had in his life. I am perfectly acquainted with those worthy gentlemen, the booksellers. Heaven help the poor authors who fall into their hands! To cheat them, is the mystery of their craft." "Nothing can be more true," replied the Cripple; "but, it appears, you have yet to become acquainted with those as worthy gentry--the authors. They are six of one and half-a-dozen of the other: it is impossible to decide on their relative merits. By the bye, I will relate to you an adventure which occurred not a century ago, in this very town, and which will enlighten you on the subject.

"Three booksellers were supping together at a tavern; and the conversation naturally turned on the scarcity of good modern authors. Thereupon, one of them said to his brethren: 'My friends, I must tell you, however, in confidence, that I have been in luck's way within these few days. I have purchased a manuscript, for which I paid rather dearly, it is true, but it is by an author--oh! it is uncoined gold.' One of those whom he addressed now interrupted him; and boasted of having been equally fortunate on the preceding day in a similar purchase. 'And I, gentlemen,' at last exclaimed the third, in his turn,--'I will not be behindhand in confidence with you; I will show you the gem of manuscripts, of which I only this morning became the happy owner.' As he finished, each drew from his capacious pocket the precious acquisition he had made; when these miracles of authorship turned out to be as many copies of a new theatrical piece, entitled the Wandering Jew, which the astonished bibliopoles found had been sold to each of them separately.

"Near the bookseller, in the next house," continued the Devil, "you may perceive a timid and respectful lover just awaking. He loves one of the most sprightly of widows; and was dreaming, but this moment, that, beside her in the covert of a dusky wood, whose shade lent courage to his modest spirit, he was so tender,--so gallant in his speech, that his fair mistress could not help exclaiming: 'Ah! you are becoming absolutely dangerous! If I were not steeled against the flattery of men, I should be lost. But you are all deceivers! I never trust to words;--actions alone can win me,'--'And what actions, madam, do you ask of me?' interrupted the gentle swain: 'must I, to prove the excess of my passion, undertake the twelve labours of Hercules?' 'Lord! no, Nicaise,' replied the lady, 'much less would content me.' Thereupon--he awoke."

"Prythee, tell me," said the Student, "why yonder man, in that dark-coloured bed, tosses about so furiously." "He," replied the Cripple, "is a talented licentiate; and his present agitation arises from a dream, in which he is disputing in favour of the immortality of the soul, with a little doctor of medicine,

Asmodeus; or, The Devil on Two Sticks

who is as good a catholic as he is a physician. In the same house, over the licentiate, lodges a gentleman of Estramadura, named Don Balthazar Fanfarronico, who has come post-haste to court, to demand a reward for having valiantly slain a Portuguese, by a musket-shot, in ambush. And of what do you imagine he is dreaming? Nothing less than that he is appointed to the government of Antequera, at which he is very naturally dissatisfied: he thinks he deserves a viceroyalty at least.

"In a furnished house close by, I discover two distinguished personages, whose dreams are far from pleasant. One of them is governor of a fortress, where he is now sustaining a fancied siege, and which, after a faint resistance, he is on the point of surrendering, with himself and garrison, at discretion. The other is the bishop of Murcia, whom his majesty has charged with the task of eulogising a deceased princess, whose funeral takes place in a day or two. He has, in imagination, just ascended the pulpit; and there has his imagination left him, for he has stopped short in the exordium of his discourse." "It is not impossible," said Don Cleophas, "that this misfortune may really befall the worthy prelate." "No, truly," replied the Devil; "for it is not very long since his grace found himself in a similar predicament on a like occasion.

"And now, if you would like to behold a somnambulist, look into the stables of this same house: what see you?" "I perceive," answered Leandro Perez, "a man walking in his shirt, and holding, what seems to me, a horse-comb in his hand." "Well!" replied the Demon, "he is a sleeping groom. Nightly does he rise in sleep to curry his pampered charge, and then betake himself to bed again. His fellow-servants look on the sleek coats of the horses as the frolic work of some wanton sprite; and the groom himself shares this opinion with them.

"In the large house, opposite, lives an aged chevalier of the Fleece, who was formerly viceroy of Mexico. He has fallen sick; and, as he fears he is about to die, his viceroyalty begins to trouble him: true it is that he exercised his functions so as to justify his present inquietude; the chronicles of New Spain, unless they be belied, make no too honourable mention of his name. He has just started from a dream, whose horrid visions float before him still, and which will probably bring about their own fulfilment in his death." "Ah!" exclaimed Zambullo, "that must be something extraordinary." "You shall hear," replied Asmodeus: "there is really something in it rather singular. The sickly lordling dreamt he was in the valley of the dead, where all the victims of his injustice and inhumanity thronged fiercely round, and heaped upon him menaces and insult. They pressed upon, and would have torn him limb from limb; but, as their hot breath seemed to burn his very brain, he thought he took to flight, and saved himself from their fury. He had no sooner escaped, than he found himself in a large hall, hung all around with black cloth, where, sitting at a table upon which were three covers, he saw his father and his grandfather. His two dismal companions solemnly beckoned him to approach; and, with all the gravity which belongs to the dead, said to him: 'We have waited for you long: come, take your place beside us.'"

"Oh! the wretched dream," interrupted the Student; "I could forgive the poor devil, for the fright he is in!" "To make up for it," resumed the Cripple, "his niece, who reposes in the apartment over his, passes the night in bliss: sleep brings to her its brightest illusions. She is a maiden of from twenty-five to thirty, ugly as myself, and not much better made. She dreams that her uncle, to whom she is sole heiress, has ceased to live; and that she sees, in swarms around her, amiable signors, who dispute for the honour of her slightest glance."

"If I do not deceive myself," said Don Cleophas, "I hear some one laughing behind us." "It is no deception," replied the Devil; "it is a widow laughing in her sleep, a few paces from us. She is a woman who affects the prude, and who loves nothing so well as a little friendly scandal: she dreams that she is chatting with an ancient devotee, whose conversation could hardly fail to delight one of her taste.

"I cannot help laughing in my turn, to see, in the room under that of the widow, an honest cit, who lives with difficulty on the little he possesses, but who dreams that he is picking up pieces of gold and silver, and that the more he gathers the more remain to glean: he has already filled a large coffer." "Poor fellow!" said Leandro; "he will not enjoy his treasure long." "No!" replied the Cripple; "and when he awakes he will be like the really rich, when dying: he will see all his wealth disappear."

"If you are curious to know the dreams of two actresses who live near each other, I will relate them to you. One is dreaming that she is catching birds with a call; that she strips them as she takes them, and then throws them to be devoured by a large tom-cat in which she delights, and which has all the profit of her skill. The other dreams that she is driving from her house greyhounds and coach-dogs, which for a long time have sunned themselves in her presence, having resolved to confine her affections to a pretty little lap-dog, which has recently gained her favour."

"Two dreams absurd enough!" cried the Student; "I fancy that if at Madrid, as formerly in Rome, there were interpreters of dreams, they would be sadly puzzled to explain these." "Not so much as you think," replied the Devil: "a very small acquaintance with the domestic habits of your syrens of the stage, would enable them to render their sense perfectly intelligible."

"Well! for myself," exclaimed Don Cleophas, "they are past my comprehension, and that troubles me little: I would rather be informed who is that lady sleeping in a bed with amber velvet hangings, bordered with silver fringe, and near which, upon a small table, I perceive a book and a wax-candle."

Alain René Le Sage

"She is a lady of illustrious family," replied the Demon, "whose establishment is mounted in gallant style, and who loves to see her livery adorned by young and handsome men. She is accustomed to read in bed, and cannot sleep without her favourite author. Last night she was indulging in the Metamorphoses of Ovid: in consequence, she is at this moment dreaming, extravagantly enough, that Jupiter has become amorous of her charms, and has entered her service in the form of a favourite page.

"Apropos of metamorphoses, there is another subject who will amuse you. You perceive that man, tasting in the calm of sleep the exquisite pleasure of imagined flattery. He is an actor, a veteran of such ancient service, that there is not a grey-beard in Madrid who can say he witnessed his first appearance. He has been so long behind the scenes, that he may be said to have become theatrified. He is not without talent, but, like most of his profession, he is so vain that he thinks the part of Man beneath him. Of what think you is this hero of the slips now dreaming. He imagines that he is on the point of death; and that round his couch are assembled all the deities of Olympus, to decide on what they are to do with a mortal of his importance. He listens while Mercury insists before the council of the gods that a comedian so famed, after having so often had the honour of mimicking themselves, and Jove's own person, on the stage, should not be subject to the common fate of man, but merits a reception as a brother god by those who now surround him. Mercury finishes by moving accordingly, and Momus seconds the motion; but the male and female members of the celestial parliament murmuring at the proposition of so extraordinary an apotheosis, Jupiter, to put an end to the debate, is about to decree, of his sovereign authority, that the aged son of Thespis shall be transformed into a theatrical statue, for the amusement of future generations."

The Devil was about to continue, but Zambullo interrupted him, exclaiming: "Hold! Signor Asmodeus, you forget that it is day. I am afraid they will perceive us from the street. If the gentle public should remark your lordship, we shall hear such an uproar as we may be glad to put an end to."

"Never fear!" replied the Demon; "they will not see us. I have the power ascribed to the fabulous deities of whom I spoke but now; and like to the amorous son of Saturn, who, upon Mount Ida, shrouded himself in a cloud, to hide from the world the blisses he shared with Juno, I am about to envelope you and myself in a misty veil which the searching eye of man cannot pierce, but which shall not prevent you from beholding those things which I wish you to observe." As he spoke, they were suddenly surrounded by a vapour, which, although dense as the smoke of a battle-field, offered no obstacle to the sight of the Student.

"So now to return to our dreamers," continued the Cripple,----"but I do not consider," he added, "that the mode in which you have consumed the night must have fatigued you. I advise, therefore, that you let me bear you to your home, and leave you to a few hours' sleep. In the meanwhile, I will just take a turn round the earth, and amuse myself after my fashion; taking care to rejoin you by the time you awake, when we will continue our laugh at the expense of the swarming world." "I have no desire to sleep, and am not in the least fatigued," replied Don Cleophas; "so, instead of leaving me, do me the pleasure to expound the various objects which occupy the yawning brains of the persons whom I see already risen, and who are preparing as it seems to me, to leave their houses: what can possibly call them out so early?" "What you ask me is well worth your knowledge," answered the Demon; "you shall gaze on a picture of the cares, the emotions, the anguish that poor mortal man gives himself during life, to occupy, with the vain hope of happiness, the little space which is granted him between the cradle and the tomb."

CHAPTER XVII

IN WHICH ORIGINALS ARE SEEN OF WHOM COPIES ARE RIFE.

"Observe, in the first place, that troop of beggars which you see already in the street. They are libertines, mostly of good birth, who, like the monks, live on the principle of community of property; and who pass their nights in debauch at their haunts, where they are at all times well supplied with bread, meat, and wine. They are about to separate, each to perform his part in the churches of this godly city; and to-night, when reassembled, they will drink to the charitable fools who piously contribute to their orgies. You cannot but admire these scoundrels, who so well know the semblances which art adopts to inspire pity: why, coquettes are less adept to elicit love. "Look at those three rogues who are walking off together. He who, leaning upon crutches, trembles as he moves, and seems to halt with pain,--who, as he hobbles on, you would momentarily think must fall upon his face,--despite his long white beard and wrinkled front, he is a youthful scamp, so strong and swift, would head the hunted deer. The one beside him, with that awful scald, is a graceful adolescent, whose head is covered with a bladder skin which hides as beauteous curls as ever adorned a courtly page. The third, who gyrates in a bowl, is a comic rascal, that can bring such lamentable noises from his stomach as to move the bowels of all ancient ladies, who even hasten from the topmost floors to his relief.

"While these mummers, under the mask of poverty, prepare to cheat the public into charity, I observe hosts of worthy artisans, who, Spaniards though they be, are on the road to earn their bread by the sweat of their careworn brows. On all sides you may behold men rising from their beds, or dressing hastily, that they may begin anew their various parts upon this busy stage. How many projects formed in the visionary night are about to be carried into execution, or to vanish with the sober light of morn! What schemes prompted by love, by interest, or ambition, are about to be attempted!"

"What see I in the street?" interrupted Don Cleophas. "Who is that woman loaded with saintly medals, who walks, preceded by a footman, in such anxious haste? She has some pressing business in hand, beyond a doubt." "Indeed she has," replied the Devil; "she is a venerable matron, hurrying to a neighbouring house where her ministry is suddenly required. She seeks a fair comedian who suffers for the fault of Eve, and near whom are a brace of cavaliers in sore perplexity. One of these is her spouse, and the other a noble friend, who is greatly interested as to the result: for the labours of your actresses resemble those of Alcmena; there being ever a Jupiter and an Amphitryon who share in their production.

"Would not one swear now, to look on that mounted cavalier, carrying a carbine in his hand, that he was a sportsman about to war with the hares and partridges who besiege the neighbourhood of Madrid? Nevertheless, it is no love of shooting which calls him forth so early: he is after other game; and is bent towards a village, where he will disguise himself as a peasant, that he may enter, without suspicion, the farm where his mistress resides, under the vigilant eye of an experienced mother.

"That young graduate, passing along with such enormous strides, is going, according to his daily custom, to inquire after the health of an aged canon, his uncle, whose prebendary he has in his eye. Do you see, in that house opposite to us, a man putting on his cloak, evidently preparing to go out? He is an honest and rich citizen, whom a matter of grave interest has kept awake all night. He has an only daughter, of marriageable years, and he is unable to make up his mind whether he shall give her hand to a young attorney who solicits it, or to a proud hidalgo who demands it; and he is therefore going to consult his friends on the subject: in truth, he may well feel embarrassed. He is justly alarmed lest, by resolving on the gentleman, he should have a son-in-law who would despise him; and on the other hand he fears, that if he decide for the attorney, he will introduce into his house a worm which will consume all that it contains.

"Look at the neighbour of this anxious parent. You may perceive, in that house so magnificently furnished, a man in a dressing-gown of scarlet brocade, embroidered with flowers of gold: there is a wit for you, who affects the lord in spite of his lowly origin. Ten years ago, he had not twenty maravedis wherewith to bless himself; and now, he boasts an annual revenue of ten thousand ducats. His equipage is in the best taste; but he keeps it on the savings of his table; whose frugality is such that he generally picks his chicken by himself. Sometimes, however, his ostentation compels him to regale his illustrious friends: to-day, for instance, he gives a dinner to some councillors of state; and, in anticipation, he has just sent for a pastry-cook, with whom he will haggle for a maravedi, before he agrees with him on the bill of fare, which it will be his next care to display to advantage." "You are describing a scaly villain, indeed!" cried Zambullo. "Oh! as to that," replied Asmodeus, "all beggars whom fortune suddenly enriches become either misers or spendthrifts: it is the rule."

"Tell me," said the Student, "who is that lovely woman at her toilet, talking with that handsome cavalier?" "Ah! truly," exclaimed the Cripple, "you have hit on a subject which well deserves your attention. The lady is a German widow, who lives at Madrid on her dower, and who visits in the best society; and the young man who is with her is the Signor Don Antonio de Monsalva.

"This cavalier, although a member of one of the noblest families in Spain, has pledged himself to the widow to espouse her; he has even given her a conditional promise of forfeiture to the amount of three thousand pistoles. He is, however, crossed in his love by his relations, who threaten to confine him if he do not immediately break off all connexion with the fair German, whom they look upon as an adventurer. The gallant, mortified to find his friends all thus opposed to his design, went yesterday evening to his mistress, who, perceiving his uneasiness, asked him its cause. This, after some hesitation, he told her, assuring her at the same time that whatever obstacles his family might raise, nothing should shake his constancy. The widow appeared delighted at his firmness, and they parted at midnight highly satisfied with each other.

"Monsalva has returned this morning, as you see, to pay his devoirs to the lady, whom finding at her toilet, he used every effort to beguile the time by new protestations of devotion. During the conversation, his Saxon mistress was releasing her auburn curls from the papers which had confined them during the night; and our cavalier, happening to take up one of these, heedlessly unfolded it, and, to his great surprise, observed therein his own hand-writing. 'What! madam,' said he, smiling, 'is this the use you make of these pledges of my affection?' 'Yes! Monsalva,' replied the lady; 'you behold the value that I put upon the promises of lovers who would marry me in opposition to their friends; they make excellent papillotes.' When, indeed, the cavalier discovered that it was his pledge of forfeiture which his mistress had thus destroyed, he was filled with admiration at this unlooked-for proof of disinterestedness, and he is now very properly vowing to her for the thousandth time, eternal fidelity.

"Cast your eyes," continued the Devil, "upon that tall man who is passing beneath us; he has a large common-place book under his arm, an ink-bottle hanging at his girdle, and a guitar slung at his back." "He is an odd-looking fellow indeed," cried the Student: "I would lay my life he is an original." "It is beyond a doubt," replied the Demon, "that he is a curious compound enough. There are such things as cynical philosophers in Spain; and there goes one. He is walking towards the Buen-Retiro, to reach a meadow in which there is a fountain, whose refreshing waters form a brook that glides like a silver serpent through the flowers. There will he pass the day, contemplating the beauties of nature, tinkling his guitar, and noting the reflections that the scene inspires in his common-place book. He carries in his pockets his ordinary food, that is to say, a piece of bread and some onions. Such is the sober life that he has led during ten years past; and were some Aristippus to say to him, as was erst spoken to Diogenes: 'If thou knewest how to pay thy court to the great, thou wouldst not eat onions;' this modern philosopher would reply: 'I could pay my court to the great as well as thou, if I would abase one man so low, as to make him cringe before another.'

"In truth, however, this philosopher formerly mixed greatly with the nobility; he even owes his fortune to their patronage; but, compelled to feel, as all must who move among persons more exalted than themselves, that the friendship of these lordlings was to him but an honourable species of servitude, he broke off all connection with them. At the time I speak of he kept his carriage; this he subsequently put down, on reflecting that, as he rolled along, the mud from his wheels was splashed perhaps upon his betters. Distributing his wealth among his indigent friends, he reserved for himself no more than would enable him to live as moderately as he does; and he kept so much, only because it appeared to him no less shameful for a philosopher to beg his bread from the people than from the aristocracy.

"Pity the cavalier who follows this philosopher, and whom you see accompanied by a dog. He can boast his descent from one of the most ancient and noble houses of Castile. He has been rich; but he ruined himself, like the Timon of Lucian, by feasting his friends every day; and, particularly, by giving splendid fêtes on the births and marriages of all the princes and princesses of Spain; in a word, on every occasion for rejoicing that he could make or find. No sooner did the discreet parasites who flocked round him see the ring slip over his purse than they abandoned his house and himself; one friend alone remains faithful to him now;--it is his dog."

"Tell me! Signor Asmodeus," cried Leandro Perez; "to whom belongs the carriage stopping before that house?" "It is the property of a rich contador, who comes here every morning to visit a frail beauty, whom this ancient sinner of Moorish race protects, and whom he loves to distraction. He learned last night that his female friend had been unfaithful, and in the fury which this intelligence induced, he wrote her a letter full of reproaches and threats. You would never guess what part the lady took on this occasion: instead of having the impudence to deny the fact, she sent to the treasurer this morning, owning that he was justly angered at her conduct; that he ought henceforth to despise her, since she had been capable of deceiving so gallant a lover; that she acknowledged and detested her fault; and that, to punish herself, she had already sacrificed those locks which he had so often admired; in short, that she had resolved to consecrate, in a nunnery, the remainder of her days to repentance.

"The old dotard was unable to withstand the well-feigned remorse of his mistress, and has risen thus early to console her. He found her in tears; and so well has she played her part that he has just assured her of a full pardon for the past: nay, more, to compensate for the sacrifice of her much-prized tresses, he is, at this moment, promising to enable her to cut a figure in the world, by purchasing for her a handsome country-house, which is just about to be sold, near the Escurial."

"All the shops are opened, I perceive," said the Student; "and I observe already a cavalier now entering a tavern." "That cavalier," replied Asmodeus, "is a youth of family, who is troubled with the prevailing mania for writing nonsense, that he may pass as an author. He is not absolutely without talent; he has even enough to enable him to detect its want in the dramas which are at present produced on your stage; but not so much as to qualify him to write a tolerable one himself. He has gone into that house to order a grand repast: he gives a dinner to-day to four comedians, whose good graces he would purchase in favour of a wretched comedy of his concoction, which he is on the point of presenting to their company. What will not money do?

"Apropos of authors," continued the Devil, "there now are two just meeting in the street. Do you notice the mocking style of their salutes? They despise each other thoroughly: and they are right. One of them writes as easily as the poet Crispinus, whom Horace compares to the bellows of a forge; and the other wastes a vast deal of time in composing works as cold and insipid as a water ice."

"Who is the little man descending from his carriage at the door of that church?" asked Zambullo. "He is a person worthy your remark," replied the Cripple. "It is not yet ten years since he abandoned the office of a notary, in which he was senior clerk, to shut himself up in the Carthusian monastery of Saragoza. At the end of a six-months noviciate, however, he left the convent, and re-appeared in Madrid; where those who had formerly known him were amazed to see him all at once become one of the principal members of the Council of the Indies. His sudden fortune is still the wonder of the town. Some say he has sold himself to the Devil; others, that he is the beloved of some rich dowager; and some, again, insist that he must have found a treasure." "Well! you know all about it, of course," interrupted Don Cleophas. "I should wonder if I did not," replied the Demon; "but I will unveil this mystery for you.

"During his aforesaid noviciate, it happened one day that our intended monk, in digging a deep hole in his appointed garden, lighted on a brazen coffer, which he opened, of course, and within which he found a golden casket containing some thirty diamonds of the purest water. Although the pious horticulturist knew little enough of precious stones, he shrewdly suspected that whoever had placed them there was wiser; so resolving on the course which, in one of the comedies of Plautus, is adopted by Gripus, who abandons fishing when he has found a treasure, he threw off his gown, returned to Madrid, and by the assistance of a friendly jeweller, transmuted his diamonds into pieces of gold, and his pieces of gold into an office which has procured for him an exalted station in society."

CHAPTER XVIII
RELATING TO OTHER MATTERS WHICH THE DEVIL EXHIBITED TO THE STUDENT.

"I must indulge you with a laugh," continued Asmodeus, "at the cost of an amusing character whom you see walking into that coffee-house, over the way. He is a Biscayan physician, and is going to sip his cup of chocolate; after which he will return to his home to pass the day at chess."

"While he is thus engaged, do not be alarmed for his patients; he has none: and if he had, the moments he employs in play would not be the worst for them. He moves from his chess-board in the evening to repair to the house of a rich and handsome widow, with whom he would be happy to mate, and for whom he affects a knightly passion. When he is with her, a rascally valet, his only domestic, and who is aware of his practice with the widow, brings him a false list, studded with the names of noble lords and ladies who have sent to seek the doctor. The lady dreams not he is playing false, and the Biscayan is therefore fast entrapping her into a false move, which will win him the game.

"But," continued the Devil, "let us stop a moment at that house close by; I would have you remark what is passing there before we look elsewhere. Run your eyes over the rooms: what do you observe?" "Why, I can discern some maidens, whose beauty dazzles me," replied the Student. "Some are just leaving their beds, and others have already risen. What charms do they present to my feasting eyes! I can fancy I behold the nymphs of Diana, but more lovely than the poets have depicted them."

"If those maidens, as you call them, and whom you admire so much," replied the Cripple, "have the graces of Diana's nymphs, they assuredly want their chastity to complete the picture. They are a parcel of good-natured females, who live upon a common fund. As dangerous as the fair damsels of chivalry who arrested, by their charms, the knights who passed before their castle walls, they seek to draw your less heroic youths within their bowers. And woe betide those whom they ensnare! To warn the passer-by of the peril which awaits him, beacons should be set before their doors, as such friendly monitors are placed on dangerous coasts to mark the places mariners should shun."

"I need not ask you," said Leandro Perez, "whither go those signors whom I see lolling in their carriages: they are doubtless going to the levée of the king." "You have said it," replied the Devil; "and if you also would attend it, I will carry you there before them: we shall have amusement enough, I promise you." "You could not have proposed a thing more suited to my taste," replied Zambullo; "and I anticipate all the pleasure you have promised me."

The Demon, although eager to satisfy Don Cleophas in his desires, carried him leisurely towards the palace, so that, in their way, the Student, perceiving some workmen employed upon a lofty doorway, asked if it were the portal of a church they were constructing. "No," replied Asmodeus, "it is the entrance to a new market; and it is magnificent as you see. However, though they raised its arch until its point were lost in clouds, it would be still unworthy of two Latin lines which are to adorn its front."

"What say you?" cried Leandro;—"what a notion would you give me of the verses that you speak of! I die with anxiety to hear them." "I will repeat them, then," replied the Devil; "and do you prepare to admire them.

'Quam bene Mercurius nunc merces vendit opimas,

Momus ubi fatuos vendidit ante sales!

"In these two lines is concealed one of the most delicate puns imaginable." "I cannot say I yet perceive its point," said the Student; "I do not clearly understand what is referred to by your fatuos sales." "You are not then aware," replied the Devil, "that on the spot where they are building this market for the sale of provisions, there formerly stood a monkish college in which youth was inducted to the humanities. The rectors of this college were in the habit of getting up plays, in which the students figured on the stage. These plays were, as you may suppose, flat enough as to effect and language; and were enlivened by ballets, so amusingly absurd, that everything danced, even to preterites and supines." "There! that is quite enough," interrupted Zambullo; "I am quite alive to the stuff of which college pieces are composed—excuse my pun—but the inscription is admirable."

Asmodeus and Don Cleophas had scarcely reached the grand staircase of the palace, when the courtiers commenced the inflating labour of mounting its polished steps. As they passed our unseen watchers, the Devil did the honour of announcing them to the Student: "There," said he, pointing with his finger as he spoke, "there is the Count de Villalonso, of the house of Puebla d'Ellerena; this is the Marquis de Castro Fueste; that is Don Lopez de Los Rios, president of the council of finance; and here is the Count de Villa Hombrosa." He did not, however, content himself thus with naming them; each had his legend: and the Demon's sardonic spirit found in the character of each some weakness to laugh at, or some vices to lay bare. None passed before him unnoted.

"That signor," said he of one, "is affable and obliging; and listens to you with an air of kindness. Do you ask his protection, he grants it freely; nay, proffers you his interest. It is pity that a man who loves so much to assist his fellow-creatures should have a memory so bad, that a quarter of an hour after you have spoken to him, he should forget all you have asked and he has promised.

"That duke," said he, speaking of another, "is one of the best characters that haunts the court. He is not, like most of his equals, one man at this moment and another the next; there is no caprice, no inequality in his disposition. I may add to this, that he pays not with ingratitude the affection that is shown for him, or the services that are rendered in his behalf. Unfortunately, again, he is too slothful to reward these kindnesses as they deserve: he leaves so long to be desired what is so rightfully expected, that when the favour is at last obtained, it is felt to have been dearly purchased."

After the Demon had thus exhibited to the Student the good and evil qualities of a great number of signors, he conducted him into a room in which there were all sorts and conditions of men, but especially so many chevaliers, that Don Cleophas could not help exclaiming: "What numberless knights! By our Lady! there must be enough and to spare of them in Spain." "I can answer for that," replied the Cripple; "and it is not at all surprising, since to be dubbed companion of St. Jago, or of Calatrava, your vigilants require no five-and-twenty thousand crowns in pocket or estate, as did formerly the knights of ancient Rome: you perceive therefore that knighthood is an article most admirably assorted.

"Observe," continued the Devil, "that common-looking fellow behind us." "Hush!" interrupted Zambullo; "speak softly, or the man will hear you." "No, no," replied Asmodeus; "the same charm which renders us invisible, prevents our being heard. Examine him well: he is a Catalonian, returned from the Philippines, where he ranged the seas as a pirate. Could you conceive, to look on him, that you beheld a thunderbolt of war? Nevertheless, he has performed, in his vocation, prodigies of valour. He is here this morning, to present a petition to the king, in which he asks, as a recompense for his services, a certain post, which is vacant. I doubt, however, if he will succeed, inasmuch as he has neglected duly to possess the prime minister with a proper notion of his merits."

"I perceive on the right of the pirate," said Leandro Perez, "a tall and bulky man, who is sufficiently impressed with an idea of his own importance: to judge of his station by the pride of his bearing, he is some wealthy grandee, certainly." "Nothing can be further from the truth," replied the Demon: "he is one of the poorest of Hidalgos, who lives on the profits of a gaming-table, under the protection of one of the ministers.

"But I see a licentiate, who must not pass without your notice: it is he whom you can perceive near the first window, in conversation with a cavalier clad in velvet of a silver grey. They are discoursing of a matter yesterday decided by the king; but I will tell you its history.

"Two months ago, this licentiate, who is an academician of Toledo, published a work on morals, which shocked the orthodox opinions of all your grey-headed authors of Castile: they found it full of vigorous expressions and words newly introduced. It required no more to unite them against so singular a production; and they therefore instantly assembled, and agreed upon a petition to his majesty, praying him to condemn the book as one written in a style dangerous to the purity and simplicity of the Spanish tongue.

"The petition appearing worthy of attention to his majesty, he named three commissioners to examine the work; and they estimating its style to be really reprehensible, and the more so from its peculiar brilliancy, upon their report the king has decreed that, under pain of his displeasure, those academicians of Toledo who write after the manner of the licentiate shall not dare to publish another book; and further that, in order to preserve the language of Castile in all its purity, such academicians, after their decease, shall be replaced by persons of the first quality alone."

"That is indeed a marvellous decision!" cried Zambullo, laughing: "the lovers of our vulgar tongue have henceforth nought to fear." "Excuse me," replied the Devil; "but your writers who endanger that noble chastity of style which forms the delight of all discerning readers, are not confined to the Toledan academy."

Don Cleophas was now curious to learn who was the cavalier in silver-grey habiliments, whom he beheld conversing with the hardy moralist. "He," said the Cripple, "is a Catalonian, an officer of the Spanish guard, and of course a younger son; but he is a youth whose tongue is pointed as the sword he wears. To give you an example of his wit, I will tell you of a repartee that he made yesterday to a lady whom he met in high society. But to enable you to enjoy its pungency, I must inform you that he has a brother, Don Andrea de Prada, who was some years since, an officer, like himself, in the same corps.

"It happened one day that a farmer of the king's revenues came to this Don Andrea, and said to him: 'Signor de Prada, I bear the same name as you, but our families are different. I am aware that you belong to one of the noblest houses in Catalonia, but at the same time that you are not rich. Now, I am of a poor family, and have lots of wealth. Can we not find a means, therefore, to communicate to each other that which we mutually want? Have you your titles of nobility?' 'Certainly!' replied Don Andrea. 'That being the case,' continued the other, 'if you will confide the documents to my hands, I will place them in those of an ingenious genealogist, who will set to work upon them, and will make us relations in spite of our ancestors. On my part, as in duty bound, I will make my kinsman a present of thirty thousand pistoles: is it a bargain?' Don Andrea, dazzled by the proposition, accepted it at once, gave the parchments to the farmer, and with the money he received purchased an estate in his native province, where he now resides at his ease.

"His younger brother, who gained nothing by the transaction, was dining yesterday at a house where the conversation turned by chance on the Signor de Prada, farmer of the king's revenues. On this, the lady of whom I spoke, turning to the young officer, asked if the wealthy signor were not related to him. 'No,' replied he, 'I have not that honour; but I believe he is a relation of my brother's.'"

The Student laughed, as well he might, at this family distinction, which appeared to him rather novel. But perceiving at the moment a little man following a courtier, he cried out: "Bah! but yon homunculus will lose nothing for the want of reverence to the signor whom he shadows. He has some precious favour to intreat, beyond all doubt." "I shall not occupy your time in vain," replied the Devil, "in telling you the object of the obsequiousness you observe. The little man is an honest citizen, who is proprietor of a country house in the suburbs of Madrid, near which are some mineral springs of fashionable celebrity. He has lent this house, rent free, for three months to this signor, that the latter may drink the waters: he is at this moment very humbly beseeching his noble tenant to serve him on a pressing opportunity which offers; and the signor is very politely declining to do so.

"I must not let yon cavalier of plebeian race escape me. See, where he wades through the expecting throng with all the air of one of note. He has become immensely rich by force of calculation, and in his proud mansion has as many servants as your first grandee; his table would put to shame for delicacy and abundance that of a minister of state. He has a carriage for himself, one for his wife, and another for his children; and in his stables may be seen the best of mules and the most splendid horses in the world. Only yesterday, he bought, and paid for on the nail, a superb train of noble animals, that the prince of Spain had partially agreed for, but had thought too dear." "What insolence!" exclaimed Leandro. "A Turk, now, who beheld that lump of arrogance, poised on so dangerous a height, would watch each instant for its sudden fall." "I know nothing of the time to come," replied Asmodeus, "but think your Turk would not be far from right.

"Ah! what is that I see?" continued the Demon with surprise. "Did I wonder at any thing, I should disbelieve my eyes. I absolutely discern within this room a poet--the last whom I should expect to see. How dares he come within these walls?--he who could write in terms offensive to their noblest visitants. He must count indeed on the contempt that he is held in!

"But mark particularly that venerable man who enters now, supported by a page. Observe with what respect the crowd divides to make way for him. That is the signor Don José de Reynaste e Ayala, chief magistrate of the police: he comes hither to inform the king of the events of last night in the capital. Methinks, signor Student, that we could assist him in his report! However, regard him with admiration, for he deserves it." "In truth," replied Zambullo, "he looks like a man of worth." "It would be well for Spain," replied the Cripple, "if all its corregidors would take him for their model. He has none of that intemperate zeal which urges those who should administer the law to violate its spirit from impetuosity or caprice; and he respects too much the sacred freedom of the person to deprive the meanest of his fellow-subjects of that blessed right on the mere information of an alguazil, a clerk, or even a secretary of police. He knows those gentlemen too well; and that, for the most of them, their venal souls will scruple not to traffic on the fund of his authority. When a man stands before him, accused of crime, he may be sure that justice will be done towards him; the evidence is sifted until truth is discovered; and thus the prisons, instead of echoing the sighs of innocence, perform their proper office of holding the guilty. Even these are not abandoned to the licence which ordinarily reigns in gaols. He visits, as a man, those whom, as a magistrate, he has condemned, and is careful that inhumanity, in its dispensers, shall not add rigour to the law."

"What an eulogium!" exclaimed Leandro; "you paint a man whom angels might agree to worship! You rouse my curiosity to witness his reception by the king." "I am annoyed," replied the Devil, "to be obliged to tell you of my inability to gratify a wish that I expected, without at least exposing myself to insult. It is not in my vocation, nor am I permitted, to intrude myself on kings; their cabinet is the domain of Leviathan, Belphegor, and Ashtaroth; I informed you, from my bottle, that these three demons preside over the councils of princes. All others of our craft are denied the entrée at court; and I know not what I could have been thinking of, when I offered to bring you here: it was a dangerous flight

Asmodeus; or, The Devil on Two Sticks

to take, I can assure you. If my three loving brethren should perceive me, they would show me no favour, I promise you, and between ourselves, I would rather avoid the conflict."

"That being so," replied the Student, "let us be off as quickly as you please: I should die with grief to see you curried by those wretched grooms, without being able to help you; for if I lent you a hand, I expect you would shine none the brighter for my assistance." "Most decidedly not," replied Asmodeus; "they would never feel the blows that you could deal them, and you would have the satisfaction of dying under theirs."

"But," he continued, "to console you for your exclusion from the cabinet of your potent sovereign, I will procure you a pleasure quite equal to the one you lose." And as he finished these words, he took the Student's hand, and away they went, as fast as the Devil could fly, toward the monastery of Mercy.

CHAPTER XIX

THE CAPTIVES.

In a moment they were on a house adjoining the monastery, at the gate of which there was a vast concourse of persons, of all ages and of both sexes. "Here's a crowd!" exclaimed Leandro Perez. "What ceremony can call so many good folks together?" "Why," replied Asmodeus, "it is one which you have never witnessed, though it may be seen from time to time within Madrid. Three hundred slaves, all subjects of the crown of Spain, are expected to arrive each minute: they return from Algiers, where they have been recently purchased by some fathers of the Redemption. Every street through which they are to pass will be lined with spectators to welcome them."

"It is true, indeed," replied Zambullo, "that I have never had the curiosity to behold a similar exhibition; and, if this be the treat which your worship has reserved to gratify my taste, I must tell you frankly that you need not have so boasted of its piquancy." "Oh! I know you well enough," replied the Devil, "not to be aware that it is no joyous spectacle for you to look upon the misery of your fellows; but when I tell you that, in bringing you here to view it under its present form, I am about to reveal certain singular circumstances attending the captivity of some, and the equally curious embarrassment in which others will find themselves on returning to their homes, I am persuaded that you will not be unthankful for the amusement I have provided." "Certainly not," replied the Student; "you put another face upon the matter; and you will afford me much pleasure by your promised revelations."

During this discussion, loud shouts were suddenly heard from the populace as they beheld the approaching captives, who marched two by two, in their slaves' dresses, each bearing his chain upon his shoulders. They were preceded by a considerable number of monks of the order of Mercy, who had been to meet them, and who rode on mules caparisoned in black serge, as if they headed a funeral: one of these good fathers carried the standard of Redemption. The younger captives came first; the more aged followed; and the procession was closed by an aged monk of the same order as the first, who, mounted on a diminutive steed, had all the air of a prophet: this was the chief of the missionary expedition. To him every eye was attracted, as much by his excessive gravity, as by a long white beard which flowed down his bosom, and gave to the features of this Moses of the Spaniards a venerable aspect, lighted as they were by a heartfelt joy at having been the instrument of restoring so many of his Christian brethren to their country.

"The captives whom you see," commenced the Cripple, "are not all equally rejoiced at their restoration to liberty. If there be some whose hearts beat with pleasure at the thought that they are about to see once more their dearest friends, there are others not a little fearful that, during the time they have been estranged from their families, events may have occurred which will bring tortures to their minds more cruel than the most refined of slavery itself.

"For instance, the two who first approach are in the latter category. The one, a native of the little town of Velilla in Aragon, after having passed ten years in bondage with the Turk, without once hearing of his much-loved wife, comes home to find her bound again in wedlock, and the mother of five little ones who can claim no kin with him. The other, son of a wool-merchant of Segovia, was carried off by a corsair nearly twenty years ago: he returns with a lively apprehension that matters have gravely changed during that time with his family, and he will find himself a prophet in his loss. His father and mother are dead; and his brothers, who shared their wealth, have dissipated it foolishly enough."

"My attention is rivetted," exclaimed the Student, "upon a slave whom, by his looks, I judge to be delighted that he is no longer exposed to the seducing influence of the bastinado." "The captive whom you speak of," replied the Devil, "has good reason to rejoice at his deliverance: he has learnt, since his return, that an aunt to whom he is sole heir has just been released from her troubles, and that he is consequently about to enjoy the free use of her brilliant fortune. This it is which now occupies his thoughts so agreeably, and gives to his appearance that air of satisfaction which you remark.

"How all unlike is he to the unhappy cavalier who walks beside him; the tortures of suspense fill his bosom incessantly: I will tell you on what they impend. When he was taken by a pirate of Algiers, as he was passing into Italy from Spain, he loved a maiden and by her was loved: he dreads lest, while he was in chains, his fair one's constancy may have failed her." "Has he been long a slave then?" asked Zambullo. "Eighteen months," replied Asmodeus. "Pooh!" exclaimed Leandro Perez, "I fancy our gallant is a prey to causeless fear; he has hardly put his mistress's fidelity to such a test as to have need for great alarm." "There you are mistaken," replied the Cripple; "his princess no sooner heard that he was captive to the Moor, than she hastened to provide herself with a more fortunate lover.

"Would you credit now," continued the Demon, "that the man who follows immediately behind the two we have been speaking of, and whom that thick and sandy beard so horribly disfigures, was once a very handsome man? Nothing, however, can be more certain; and you see, in that bent and hideous figure, the hero of a story remarkable enough to induce me to relate it to you.

"His name is Fabricio, and he was hardly fifteen years of age when his father, a wealthy cultivator of Cinquello, a large village of the kingdom of Leon, died. He lost his mother shortly afterwards; so that, being an only son, he became thus early the master of a considerable property, the management of which was confided to an uncle, who happened to be honest. Fabricio completed his studies at Salamanca, where he had been previously placed; he then particularly devoted himself to the noble accomplishments of riding and fencing; in a word, he neglected nothing which might concur to render him worthy the sweet regards of Donna Hippolita, sister of a vegetating signor, whose cottage was about a couple of gun-shots from Cinquello.

"This lady was beautiful in the extreme, and about the age of Fabricio, who, having seen her from his infancy, had, to speak vulgarly, sucked in with his mother's milk the love which occupied his soul in manhood. Hippolita, on her side, could not help perceiving that Fabricio was not ill-made; but, knowing him to be the son of a husbandman, she had never deigned to look on him with attention. Her pride was only equalled by her loveliness, and by the haughty bearing of her brother, Don Thomaso de Xaral, who was probably unsurpassed, even in Spain, for his lordly want of money, and his beggarly pride.

"This inflated country gentleman lived in a small house which he dignified by the name of castle, but which to speak properly was a ruin, so little had the winds respected his nobility. However, although his means did not enable him to repair his mansion, and although he had hardly enough to sustain himself, he must needs keep a valet to attend upon his person; nay, he even kept a Moorish female to wait upon his sister.

"It was a refreshing sight to witness, in the village, on Sundays and at every festival, Don Thomaso habited in crimson velvet, but sadly faded, and a little hat, overshadowed with an ancient plume of yellow feathers, which were carefully enshrined, like relics, on the common days of the year. Disporting this frippery, which to him was proof apparent of his noble birth, he would affect the grandee, and seemed to think that he amply repaid the reverence that was offered to him when he condescended to notice it by an approving smile. His fair sister was not less vain than himself of the antiquity of her race; and she joined to this folly that of such self-congratulation on her charms, that she lived in the most perfect confidence that ere long some noble signor would come to beg the honour of her hand.

"Such were the characters of Don Thomaso and the beauteous Hippolita. Fabricio, aware of their foibles, and in order to insinuate himself into the estimation of persons so exalted, lost no opportunity of flattering their pride by the most respectful seeming; and so well did he manage, that the brother and sister at last were graciously pleased to allow him frequent occasions for paying his homage to them. As he was as well informed of their poverty as of their vanity, he was tempted every day to make offer of his purse; and was only withheld from doing so by the uncertainty as to which of their failings was the greater: nevertheless, his ingenious generosity found a way of relieving the one without causing the other to blush. 'Signor,' said he one day to Don Thomaso in private, 'I have a thousand ducats which I would entrust in safe hands: have the kindness to take care of them for me;--permit me to owe this obligation to you.'

"I need hardly tell you that Xaral consented; but besides being short of money, he had the very soul for a trustee. He therefore made no scruple of taking charge of the sum proposed; and no sooner was it in his possession, than, without ceremony, he employed a good part of it in putting his house in order, and adding thereto sundry little conveniences. A new dress of splendid light blue velvet was bought, and made at Salamanca; and a green plume, also purchased there, came to snatch from the olden plume of yellow the glory which had pertained to it from time immemorial, of adorning the noble front of Don Thomaso. The lovely Hippolita had also her compliment, and was entirely new-rigged. And thus did Xaral quickly melt the ducats which had been confided to him, not once reflecting that they did not belong to him, or that he would never be able to restore them. Indeed, he would not have scrupled thus to use them, had such extraordinary thoughts occurred to him; he would have felt that it was perfectly proper a plebeian should pay for the patronage of so noble a person as himself.

"Fabricio had foreseen all this; but had at the same time flattered himself, that out of love for his money, if not for himself, Don Thomaso would live with him on terms of greater intimacy; that Hippolita by degrees would become accustomed to his attentions, and finally pardon the audacity which had inspired him to elevate his thoughts to her. In effect, his intercourse with them certainly increased, and they displayed for him a consideration that he had never before appeared to deserve: a rich man is ever appreciated by the great, when he will consent to act for them the part of the wolf to Romulus and Remus. Xaral and his sister, who until now had nothing known of riches but the name, had no sooner tasted the intoxicating draught, than they deemed Fabricio, the source whence it flowed, an object not to be neglected; and they therefore exhibited towards him such marks of respect, and almost affection, as made him think his money well bestowed. He was soon convinced that he had really won upon them; and that wisely reflecting it is the lot of the proudest signors to be obliged, in order to sustain their pretensions, to graft their noble scions on the stocks of the fortunate vulgar, they now looked on him without disdain. With this notion, which flattered his own self-love, Fabricio resolved to propose for Hippolita to her brother.

"On the first favourable opportunity which offered to speak with Don Thomaso on the subject, he informed him that he had dared aspire to the honour of becoming his brother-in-law; and that, as the price of such concession, not only would he abandon all claim to the money deposited in his hands, but that he would add to it a present of a thousand pistoles. The haughty Xaral coloured at this proposition, which awakened his slumbering pride; and in the excitation of the moment, could scarcely refrain from displaying the utter contempt in which he held the son of an industrious father. But, however insulted he felt at the temerity of Fabricio, he constrained himself; and, as respectfully as his nature would permit, replied that in a matter of such importance he could not at once determine; that he must consult Hippolita, and that it would even be necessary to summon a conclave of his noble relatives thereupon.

"With this answer he dismissed the gallant, and forthwith convoked a diet composed of certain hidalgos of his neighbourhood, with whom he claimed affinity, and who, like himself, were all infected with demophobia. With these he consulted, not as to whether they were of opinion that he should bestow his sister upon Fabricio, but on the most proper steps to be adopted in order sufficiently to punish the insolent young man, who, forgetful of the meanness of his origin, had dared pretend to the hand of a lady of the rank of Hippolita.

"As soon as he had exposed to the assembly this presumptuous demand,--as he mentioned the name of Fabricio, and uttered the words, 'Son of a husbandman,'--you should have seen how the eyes of all the nobles lighted up with fury. Each of them vomited fire and flame against the audacious groundling; and with one voice they all insisted, that his death beneath the cudgels of their domestics alone could expiate the vile affront he had offered to their family by the proposal of so scandalous an union. However, on mature consideration, the offended members of the diet agreed to spare the culprit's life; but, in order to teach him that first and far most useful knowledge--of himself, they resolved to play him such a trick as he should have reason to remember while he lived.

"Various were the schemes proposed: the one on which they at last decided was as follows. Hippolita was to feign a sensibility for the passion of Fabricio; and, under pretence of consoling her unhappy lover for the refusal which Don Thomaso would have given to his proposal for her hand, she was to make an assignation for some particular evening to receive him at the castle; where, at the moment of his introduction by the Moorish female, the friends of the signor would surprise him with the waiting-maid, and compel him to espouse her.

"The sister of Xaral at first inclined to favour this piece of rascality; she even joined in thinking that her reputation demanded of her to consider as an insult the addresses of a person in a station so inferior to her own. But these haughty feelings soon yielded to others more gentle, prompted by pity; or rather, love suddenly vanquished all pride of heart in the bosom of Hippolita.

"From that moment, she looked on all things with a different eye. The obscure origin of Fabricio now appeared to her more than compensated by a nobility of disposition; and she perceived in him but a cavalier worthy of her tenderest affection. Remark again, Signor Student, and with all due admiration, how prodigious are the changes which this passion can effect: the very girl who yesterday imagined that a monarch's heir scarce merited the honour of possessing her, to-day is all enamoured of a ploughman's son, and is flattered by pretensions which before she had regarded as disgraceful.

"Far therefore from assisting her brother in his purposed revenge, and yielding to the new-born passion which now reigned supreme within her soul, Hippolita entered into secret correspondence with Fabricio, by means of her Moorish attendant, who frequently of an evening introduced the gallant into the cottage. Thus baffled in his design, Don Thomaso soon became suspicious of the truth; and watching his sister, he was convinced by his own eyes that, instead of fulfilling the wishes of her relations, she had betrayed them.

"He instantly informed two of his cousins of the discovery he had made: 'Vengeance! Don Thomaso, vengeance!' they exclaimed, infuriate at such baseness in one of their illustrious race. Xaral, who did not require urging to exact satisfaction for an indignity of this nature, replied, with true Spanish modesty, 'that they should find he knew well how to use his sword when its employment was called for to avenge his honour;' and he entreated them to come to his house on a particular night.

"They came at the appointed time, and were secretly received and concealed in a small room by Don Thomaso; who left them, saying that he would return the instant the lover entered his doors, should he think fit to come at all that evening. This did not fail to happen; the unlucky stars of our lovers had decreed that they should choose that very night for their meeting.

"Don Fabricio was already with his dear Hippolita, listening to and repeating for the hundredth time those sweet avowals which make up the dialogue of lovers, but which, though spoken from eternity, have still the charm of novelty, when they were disagreeably interrupted by the cavaliers who waited to surprise them. Don Thomaso and his cousins, with all the courage of three against one, rushed upon Fabricio, who had scarcely time to draw in his defence; but perceiving at once that their object was to assassinate him, he fought with a courage which makes one equal to three; he wounded all his assailants, and exerting the skill he had acquired at Salamanca, managed to keep them at his sword's point till he had gained the door, when he made off at full speed.

"Upon this, Xaral, maddened with rage at beholding his enemy escape him, after having with impunity dishonoured his house, turned all his fury against the unfortunate Hippolita, and plunged his sword into her heart. After which his two relatives returned to their homes, extremely mortified at the bad success of their plot, and with no other consolation than their wounds. There we will leave them," continued Asmodeus. "When we have passed in review the other captives, I will finish the history of this one. I will relate to you how, after justice, or rather the law, had possessed itself of his effects on account of this mournful event, the pirates seized his person, with about as good reason, when he happened to be making a voyage."

"While you were telling me this story of love and pride," said Don Cleophas, "I observed a young man whose countenance bespeaks such sorrow at his heart, that I wonder I did not interrupt you to inquire its cause." "You will lose nothing by your discretion," replied the Demon; "I can tell you now all you desire to know. The captive whose dejection attracted your notice, is a youth of family from Valladolid. Two years was he in slavery, but with a patron who possessed a very pretty wife. The lady looked with favour on the slave, and the slave, as in duty bound, repaid the lady's favours with interest. The patron, becoming suspicious as to the nature of his slave's labours, hastened to sell the Christian to the brothers of the Redemption, lest he should be irreligiously employed in the propagation of Mahometanism. The tender Castilian, ever since, has done nothing but weep for the loss of his patroness; liberty itself cannot console him."

"An old man of good appearance attracts my attention there," said Leandro Perez; "who, and what, is he?" The Devil replied: "He is a barber, of Guipuscoa, who is about to return to Biscay after a captivity of forty years. When he fell into the hands of a corsair, in going from Valencia to the island of Sardinia, he had a wife, two sons, and a daughter. Of all these, one son alone remains; and he, more lucky than his father, has been to Peru, whence he has safely returned with immense wealth to his native province, in which he has recently purchased two handsome estates." "What pleasure!" exclaimed the Student, "what delight awaits this happy son, to behold again his long-lost parent, and to be enabled to render his declining years peaceful and agreeable!"

"You," replied the Cripple, "speak like a child whom tenderness and duty prompt; the son of the Biscayan barber is of a sterner mould: the unlooked-for coming of his sire to him will bring more grief than joy. Instead of welcoming him to his mansion at Guipuscoa, and sparing nothing to mark the bliss he feels at pressing him once more to his bosom, he will probably be filial enough to make him steward of one of his estates.

"Behind this captive, whose good looks you admire so much, is another as like an old baboon as are two drops of water to each other: he is a little Aragonese physician. He has not been a fortnight in Algiers; for as soon as the Turks knew what was his profession, they resolved, rather than suffer him to remain among them, to place him without ransom in the hands of the fathers of Mercy, who would certainly never have purchased him, and who bring him back with compunction to Spain.

"You who feel so sensibly the woes of others, ah! how would you grieve for that other slave, he who wears upon his head that little cap of brown cloth, did you but know the ills he has endured during twelve years, in the house of an English renegade, his patron." "And who is this unhappy captive?" asked Zambullo. "He is a cordelier of Navarre," replied the Demon. "I must own, however, that for myself, I rejoice that he has suffered so severely; since, by his eternal preaching, he has prevented more than a hundred Christian slaves from adopting the turban."

"Well! to imitate your frankness," replied Don Cleophas, "I must say that I am really afflicted to think that this good father should have been so long at the mercy of the barbarian." "As to that," replied Asmodeus, "you are as unwise to regret it, as I to rejoice. The good monk has turned his dozen years' captivity to so good account, that he will find his advantage in having passed that time in suffering instead of in his cell, where he would have striven with temptations that he would not at all times have vanquished."

"The first captive after the monks," said Leandro Perez, "has a most complacent air for a man who returns from slavery: he excites my curiosity to know his history." "You anticipate me," replied the Cripple; "I was just about to tell you all about him. You see in him, a citizen of Salamanca, an unfortunate father, a mortal rendered insensible to misfortune by the weight of those he has experienced. I am tempted to relate to you the painful details of his life, and to leave the rest of the captives to their fates; besides, there is scarcely another whose adventures are worth the trouble of telling."

Alain René Le Sage

The Student, who began to tire of this sombre procession, stated that he asked for nothing better; whereupon, the Devil began the history contained in the following chapter.

CHAPTER XX

OF THE LAST HISTORY RELATED BY ASMODEUS: HOW, WHILE CONCLUDING IT, HE WAS SUDDENLY INTERRUPTED; AND OF THE DISAGREEABLE MANNER, FOR THE WITTY DEMON, IN WHICH HE AND DON CLEOPHAS WERE SEPARATED.

"Pablos de Bahabon, son of an alcade of a village in Old Castile, after having divided with his sister and brother the small inheritance which their father, although one of the most avaricious of men, had left them, set out for Salamanca with the intention of increasing the number of students in its university. He was well made, not without wit, and was just entering upon his twenty-third year.

"With a thousand ducats in his possession, and a disposition fitted to get rid of them, it was not long before he was the talk of the town. The young men, without exception, were eager to cultivate his friendship; the strife, was who were to be included in the joyous parties which Don Pablos gave every day. I say Don Pablos, because he had assumed the Don, that he might live on equal terms with the students whose nobility would otherwise have demanded a formality in his intercourse with them, anything but pleasant. So well did he love gaiety and the good things of this world, and so badly did he manage the only thing which can always command them,--his purse, that at the end of fifteen months he found it one morning empty. He contrived, however, to get on for some time longer, partly by credit and partly by borrowing; but he soon found that these are resources which speedily fail when a man has no other.

"This having come to pass, his friends perceiving that their visits were anything but agreeable,--to themselves, they ceased to call; and his creditors commenced paying him their respects, with an assiduity which was anything but delightful to poor Don Pablos. For although he assured the latter that he was in daily expectation of receiving bills of exchange from his relations, there were some who were uncivil enough to decline waiting their arrival; and they were so sharp in their legal proceedings that our hero was on the point of finishing his studies in jail, when one day he met an acquaintance while walking on the banks of the Tormes, who said to him: 'Signor Don Pablos, beware! I warn you that an alguazil and his archers are on the look-out for you, and they intend to pay you the honour of a guard on your return to the city.'

"Bahabon, alarmed at this intended public attention to his person, which suited so ill to the state of his private affairs, resolved to shun this demonstration of respect, and instantly took to flight and the road to Corita. In his anxiety for privacy, he had not walked far before he turned off to plunge into a neighbouring wood, in which he resolved to conceal himself until night should lend her friendly shades to enable him to travel more secure from observation. It was at that season of the year when the trees are decked in their proudest apparel, and he therefore chose the best dressed in the forest, that it might spare a covering for him: into this he mounted, and arranged himself upon a branch whose wavy ornaments shrouded him from sight.

"Feeling secure in his elevated seat, he by degrees soon lost all fear of the too attentive alguazil; and as men usually make the best reflections on their conduct when thought is too late to avail them, he recalled all the follies he had committed, and promised to himself, that if ever he again should be in fortune's way, he would make a better use of her favours. Most especially he vowed to be no more the dupe of seeming friends, who lead young men into dissipation, and whose attachment finishes with the last bottle.

"While thus occupied with the busy thoughts which come like creditors into the distressed mind, night recalled him to his situation. Disengaging himself from the sheltering leaves, and shaking hands with the friendly branch, he was preparing to descend, when, by as much light as the moon could throw into the forest, he thought he could discern the figure of a man. As he looked, his former fears returned: and he imagined it must be the alguazil, who, having tracked his footsteps, was seeking him in the wood. His fears redoubled when he saw the man, after walking round it two or three times, sit himself down at the foot of the very tree in which he was."

Asmodeus interrupted the course of his narrative in this place: "Signor Don Cleophas," said he, "permit me to enjoy for a while the perplexity I occasion in your mind at this moment. You are desperately anxious to know now, who can this mortal be that comes so inopportunely, and what can have brought him thither. Well, that is what you shall learn: I will not abuse your patience.

"After the man had seated himself at the foot of the tree, whose thick foliage almost hid him from the sight of Don Pablos, he reposed for a few seconds, and then rose and began digging the ground with a poniard. Having made a deep hole, and placed therein a leathern bag, he refilled it, covered it over carefully with the moss-grown turf he had removed, and then retired. Bahabon, who had strained his eyes to watch these operations, and whose fears were changed to anxious joy during their progress, scarcely waited until the man was out of sight ere he descended from his hiding-place to disinter the sack, in which he doubted not to find a good store of silver or of gold. His knife was sufficient for the purpose; but, had he wanted that, he felt such ardour for the work, that he would have penetrated with his nails into the bowels of the earth.

"The instant that he had the bag in his possession, just handling it sufficiently to feel convinced that it contained good sounding coin, he hastened to quit the wood with his prey, less fearing to meet the alguazil in his altered state, than the man to whom the bag of right belonged. Intoxicated with delight at having made so good a stroke, our student walked lightly all the night, without caring whither he went, or feeling in the least degree incommoded with his burden. But, as day broke, he stopped under some trees near the village of Molorido, less, in truth, to repose, than to satisfy at last the curiosity which burned within him to know what it was indeed the sack enclosed. Untying it with that agreeable trembling which you experience at the moment you are about to enjoy an anticipated but unknown pleasure, he found therein honest double-pistoles, and, to his unspeakable delight, counted no less of these than two hundred and fifty.

"After having contemplated them for some time with a voluptuous eagerness, he began seriously to reflect on what he ought to do; and having made up his mind, he stowed away the doubloons in his pockets, threw the bag into a ditch, and repaired to Molorido. He entered the first decent inn; and then, while they were preparing his breakfast, he hired a mule, upon which he returned the same day to Salamanca.

"He clearly perceived, by the surprise which his acquaintances displayed at seeing him again, that they were in the secret of his sudden evasion; but he had his story by heart. He stated that, being short of money, and not receiving it from home, although he had written twenty times to relate his pressing need, he had determined to go for it himself, and that, the evening previous, as he entered Molorido, he had met his steward with the needful, so that he was now in a situation to undeceive all those who had decreed him a man of straw. He added, that he intended to convince his creditors that they were wrong in distressing an honest man who would have long since satisfied their claims, had his steward been more punctual in the remittance of his rents.

"In reality, on the following day he called a meeting of his creditors, and paid them all to the last maravedi. No sooner did the very friends who had abandoned him in poverty hear of these extraordinary proceedings, than they quickly flocked around him, to flatter him by their homage, hoping to enjoy themselves again at his expense; but he was not to be caught a second time. Faithful to the vow he had made in the forest, he treated them with disdain, and changing entirely his course of life, he devoted himself to the study of the law with zeal and assiduity.

"However, you will say, he was all this while conscientiously expending double-pistoles not very honestly acquired. To this I have no reply to make than that he did what nine-tenths of the world are daily doing in similar circumstances. He of course intended to make proper restitution at some future time; that is, if he should chance to discover to whom the doubloons belonged. In the meantime, tranquillizing himself with the goodness of his intentions, he disposed of the money without scruple, patiently awaiting this discovery, which nevertheless he made before twelve months were over.

"About this time, it was reported in Salamanca that a citizen of that town, one Ambrosio Piquillo, having gone to the neighbouring wood to seek for a bag, filled with gold and silver coin, which he had there deposited nearly a year before, had turned up only the earth in which he had buried it, and that this misfortune had reduced the poor man to beggary.

"I must say, in justice to Bahabon, that the secret reproaches of his conscience were not made in vain. He ascertained the dwelling of Ambrosio, whom he found in a wretched chamber whose entire furniture consisted of a truckle-bed and a single chair. 'My friend,' said he with admirable hypocrisy as he entered, 'I have heard the public report of the cruel accident which has befallen you, and, charity obliging us to aid one another according to our means, I have come to bring you a trifling assistance; but I should like to hear from yourself the story of your misfortune.'

"'Signor cavalier,' replied Piquillo, 'I will relate it to you in a few words. I had the misfortune to have a son who robbed me. Discovering his dishonesty, and fearing that he would help himself to a leathern sack in which there were two hundred and fifty doubloons, I thought I could not do better than bury them in the wood to which I had the imprudence to take them. Since that unlucky day, my son has stripped me of all else that I possessed, and he at last disappeared with a woman whom he had carried off by force. Finding myself thus reduced by the libertinage of my worthless child, or rather by my misplaced indulgence for his faults, I determined on recourse to the leathern bag; but alas! my only remaining means of subsistence had been cruelly carried away.'

"As the poor man recounted his loss, his grief was renewed, and his tears fell fast as he spoke, Don

Pablos, affected at beholding them, said to him: 'My dear Ambrosio, we must console ourselves for all the crosses we encounter during life. Your tears are useless; they cannot bring back your double-pistoles, which, if some scoundrel has laid hands on them, are indeed lost to you. But who knows? They may have fallen into the possession of some worthy man, who, when he learns that they belong to you, will hasten to restore them. You may yet see them again: live at least in that hope; and, in the meanwhile,' added he, giving him ten of his own doubloons, 'take these, and come to me in a week from this time.' He then gave his name and address, and went out overwhelmed with confusion at the benedictions heaped upon him by Ambrosio, who could not find words to express his gratitude. Such, for the most part, are your generous actions: you would find little cause for admiration, could you but penetrate their motives.

"At the week's end, Piquillo, mindful of what Don Pablos had said to him, went to his house. Bahabon received him kindly, and said to him: 'My friend, from the excellent character I everywhere hear of you, I have resolved to contribute all in my power to set you on your feet again: my interest and my purse shall not be wanting to effect this. As a beginning in the business,' he continued, 'what think you I have already done? I am intimate with several persons as much distinguished by their charity as their station: these I have sought; and I have so effectually inspired them with compassion for your situation, that I have collected from them two hundred crowns, which I am about to give you.' As he finished, he went into his cabinet, whence he returned in a moment with a linen bag, in which he had placed this sum in silver, and not in doubloons, for fear that the citizen, on receiving so many double-pistoles, should begin to suspect the truth; whereas, by this piece of management, he effectually secured his object, which was to make restitution in such a manner as might conciliate his reputation with his conscience.

"Ambrosio, far from thinking that these crowns were a portion of his money restored, took them, in good faith, as the product of a collection made on his behalf; and, after repeatedly thanking Don Pablos for his kindness, he returned to his habitation, grateful to Heaven for having created a cavalier who took so much interest in his misfortunes.

"On the following day he met one of his friends, who was in no better plight than himself, and who said to him: 'I leave Salamanca to-morrow, to set out for Cadiz, where I intend to embark in a vessel bound for New Spain. I have no great reason to be contented with my position here, and my heart tells me I shall be more fortunate in Mexico. If you will take my advice, you will go with me; that is, if you have but a hundred crowns.' 'I should not have much trouble to find two hundred,' replied Piquillo; 'and I would undertake this voyage willingly, were I sure to gain a living in the Indies.' Thereupon, his friend boasted of the fertility of New Spain, and represented to him so many ways of there enriching himself, that Ambrosio, yielding to his powers of persuasion, now thought of nothing but the necessary preparations for setting out with his friend to Cadiz. But before he left Salamanca, he took care to address a letter to Bahabon, informing him that, finding a promising opportunity of going to the Indies, he was anxious to profit by it, in order to see whether Fortune could be induced to smile more kindly on him in another country than in his own; that he took the liberty of stating this to him, assuring him that he should gratefully preserve during life the remembrance of his goodness.

"The departure of Ambrosio somewhat annoyed Don Pablos, as it disconcerted the plan he had formed for discharging the debt he owed him. But, when he reflected that the poor citizen might in a few years return to Salamanca, he became gradually reconciled to what had happened, and applied himself more diligently than ever to master the complications of civil and ecclesiastical legalities. So great was the progress he made, as much by the powers of his mind and its aptitude for his profession, as by the application I have spoken of, that he became a shining light in the university, of which he was ultimately chosen rector. In this position he was not contented to sustain its dignity by the extent and solidity of his scientific acquirements; he searched so deeply into his own heart, that he acquired all those habits of virtue which constitute a man of worth.

"During his rectorship, he learned that in one of the prisons of Salamanca there was a young man accused of rape. On hearing this, he remembered that Piquillo's son had carried off a woman by force. He therefore made inquiries as to this prisoner, and, finding that it was indeed the son of Ambrosio, he generously undertook his defence. What deserves most to be admired in the science of the law, Signor Student, is, that it furnishes arms for offence and defence equally; and as our rector was an adroit fencer with these deadly weapons, he used them to good effect on this occasion in favour of the accused. It is true, that he joined to his legal skill the interest of his friends, and the most pressing solicitation, which, probably, as in most cases, did more than all the rest.

"The guilty youth, therefore, came out of this affair whiter than snow. On going to thank his liberator, the latter said to him: 'It is out of respect for your father that I have rendered you this service. I love him; and to give you a further proof of my affection for him, if you will live in this town, and here lead the life of an honest man, I will take care of your welfare; if, on the contrary, you desire, like Ambrosio, to seek your fortune in the Indies, you may reckon on fifty pistoles for your outfit: I present them to you.' The young Piquillo replied: 'Since I am honoured by the protection of your lordship, I should be wrong to quit a place where I enjoy so great an advantage. I will not leave Salamanca, and I promise you solemnly that I will conduct myself to your satisfaction.' On this assurance, the rector placed in his hands twenty pistoles, saying: 'Take this, my friend; embrace some honest profession; employ your time well, and rely on it that I will not abandon you.'

"Two months afterwards, it happened that the young Piquillo, who from time to time paid his respects to Don Pablos, one day appeared before him in tears. 'What ails you?' asked Bahabon. 'Signor,' replied the son of Ambrosio, 'I have just heard news which cuts me to the soul. My father has been taken by a corsair of Algiers, and is at this moment in chains: an old Salamancan, lately returned from Barbary, where he was ten years in captivity, and whom the fathers of Mercy have redeemed, told me not an hour since that he had left Ambrosio in slavery. Alas!' he added, striking his breast and tearing his hair, 'wretch that I am! it was my infamous behaviour which reduced my father to the necessity of burying his money, and afterwards to leave his country! It is I who have delivered him to the barbarian who loads him with fetters. Ah! Signor Don Pablos, why did you shield me from the vengeance of the law? Since you love my father, you should have avenged him, and have suffered me to expiate, by an ignominious death, the crime of having caused all his misfortunes.'

"These exclamations, evidently betokening an erring mind's return to virtue, together with the natural expressions of the young Piquillo's sincere grief, greatly affected the rector. 'My child,' he said to him, 'I see with pleasure that you repent of your past transgressions. Dry up your tears: it is enough for me to know what has become of Ambrosio to give you assurance of beholding him again. His deliverance depends but on an easy ransom, which I shall cheerfully provide; and how great soever may have been the sufferings he has endured, I feel persuaded that on his return, to find in you a son restored to virtue, and filled with tenderness for him, he will not complain of the rigour of his destiny.'

"Don Pablos, by this assurance, dismissed the son of Ambrosio with a lightened heart; and, a few days afterwards, he set out for Madrid. On his arrival in this capital, he placed in the hands of the fathers of Mercy a purse containing a hundred pistoles, to which was attached a label bearing these words: 'This sum is given to the fathers of the Redemption, for the ransom of a poor citizen of Salamanca, named Ambrosio Piquillo, now captive in Algiers.' The good monks, in their recent voyage, acting in pursuance of the directions of the rector, did not fail to purchase Ambrosio, and you beheld him in that slave whose tranquil air excited your attention."

"In my opinion," said Don Cleophas, "Bahabon has worthily repaid the debt he owed to this luckless citizen." "Don Pablos, however," replied Asmodeus, "thinks differently. He will not be contented until he has restored to him both principal and interest; the delicacy of his conscience even extends so far as to scruple at his retention of the wealth he has gained since he has become rector of the university; and when he sees Ambrosio, he intends saying to him: 'Ambrosio, my friend, do not regard me as your benefactor; you behold in me the scoundrel who disinterred the money you had buried in the wood. It is not enough that I restore to you the doubloons I robbed you of, since by their means it is that I have raised myself to the station I now enjoy: all that I possess belongs to you; I will retain so much alone as you shall please to----'" Asmodeus suddenly stopped in his relation; a trembling seized him as he spoke, and an unearthly paleness overspread his visage.

"Why, what's the matter now?" exclaimed the Student; "what wonderful emotion agitates you thus, and chains your willing tongue?" "Ah! Signor Leandro," answered the Demon with tremulous voice, "what misery for me! The magician who kept me prisoned in my bottle, has discovered that I am absent without leave; and prepares e'en now such mighty spiritings, to call me back to his laboratory, as I must fain obey." "Alas!" exclaimed Zambullo, quite affected, "I am mortified beyond expression! What a loss am I about to suffer! Must we, then, my dear Asmodeus, separate for ever?"

"I trust not," replied the Devil. "The magician may require some office of my ministry; and if I have the fortune to assist him in his projects, perhaps, out of gratitude, he may restore me to liberty. Should that arrive, as I hope it may, rely on my rejoining you at once; on condition, however, that you reveal not to mortal ears what has this night passed between us. Should you be weak enough to confide this to any one, I warn you," continued Asmodeus emphatically, "that you will never see me more.

"I have one consolation in leaving you," he resumed, "which is, that at least I have made your fortune. You will marry the lovely Seraphina, into whose bosom it has been my business to instil a doting passion for your lordship. The Signor Don Pedro de Escolano, too, has made up his mind to bestow her hand upon you: and do you take care not to let so splendid a gift escape your own. But, mercy on me!" he concluded, "I hear already the potent master who constrains me; all Hell resounds with the echoes of the fearful words pronounced by this redoubtable magician: I dare not stay a moment longer. Farewell, my dear Zambullo! We may meet again." As he ceased, he embraced Don Cleophas, and, after having dropped the Student in his own apartment on his way to the laboratory, disappeared.

CHAPTER XXI

OF THE DOINGS OF DON CLEOPHAS AFTER ASMODEUS HAD LEFT HIM; AND OF THE MODE IN WHICH THE AUTHOR OF THIS WORK HAS THOUGHT FIT TO END IT.

Upon the retreat of Asmodeus, the Student, feeling fatigued at having passed all the night upon his legs, and by the extraordinary bustle in which he had been occupied, undressed himself and went to bed. Agitated as his mind may be supposed to have been, it is no wonder that he lay for some time restless; but at last, paying with compound interest to Morpheus the tribute which all mortals owe to his sombre majesty, he fell into a deathlike sleep, in which he passed the whole of that day and the following night.

Twenty-four hours had he been thus lost to the world, when Don Luis de Lujana, a young cavalier whom he numbered among his friends, entered his chamber, singing out lustily, "Hollo! Signor Don Cleophas, get up with you!" At this salutation, Zambullo awoke. "Are you aware," said Don Luis to him, "that you have been in bed since yesterday morning?" "Impossible!" exclaimed Leandro. "Not the less true for that," replied his friend; "twice have you slept the clock's dull round. All the inmates of the house assure me of this fact."

The Student, astonished at the trance from which he emerged, feared at first that his adventures with Asmodeus were but an illusion. He could not, however, persist in this belief; and when he recalled to himself certain circumstances of his intercourse with the Demon, he soon ceased to doubt of its reality. But, to make assurance doubly sure, he rose, dressed himself quickly, and went out with Don Luis, whom he took, without saying why, in the direction of the Gate of the Sun. Arrived there, and perceiving the mansion of Don Pedro almost reduced to ashes, Don Cleophas feigned surprise. "What do I behold?" he cried. "What dreadful ravages has fire made here! To whom did this unlucky house belong, and when was it thus consumed?"

Don Luis de Lujana, having replied to these two questions, thus continued: "This fire is less spoken of in the town on account of the great damage it has done, than for a circumstance which attended it, and of which I will tell you. The Signor Don Pedro de Escolano has an only daughter, who is lovely as the day: they say that she was in a room all filled with fire and smoke, in which it seemed certain she must perish; but that nevertheless her life was saved by a youthful cavalier, whose name I have not heard;--it forms the subject of conversation throughout Madrid. The young man's daring is lauded to the skies; and it is believed that, as a reward for his success, however humble my gentleman may be, he may well hope to gain a life interest in the daughter of the Don."

Leandro Perez listened to Don Luis without appearing to take the slightest interest in what he heard; then getting rid of his friend, under some specious pretext, he gained the Prado, where, seating himself beneath a tree, he was soon plunged in a profound reverie. The Devil first came flitting through his mind. "Ah! my dear Asmodeus," he exclaimed, "I cannot too much regret you. You, in a moment, would have borne me round the world; and, with you, should I have journeyed without any of the usual devilries of travelling: gentle spirit, you are a loss indeed! But," he added a moment afterwards, "my loss, perhaps, is not quite irreparable: why should I despair of seeing the Demon again? It may fall out, as he himself suggested, that the magician will shortly restore him to freedom and to me." As the Devil left his mind the lady entered it; upon which he resolved at once to seek Don Pedro in his temporary abode, moved principally by curiosity to see the lovely Seraphina.

As soon as he appeared before Don Pedro, that signor rushed towards him with open arms, and embracing him, exclaimed: "Welcome! generous cavalier, I began to feel angry at your absence. 'What!' said I, 'Don Cleophas, after the pressing invitation which I gave him to my house, still to shun my sight! He ill indeed repays the impatience of my soul to testify for him the friendship and esteem which fill it.'"

Zambullo bowed respectfully at this kindly objurgation; and, in order to excuse his seeming coldness, replied to the old man, that he had feared to incommode him in the confusion which the event of the preceding day must have occasioned. "I cannot listen to such an excuse," resumed Don Pedro; "you can never be unwelcome in a house which but for your noble conduct would have been a house of mourning indeed. But," he added, "follow me, if you please; you have other thanks than mine to receive." And taking the Student's hand, he led him to the apartment of Seraphina.

"My child," said Don Pedro, as he entered the room, where this lady was reposing from the noon-day heat, "I present to you the gentleman who so courageously saved your life. Show to him now, if you can, how deeply sensible you are of the obligation he conferred, since the danger from which he rescued you deprived you of the power to do so on the spot." On this, the Signora Seraphina, opening a mouth of roses to express the gratitude of her heart to Leandro Perez, paid him in compliments so warm and graceful, as would charm my readers as much as they did their blushing object, could I repeat each honeyed word; but as they have not been faithfully reported, I think it better to omit them altogether, than chance to spoil them by my own imperfect knowledge in such matters.

I will only say, that Don Cleophas thought he beheld and listened to some bright divinity, and that he was at once the victim of his eyes and ears. To say that he loved her, is a thing of course; but, far from regarding the beauteous form before him as a possession to which he might aspire, his heart foreboded, despite all that the Demon had assured him, that they would never pay at such a price the service they imagined him to have rendered. As her charms increased in their effect upon his mind, doubts, teasing doubts, came threatening to destroy the infant Hope, first-cherished child of Love.

What completed his mystification on the subject, was, that Don Pedro during the lengthened conversation which ensued, not once e'en touched upon the tender theme; but contented himself with loading him with civilities, without hinting in the slightest degree that he had any desire for the honour of his relationship. Seraphina, too, as polite as her father, while she did not fail in expressions of the deepest gratitude, dropped no one word whose magic charm would serve Zambullo to conjure visions of wedding joys; so that our Student left the Signor Escolano and his daughter with Love as his companion, but leaving Hope behind him.

"Asmodeus, my friend," he muttered as he walked along, as though the Devil still were by his side, "when you assured me that Don Pedro was disposed to adopt me as his son-in-law, and that Seraphina burned with passion lighted in her heart by you for me, it must have pleased you to make merry at my cost, or else you know as little of the present time as of that which is to come."

He now regretted that he had ever seen the dangerous beauty; and looking on the love which filled his breast as an unhappy passion which he ought to stifle in its infancy, he resolved to set about it in earnest. He even reproached himself for having desired to gain his point, supposing he had found the father all disposed to give his daughter to him; and represented to himself that it would have been disgraceful to have owed his happiness to a deception like that he had projected.

He was yet occupied with these reflections, when Don Pedro, having sent to seek him on the following day, said to him: "Signor Leandro Perez, it is time I proved to you by deeds, that in obliging me you have not to do with one of those who repay a benefit in courtly phrases. You saved my daughter: and I wish that she, herself, should recompense the peril you encountered for her sake. I have consulted Seraphina thereupon, and find her ready to obey my will; nay, I can say with pride, I recognized her for my child indeed when I proposed that she should give her hand to him who saved her life. She showed her joy by transports which at once convinced my soul her generosity responds to mine. It is settled therefore that you shall marry with my daughter."

After having spoken thus, the good Signor de Escolano, who reasonably expected that Don Cleophas would have gone down on his knees to thank him for so great a boon, was sufficiently surprised to find him speechless, and displaying an evident embarrassment. "Speak, Zambullo!" he at length exclaimed. "What am I to infer from the confusion which my proposition to you has occasioned? What possible objection can you have? What! a private gentleman--although respectable--to refuse an alliance which a noble would have courted! Has then the honour of my house some blemish of which I am ignorant?"

"Signor," replied Leandro, "I know too well the space that Heaven has set between us." "Why then," returned Don Pedro, "seem you to care so little for a marriage which does you so much honour? Confess! Don Cleophas, you love some maiden, and have pledged your faith; and it is your honour now which bars your road to fortune." "Had I," replied the Student, "a mistress to whom my vows had bound my future fate, it is not fortune that should bid me break them; but it is no such tie that now compels me to reject your proffered bounty. Honour, it is true, compels me to renounce the glorious destiny that you would tempt me with; but, far from seeking to abuse your kindness, I am about to undeceive you to my own undoing. I am not the deliverer of Seraphina."

"What do I hear!" exclaimed Don Pedro, in utter astonishment. "It was not you who rescued Seraphina from the flames which threatened her with instant death! It was not Don Cleophas who had the courage to risk his life to save her!" "No, Signor," replied Zambullo; "mortal man would have vainly essayed to shield her from her fate; learn that it was a devil to whom you owe your daughter's life."

These words only increased the astonishment of Don Pedro, who, not conceiving that he was to understand them literally, entreated the Student to explain himself. Upon which Leandro, regardless of the loss of the Demon's friendship, related all that had passed between Asmodeus and himself. Having finished, the old man resumed, and said to Don Cleophas: "The confidence you have reposed in me confirms me in my design of giving you my daughter. You were her chief deliverer. Had you not thus intreated the Devil whom you speak of to snatch her from the death which menaced her, it is clear that he would have suffered her to perish. It is you then who preserved the life of Seraphina, which cannot be better devoted than to the happiness of your own. You deserve her; and I again offer you her hand with the half of my estate."

Leandro Perez at these words, which removed all his conscientious scruples, threw himself at the feet of Don Pedro to thank him for his generosity. In a few weeks, the marriage was celebrated with a magnificence suitable to the espousal of the heir of the Signor de Escolano, and to the great satisfaction of the relations of our Student, who was thus amply repaid for the few hours' freedom he had procured for the Devil on Two Sticks.

www.ingramcontent.com/pod-product-compliance
Lightning Source LLC
Chambersburg PA
CBHW071900070526
44583CB00016B/1781